The Story of Swimming

for Martin and Ellen

Susie Parr

The Story of Swimming

A social history of bathing in Britain

dewi lewis media

The Story of Swimming
by Susie Parr

First published in the United Kingdom in 2011 by

Dewi Lewis Media
8 Broomfield Road, Heaton Moor
Stockport SK4 4ND, England

www.dewilewismedia.com
www.dewilewispublishing.com

© 2011
for the text: Susie Parr
for this edition: Dewi Lewis Media
for the photographs: see credits page 191

ISBN: 978-1-905928-07-1

Design and Layout: Dewi Lewis Publishing
Print: EBS, Verona, Italy

Contents

Introduction

It is a Sunday in late September, about 5 in the afternoon. It has been a warm day, but now the sun is low and the air is clear and fresh – a chilly night to come. I walk from the car park down the sandy track to the beach, passing families straggling back to their cars, loaded with all the paraphernalia of an afternoon at the beach – umbrellas, wind-breaks, carrier bags, kites, buckets and spades – and trailing cranky children. There's a real end-of-the-summer feel.

I walk along the shingle to my favourite spot beneath the yellow sandstone cliffs. I'm carrying a bag containing towel, swimsuit, jumper and a flask of tea. I put down my bag on a flat rock, wrap the towel round me and start to wriggle out of my clothes and into my costume. Then I spread the towel out across the warm stones, and head down towards the sea. It is high tide, and the water is full and smooth. There is a long sigh as each swell breaks, then the water slowly pulls back on the stones and shells. The stones hurt my feet as I make my way down to the water's edge. The beach shelves steeply into the water. I wade in up to thigh depth, then launch myself out, gliding smoothly through the water. The cold makes me gasp, then the shock subsides and a tingle spreads all over my body.

I move out into deeper water looking down through clear green to the dim shapes of the rocks beneath, wafting seaweed. The water sucks and blows at the shingle. I swim along parallel to the shore about twenty yards out, then float on my back, toes pointing to the horizon, lifting and lowering in the swell, watching the distant progress of tankers heading out to France. No-one else is swimming, even though there are still plenty of people on the beach. I paddle myself round so I can look at the cliffs and watch the ravens and gulls wheeling in the red light. There is a melancholy feel to these late summer swims. I always wonder will this be the last bathe of the year. I move further out, the water becoming a darker silky grey. I feel cold and yet I want to stay here, suspended, gently lifting and lowering.

My fingers look a livid white through the water, I can't feel them any more – it's time to get out. I move reluctantly towards the shore and try to judge my exit so that I won't be surprised by one of those waves that can push your face against the shingle, spinning you round in an abrasive undertow of sand and stones. A gentle swell carries me to the right spot and I emerge, dripping and shivering and

About to swim, Raasay © Martin Parr/Magnum.

clamber with difficulty up the shingle shelf. A rub-down with the towel and then clothes are pulled onto sticky skin. Jumper on, I sit on the towel and pour myself tea, holding the cup with both hands to catch the warmth. My fingers are numb but my whole body still tingles. A late wasp drones by, zig-zagging towards the litter bin. A couple walking their dog along the beach pass close by. The man says: *'You're brave. Isn't it very cold? You wouldn't catch me in there.'*

Warming my hands, sipping hot tea and looking out to sea I think about his comment. Why do I love to do this, when so many people plainly think it is mad and I am often the only one in the water? I'm sure I remember more people bathing in the sea and in rivers and lakes when I was a child. In fact I learned to swim in a river pool in Cumberland, a pink rubber ring round my waist, watching my brother and sister diving off white boulders into deep peaty brown water. Even my mum, who was not at all sporty because she was so short-sighted, told me how she used to swim in the cold water of the Tay across the harbour at Broughty Ferry when she was a girl. But these days it is rare to see anyone enter the water unless zipped into a wetsuit and wielding a surf-board. It is unusual to see families swimming together in the sea. Children paddle and play in the shallows, but always with a watchful parent nearby, usually fully dressed, arms crossed, supervising but not taking part in the fun.

When I bathe, I feel as if am following a thread back to some long-established tradition that feels completely fundamental to who I am. Thinking about this makes me want to know where the urge to immerse myself in water comes from. How did open water bathing start in the UK? What shaped it? Why did it become so popular? And is it really in decline?

I need to understand more about what compels me to wade into the sea at West Bay, launch myself into the dim depths of Henleaze Lake or icy brown pool at Lumb Falls, and float on my back in the blue-green waters of Raasay. How do the things I'm feeling and thinking when I swim relate to what other bathers have thought and felt over the centuries? What can paintings, woodcuts, postcards, literature, cartoons, diary entries and photographs tell me about the social history of sea, river and lake bathing in the UK?

In this book I find the earliest records of swimming in

Britain, look at accounts written by the Romans, explore Anglo Saxon poetry and delve into stories about the Viking invaders. I search for references to bathing in medieval and Elizabethan literature and describe how medicinal sea-bathing flourished in the 18th century, leading to the rise of Georgian and Regency watering holes like Brighton, Weymouth, Tenby and Scarborough.

Romantic artists and writers including Wordsworth, Byron and Shelley were mesmerised by natural water and drawn to immerse themselves in it. I want to understand the Romantic reconfiguration of the relationship between man and the natural world and trace its impact through a whole line of literary swimmers including Algernon Swinburne, Rupert Brooke, D.H. Lawrence and Iris Murdoch. Swimming and bathing was not always for the rich and fashionable. The advent of rail travel made the seaside accessible to the masses and sea-bathing something everyone could enjoy. Britain's seaside resorts, thronged with bathers and revellers, became sites where class tensions were played out on the sand. I explore the impact of seaside excursions and outings on Britain's once quiet watering places.

I am a member of Henleaze Swimming Club in Bristol (which was founded in 1919) and want to understand the origins of venerable organisations like this and of my mother's club – Ye Amphibious Ancients in Broughty Ferry near Dundee, founded in 1889 and still going strong. I will find out how these clubs evolved and trace the developments in swimming and bathing in the UK around the turn of the last century and during the war years. Why did swimming and bathing in the UK's open water seem to decline in the second half of the 20th century? Was this due to the building of indoor municipal pools? Holidays in the sun? The growth of surfing and water sports?

In recent years, a new passion for open water bathing has become apparent, a movement that seems to have its roots in Romanticism. In particular, the late Roger Deakin sought out wild and natural places to swim, celebrated swimming traditions and asserted the swimmer's right to bathe in Britain's lakes and rivers. The movement has grown and now attracts thousands of followers. In keeping with this new Romanticism, interest in the adventurous and heroic aspects of swimming seems to be reviving. A budding tourist industry now invites bathers to sign up for endurance holidays involving long-distance swims in exotic or challenging waters including the Hellespont, once swum by Lord Byron. Modern day heroes like David Walliams and Lewis Gordon Pugh undertake swimming feats for charity or to make a point about pollution and global warming. And the growing popularity of triathlon and open water distance swimming events, which now have Olympic status, inspires many athletes to zip themselves into state of the art wetsuits and head for the water.

Despite such hopeful signs, when I talk to people about swimming in Britain's seas, rivers or lakes I am astonished by how many seem fearful of open water. What puts them off? Worries about pollution; concerns about depth, tides, currents and lurking creatures; fears about lack of fitness and, of course, the cold. It seems to me that something very ancient and deep in our culture may be in danger of dying and fading away, almost without anyone noticing.

In this book, I take a broadly chronological look at the social history that has shaped British swimming and trace the overlapping themes that emerge in each period. I swim at places that have played a part in this social history. I interview present day swimmers, both heroic and humble, in order to find out about what drives them into the water and to show how they are connected with each other and with bathers from the past. This book is my celebration of bathing and of the history that compels me to enter the water and stay there for as long as I can, floating, feeling the cold on my skin.

Might, method, medicine and magic: early British bathing and swimming

Around 8200 BC, the bridge of dry land linking East Anglia with Holland started becoming marshy and prone to flooding. By 6000 BC, the marshes themselves had become sea. From that point on, Britain was a cluster of islands – the largest with over 11,000 miles of coastline – whose civilisations would be shaped by the presence of sea, estuary, river, lake and spring.

Archaeological evidence can tell us something of what coastal and inland waters meant for the people who lived in Britain after the Ice Age. Excavations at Goldcliff – an important Mesolithic site in Wales, which around 7,500 years ago sat on a small wooded island surrounded by salt marshes – have uncovered stone tools, pollen, animal and fish bones. It is believed that fish was plentiful in the Mesolithic diet and was caught using stone barbs attached to wooden spears and harpoons made of antler. Erosion in the Severn Estuary has revealed a trail of human footprints, baked into the mud by the sun and then preserved by layers of peat, heading out towards the sea at Uskmouth. They tell us that around 6,250 years ago, a Mesolithic man was walking barefoot towards the water, perhaps on his way to catch some fish. Similar footprint trails have been revealed in estuary mud around the coastline of Britain. Some were left by women and children, who might have been gathering shellfish. On the Isle of Oronsay, five shellfish middens have been excavated, showing that the Mesolithic people – who are thought to have travelled from island to island – enjoyed a diet of dog whelks and periwinkles.

The first written accounts of Britain's civilisations, supplemented by artefacts, literature and folklore, suggest that from the earliest days water was of symbolic as well as functional importance. The relationship between the British peoples and water was itself fluid, shaped by the customs and practices brought by waves of invaders and settlers – strangers who always arrived by boat.

The story of early British bathing and swimming is untidy, pieced together from scraps of reference and fragments of artefact. Amongst the flotsam of evidence, four distinct yet interconnected strands emerge. These stretch across decades, centuries, and millennia, linking the recent and far distant past with the present. The four intertwining themes that characterise early British swimming are might, method, medicine and magic.

Early British swimming & military might

The first recorded accounts of swimming in Britain occur at the time of the Roman invasions. For a Roman soldier, swimming was as important a part of military training as marching, sword practice, archery and vaulting. Vegetius, who between AD 383 and 395 wrote *Epitoma Rei Militaris*, an account of Roman military practice that was to influence British education in the Middle Ages, underlined the importance of teaching soldiers to swim. If there were no bridges, troops could swim across rivers and surprise the enemy. They could also escape quickly from danger, unlikely to be pursued.

Roman soldiers were trained not only to swim but to manage currents and deep water whilst wearing armour.

Strong swimmers were lauded. Plutarch describes how, retreating from a battle with Germanic tribes in 105 BC, commander Quintus Sertorius, having lost his horse, swam across the Rhone against the current. The wounded soldier carried a shield and wore a breastplate, both of which must have weighed him down. Yet he reached the bank, the sole survivor of an entire Roman legion and was from that point on regarded as a hero.

The Romans used swimming as a military strategy in the expeditions to Britain led by Julius Caesar in 55 and 54 BC. Biographies of Caesar describe him as a formidable swimmer. He would lead his troops across rivers, the soldiers either swimming or using inflated animal skins as floats. In one account, Caesar and his men were locked in combat with the native Britons on the banks of a river.

Roman soldiers swimming into battle.

The Romans were struggling and eventually retreated, half swimming, half wading across the river in their armour.

Tacitus describes an earlier battle in AD 43 in which an invading force, led by Aulus Plautius, landed on the Kent coast at Richborough and advanced towards the downs, crossing the Medway at Snodland. Roman soldiers swam the river undetected, then mounted a surprise attack on the Britons on the far bank, maiming their chariot horses and forcing them to retreat.

According to Tacitus, by AD 69 the Romans were using Germanic mercenaries in their efforts to quell the Britons. In particular they employed Batavi warriors, people from the Rhine region, who were known to be accomplished swimmers. The Batavi trained their horses to swim across rivers and to cope with deep water and strong currents. Paulinus ordered Batavian cavalry, supported by infantry-men in boats and *ballistae* (catapults) situated on the mainland, to swim across the Menai Straits to Anglesey. The waiting Celts, thinking they would be protected by a treacherous stretch of water that could only be crossed by boat, were routed and butchered.

In the fenlands of the East, native British troops were more accustomed to managing the marshy conditions. Herodian writes that Septimus Severus, the Roman emperor who died at York in AD 211, tried to secure safe passage for his own soldiers across treacherous terrain:

He endeavoured to render the marshy places stable by means of causeways, that his soldiers treading with safety might easily pass them and, having firm footing, might fight to advantage. For many parts of the British country, being constantly flooded by the tides of the ocean, became marshy. In these the natives were accustomed to swim and traverse about as high as their waists.

The battles and bloodshed of invasion eventually gave way to a long period of peaceful settlement, during which time the Romans introduced their native customs into their British location and lifestyle. One of the most important features of Roman civilisation was bathing. Elaborate baths, comprising series of heated rooms and cold plunge pools, were built in most British towns, in military barracks and in the many grand villas erected in the countryside. Remains of large artificial swimming pools, or *piscinae* have been found at Bath and Buxton spas, at Wroxeter in Shropshire and at Well in Yorkshire.

In the South West, the Romans found a remarkable hot water spring that brought over one million litres of water to the surface every day at a temperature of 48 degrees centigrade. A reservoir was built and pipes laid to control the water flow, and baths and a temple erected nearby. A town, Aquae Sulis – now known as Bath – quickly grew around this complex and the waters soon gained a reputation for their curative powers. As a result, people travelled from all over the Roman Empire to bathe in Britain. The bathers, relishing the hot, health-giving water, probably behaved as rowdily as the Roman citizens who disturbed Seneca's peace in AD 50:

I live over a public bath-house. Just imagine every kind of annoying noise! The sturdy gentleman does his exercise with lead weights; when he is working hard (or pretending to) I can hear him grunt; when he breathes out, I can hear him panting in high pitched tones. Or I might notice some lazy fellow, content with a cheap rub-down, and hear the blows of the hand slapping his shoulders. The sound varies, depending on whether the massager hits with a flat or hollow hand. To all of this, you can add the arrest of the occasional pickpocket; there's also the racket made by the man who loves to hear his own voice in the bath or the chap who dives in with a lot of noise and splashing.

The Romans did not just bathe and swim in man-made baths but also used natural pools, rivers and lakes. There are many accounts of youths bathing in the Tiber in Rome and it is likely that this practice was continued in the great rivers of Roman Britain. Broomlee Lough, a moorland tarn close to Housesteads Fort on Hadrian's Wall, was a likely swimming hole for Roman soldiers and was probably used for training as well as for refreshment and relaxation on warm days.

Following the collapse of Roman civilisation in Britain, new invaders – the Anglo Saxons – arrived from North Germany early in 5th century, their advent documented by Bede in his ecclesiastical history of the English. Decades of bloody battles ensued. There is no doubt that these new invaders also practised and honoured the art of swimming, and were no strangers to cold water. Caesar himself had commented on the hardiness of the Germanic tribes whom he had defeated in AD 58. He wrote: *They have trained themselves to wear nothing except skins, even in the coldest places, and they bathe in the rivers.*

We know that swimming was important to the invaders because it features in the great Anglo Saxon poem *Beowulf*, which was probably composed in Mercia or Northumbria in the 7th century. The epic poem would originally have been recited aloud in instalments. The first written copy was made in Wessex in around AD 1000. Although written in England, the poem is actually set in Denmark and Sweden. The hero of the story is Beowulf, a warrior who takes on various enemies that threaten the Danish people.

Great swimming feats are described in the poem, the first when the young Beowulf and his friend Breca venture out to compete in the open sea:

> It was in early manhood that we undertook
> with public boast – both of us still
> very young men – to venture our lives
> on the open ocean; which we accordingly did.
> Hard in our right hands we each held a sword
> as we went through the sea, so to keep off
> the whales from us.
> Thus stroke for stroke we stitched the ocean
> five nights and days, drawn apart then
> by cold storm on the cauldron of waters;
> under lowering night the northern wind
> fell on us in warspite: the waves were rough!

The final swimming episode in the poem involves an unsuccessful raid on the Frisians and the Franks, in which Beowulf's lord, Hygelac, is killed and Beowulf has to swim back to Sweden, solitary and wretched, carrying the mail coats of thirty men.

Beowulf's struggles with the wind, waves and cold of the northern seas would ring true for any British open water swimmer today, but the poem invests him with superhuman strength and supernatural swimming powers. This was a standard feature of epic poems and suggests that swimming was a worthy skill for an Anglo Saxon warrior to acquire, one through which powers of strength and endurance could be demonstrated. So there are similarities between the heroic swimming of the Romans and that of the Anglo Saxons. Two entirely different cultures and civilisations honoured warriors who were able to swim great distances, even when exhausted or wounded, wearing armour, carrying weapons and ready to fight.

Following the settlement of England by the Anglo Saxons, another war-like people invaded from the north: the Vikings sacked Lindisfarne in 793. Waves of attacks and

settlement across the British Isles followed. Shetland and Orkney were annexed by Norway and remained in Norwegian hands until the 15th century. As with the Anglo Saxons, much evidence of the practice of swimming during this period can be found in lengthy sagas and epic poems transcribed in the 13th century, which describe people and events from the Viking era in Britain, Norway and Iceland.

According to the sagas, competitive swimming was commonly practised. Nordic leaders who raided, visited or settled in Britain – including Olaf Tryggvason, Olaf Haraldsson, Earl Magnus of Orkney and his nephew Kali Ragavald – were all able to swim. While some references to swimming in Norse literature are fantastical and, as in *Beowulf*, refer to warriors battling with sea and water monsters, others may be grounded in fact. For example, Magnus is described in the *Orkneyinga Saga* as having escaped from the King of Norway's fleet, anchored off the Scottish coast, by swimming ashore. As well as using swimming as a means of escape, Nordic settlers were also fond of engaging in vigorous competitive swimming feats, similar to that undertaken by Beowulf and Breca. Sigurd the Stout, Magnus's son, who became King of Orkney in 1098, was no stranger to the competitive spirit:

It was a day of beautiful weather and warm sunshine and many went out to swim from the long-ship and the merchant vessel. An Icelandic man who was among the swimmers, amused himself by drawing those under water who could not swim as well as himself. And at that the spectators laughed. When King Sigurd heard and saw this he cast off his clothes, sprang into the water, swam to the Icelander, seized him and pressed him under the water.

Olaf Tryggvason, who brought Christianity to Orkney and to the Viking communities on the British mainland, is said to have entered into an underwater wrestling match with Kjartan, the hero of one of the sagas. He also punished citizens who practised sorcery by chaining them to rocky outcrops in a rising tide. He himself died in 1000, having leapt into the sea following his defeat in the Battle of Svold in the Baltic, although rumours that he had swum safely to shore persisted for many years.

Warriors didn't only use swimming as a military tactic or as part of their training. The Vikings continued to raid and trade along the western coast of the British Isles, reaching Pembrokeshire. There, they engaged local men as mercenaries. Together with their Welsh reinforcements,

Shetland helicopter pilots re-enact the Haagdyve © Flo Bragg.

the raiders returned to the Northern Islands of Orkney and Shetland, a stopping off point on their way home. While their employers were away, the Welsh soldiers remained on Shetland and set about trying to win the favour of the local women, who initially rejected the mercenaries because they were dirty. To address this problem, the men engaged in a cleansing ceremony in which they bathed in the icy sea. The ritual became known as *Haagdyve* and is understood to have taken place at Mavis Grind, a point where the Atlantic Ocean meets the North Sea.

The Haagdyve ceremony has been re-instated by Shetland helicopter pilots, who are led into the water every Boxing Day by Captain Alan Price, himself a Welshman.

The idea that swimming was an essential military skill and a means of demonstrating manly strength and prowess

re-surfaces in the knightly literature of the Middle Ages (roughly the period between 1066 and 1500). Instruction for knights (warriors encased in full body armour and mounted on horseback) was drawn almost exclusively from Vegetius's *Epitoma Rei Militaris*, originally written for the training of Roman soldiers. This was first read, in Latin, by a member of the Anglo Norman aristocracy, Geoffrey of Anjou, the father of Henry II, then translated into French in 1284. In the 15th century, an English translation, of which ten copies still exist, made it much more widely used by English aristocracy.

The English translation adapts the guidelines originally developed for Roman warriors to the world view of medieval knights:

*New chosen knyghtes in somer sesun schul ben taught
and used to swymme, for thei school not fynde alwey
redy brugges over reveres and flodes.*

According to the text, the knight: *what with grete schoures
and reynes, what with sodeyn snowes throw rising and
encreesing of ryvers and flodus and unkonnyngnesse of
swymmynge, putteth himself in greet peril, what of enemy
us on the on side, what of peril of waterus on the other
side.*

The text supports the 'old romayns' opinion that swimming
was an important skill for warriors to acquire. It could save
their lives in battle and then revive them so that *after here
labor and travaille of dedes of armes might with swym-
myng wesche awey the swoot and the dust and poudre
that thei hadde caught with rennyng and rydyng.*

Vegetius's recommendations were incorporated into new
manuals on military training and education that were
widely read throughout medieval Europe. However, despite featuring in instructional literature, it seems doubtful
that swimming was much practised by knights and warriors. Other than references to the exploits of Greek and
Roman soldiers, swimming rarely appears in the knightly
narratives, the romances and *chansons de geste* that were
the dominant literary forms of the period. The reason is
obvious: the bulky and all-encapsulating body armour
favoured by mounted knights would have made it impossible to stay buoyant. In *Lancelot, The Knight of the Cart*
written by Chrétien de Troyes in 1170, the hero rides
across a drawbridge to reach a castle, while his companion Sir Gawain tries swimming the moat. The weight of
Gawain's helmet, hauberk and iron greaves leads to
predictable – and somewhat comic – consequences:

*One moment he rises, the next he sinks; one moment
they see him, the next they lose him from sight.*

Such practical difficulties aside, swimming continued to
be regarded as a desirable knightly skill. In The *Faerie
Queene*, Spenser describes a Saracen knight fighting
Artegall in a river, both mounted on swimming horses.
The episode ends with both knights having to rely on
their own skills in the water:

*So ought each knight, that use of peril has,
In swimming be expert through water's force to pass.*

Shakespeare continues the tradition of admiration for
the strength and bravery of swimmers. In *Julius Caesar*,

Sir John Luttrell escaping from a shipwreck, by Hans Eworth (1550).

Cassius describes a swimming competition with Caesar
in which both men, wearing armour, jump into a turbulent
river:

*Accoutred as I was, I plunged in
And bade him follow; so indeed he did.
The torrent roared and we did buffet it
With lusty sinews, throwing it aside
And stemming it with hearts of controversy.*

This image of a powerful swimmer locked in combat with
water is re-visited in *The Tempest* when Ferdinand escapes
the shipwreck:

*I saw him beat the surges under him
And ride upon their backs; he trod the water,
Whose enmity he flung aside, and breasted
The surge most swoll'n that met him; his bold head*

*'Bove the contentious waves he kept, and oared
Himself with his good arms in lusty stroke
To the shore.*

Shakespeare's sense of awe for the strong swimmer finds an equivalent in Hans Eworth's portrait of Sir John Luttrell (painted in 1550). Sir John is depicted escaping, Ferdinand-like, from a shipwreck that occurred while commanding an English garrison during military operations leading up to the Treaty of Boulogne. But the portrait has little realistic detail, unlike Shakespeare's description of someone fighting for their life in heavy seas. Sir John's unblemished appearance and upright posture in the water, together with the presence of the Three Graces hovering in the stormy sky above him, make the portrait allegorical, a symbol of the nobleman's domination over the forces of nature and England's command of the waves.

In *Henry IV*, Shakespeare uses the image of diving to convey Hotspur's impetuous, overblown nature. There is a resonance here with the superhuman feats of Beowulf. But while Beowulf's dive demonstrates his heroism, the swimming analogy makes Hotspur seem rash and deluded, suggesting Shakespeare's wariness of water:

*By heaven, methinks it were an easy leap
To pluck bright honour from the pale-faced moon
Or dive into the bottom of the deep
Where fathom-line could never touch the ground
And pluck up drowned honour from the deep.*

Swimming & bathing: method & medicine

Having declined during the Middle Ages, the practice of swimming revived somewhat in the 16th century. A reawakened interest in the classics generated a new genre of educational literature, developed to guide the behaviour of young gentlemen. Works such as *The Governor* (Thomas Elyot, 1531) and *Positions* (Richard Mulcaster, 1581) drew strongly on classical sources, particularly *Epitoma Rei Militaris*. Swimming was advocated as a generally useful, albeit, neglected skill. Primarily seen as a military accomplishment, swimming and immersion were also starting to be recognised as having health-promoting properties. In particular, Mulcaster anticipates the work of later scientists by listing the ailments alleviated by swimming in cold water, amongst them headaches, dropsies, scabs, scurf, smallpox and leprosies.

The most significant early work on swimming was written in Latin by Cambridge scholar Sir Everard Digby, in 1587. *De Arte Natandi* was created in order to raise swimming *from the depths of ignorance and the dust of oblivion*. It was also intended as a manual for youths of good birth, presumably students at Cambridge, whose custom it was to cool off in rivers during the summer. The treatise describes the many benefits of learning to swim. Not only enabling the swimmer to escape from dangerous situations, it can also bring many health benefits, purging poisonous humours and driving away contagious diseases, thereby extending life.

Written in Latin, Digby's work has a degree of gravitas that suggests it was intended for the educated rather than the general public. In keeping with this, Digby takes an elevated view of his enterprise. For him, writing the first treatise on the subject ranks him amongst the great classical thinkers who have addressed other important topics: Virgil on agriculture, Vegetius on war, Hippocrates on medicine and so on. *De Arte Natandi* made for esoteric reading and sadly the Latin version was never re-printed. But in 1595, the treatise was re-structured, abridged and translated into English *(for the better instruction of those who understand not the Latine tongue)* by Christopher Middleton. Although the translation retains much of the original content and the illustrations, many literary flourishes are removed and the work is given a more down to earth title: *A Short Introduction for to Learne to Swimme*. The translation and simplification of the book made it accessible to a wider range of readers. Middleton's aim was to *uncurtain that to the view of all which was only appropriated to a few*.

Both Latin and English versions depict the art of swimming as a most desirable skill, being a sign of man's superiority over other forms of life and his position near the top of the *chain of being*. This concept of the order of the universe had its roots in medieval philosophy and provided a means of ranking all forms of life. God, the angels and man are placed at the top of the ladder with various animal and plant species listed beneath them. According to Digby, the most noble or highest ranking animals (the lion for example) swim well, whereas humbler creatures, like the toad, are unable to swim. The ability to swim makes men superior to fish, because they can survive in water, whereas fish cannot survive in air. Although swimming is a natural skill for man, many drown because they have not practised the art sufficiently to prevent them from succumbing to fear. Also they do not deal properly with the many hazards that may arise when swimming in ponds, lakes and rivers.

Having established a philosophical framework, the treatise then takes a practical turn, advising on the best conditions for swimming and providing instruction on how to enter the water, propel oneself through it, float and even perform tricks such as turning, dancing, swimming like a dolphin, or paring toe nails while floating on one's back. The swimmer is urged to avoid swimming in cold winds and on rainy days, to find banks that are not overgrown where *oft-times do lie and lurk many stinging serpents and poisoned toads* and taking care to avoid *thorns, briars, stubs and thistles which may offend the bare feet.* He should find clear water, as cloudy water has *slimy filth that is infectious to the skin* and may conceal *any old stakes or sharp stones.* He must make sure he knows the dimensions of his swimming hole, particularly the depth (which he can plumb using a rod) and that he avoids *swift or violent streams.*

The practical nature of this work brings the experience of swimming in the Elizabethan landscape vividly to life. One can imagine Everard Digby or Christopher Middleton undressing on the bank of a favourite swimming hole on a bright May morning, then plunging into the water. And we do not have to rely upon words alone, for *De Arte Natandi* is abundantly illustrated. Forty three woodcuts depict a male figure swimming in a river and performing the moves that are described in the text. Each illustration has a frame or template showing the surrounding landscape and a central panel depicting the swimmer. The reader can see trees, grass and rushes, a thatched cottage with a picket fence, a windmill, a stile, fields with grazing cattle, while a magnificent sun sending its rays flickering across the scene. In many of the images a bearded male figure – wearing hat, ruff and doublet – sits pulling on his hose while watching the swimmer. Beside him, a naked figure runs across the grass towards the river, clearly about to dive in. The illustrations afford detailed glimpses of the day-to-day life of an Elizabethan gentleman: a knife is used to pare the toe-nails, a hawk is carried across the river perched on the swimmer's wrist.

With this work, swimming terminology begins to concern technique rather than strength. Digby coins some Latin terms to describe various manoeuvres ('convolutio'; 'retrogradatio'; 'prolapsio') but also uses more straightforward

phrases, for example 'bell turn' and 'swimming like a dog', in order to describe the correct movement. Middleton charmingly extends the use of analogy to convey technique when he describes how to change direction in the water:

This is commonly called 'the roach turn' since it resembles the roach when in the pleasant heat of the summer they wantonly frisk to and fro.

Interestingly, although Middleton uses the verbs: 'strike' 'beat' and 'thrust' when describing the motion of swimming, the word 'stroke' as a noun is not used. This early language for swimming methods foreshadows the extensively technical terminology that was to emerge in the nineteenth century. Digby's work formed the basis, not only for Middleton's translation, but for two subsequent treatises: *The Compleat Swimmer* (1658) by William Percey and a French version of *The Art of Swimming* by Melchisedech Thevenot, published in Paris in 1696 and then, in 1699, translated back into English, with hardly any acknowledgement of Digby's original material.

The Art of Swimming was extraordinary in focussing on the details and practicalities of swimming, and – in the case of Middleton's version at least – for its democratic spirit. Nothing similar would be published until the mid-Victorians, fired with the ethos of self help, produced detailed instructional manuals with the aim of enabling ordinary people to swim. In contrast, educational literature published in the early 17th century continued to focus on the elite. Educational works for young noblemen alluded to swimming as a desirable form of exercise, akin to riding and running. These works include James Cleland's *Hero-Paideia* (1607) and *The Compleat Gentleman* by Henry Peacham (1622), both of which draw on classical references in declaring swimming to be a useful skill for self-preservation in war or other dangers.

These instructional works suggest that swimming was an increasingly common and pleasurable practice, despite its attendant dangers. The swimming image used in Shakespeare's *Henry VIII* suggests that in hot weather British children would take to the water to cool off, oblivious to the hazards:

I have ventured,
Like little wanton boys that swim on bladders,
This many summers in a sea of glory,
But far beyond my depth.

From *The Art of Swimming* by Christopher Middleton (1595).

In keeping with this, in his introduction to *The Compleat Swimmer* (1658), William Percey describes a traumatic childhood experience:

I remember when I was a school boy, delighting much in hot weather to bath in our country rivulets. I once was in danger of drowning; but by the help of another that could swim was saved… which danger wrought in me such an earnest desire to learn to swim that I seldom did forbear the exercise a day, til I was become a perfect swimmer.

Millerd's *Map of Bristol* (1673) bears a Latin inscription that paints a summery picture of everyday life on the banks of the River Frome, in which swimming plays a part:

Hither each man's pleasure draws him, young and old alike. Some demand the grass, some the water. Here slow and swift fish are caught with the rod, here the limbs of the weary are refreshed with gentle swimming. Here, too, the student wanders meditating the arts, and the happy lover walks with his darling.

There are records of students swimming in Merton Pool and Scholler's Pool in 1667, and in Parson's Pleasure on the River Cherwell in 1689. Several accounts suggest that hot weather made the delights of cool rivers and ponds irresistible, sometimes with fatal consequences. Henry Prince of Wales, who had a house in Richmond by the Thames, would swim there during summer evenings. Unfortunately, in 1612, he contracted typhus following a swim and died, his demise meeting with an unprecedented outpouring of public grief. Nevertheless, swimming lessons grew in popularity, particularly in London.

Women also enjoyed bathing and swimming. *A Wanton Discovery* (1701).

soon exercised ourselves till the sweat ran; upon which, I being in a sweat as well as the rest, went to the River and leapt in. The Benefits of Bathing in Rivers is very great, and this is chiefly practised by Young Men and Boys. All Creatures being disturbed by the Summer's Heat go into Rivers and Ponds to cool them.

There is some evidence, too, that bathing and swimming were not just a male preserve. *The Swimming Lady*, or *A Wanton Discovery* was a popular ballad printed in 1701. It is prefaced with a charming woodcut showing a young lady, naked, enjoying a dip in a river near Oxford, while her lover spies on her from behind a tree:

> The four and twentieth day of May
> Of all the times in the year
> A Virgin-Lady bright and gay
> Did privately appear
> Close by the river-side which she
> Did single out the rather,
> Cause she was sure she was secure
> And had an Intent to bath her.

Another ballad, written around the same time, describes three pretty, 'wanton' girls who took a moonlight dip in their father's garden pond during the fine summer weather, secretly watched by the house servant. In both ballads, the sight of naked women bathing has clear erotic impact:

> Each Fish did wish himself a Man
> About her all were drawn
> And at the Sight of her began
> To spread abroad their Spawn.
> She turned to swim upon her back
> And so displayed her Banner,
> If Jove had been in Heaven then
> He would have dropped upon her.

The ballads anticipate the episode in John Cleland's *Fanny Hill* (1749) in which 'woman of pleasure' Harriet describes to Fanny how, as a young virgin, she watched her neighbour's son swimming in a stream on a hot day. Fearful for his safety as he dived down, she fell into a faint. He emerged from the water to find her insensible on the shore and promptly ravished her. Harriet's description of the swimmer is unashamedly erotic:

He had changed his posture and swam prone on his belly, striking out his legs and arms, finer modell'd than which could not have been cast, whilst his floating locks played over a neck and shoulders whose whiteness they

Sir John Floyer's treatise on cold water bathing, written in 1715, was mainly concerned with the medical benefits of immersion. But it contains many incidental descriptions of boys and men bathing and swimming in pools and rivers, particularly in hot weather. These are further evidence that inland swimming was as common in the early 18th century, as it had been in Everard Digby's time:

About Eleven Years ago in the Summer time, when Grass was ready to be mown, I being a school boy, went down to a River with four or five more, where after we had all been in the Water, we ran about the Meadows all naked, to dry ourselves: but the Weather being excessive hot, we

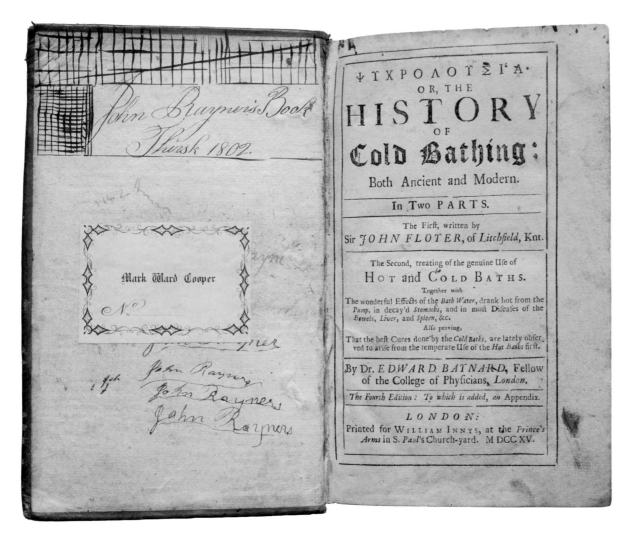

A scientific look at bathing. *The History of Cold Bathing, both Ancient and Modern* by Sir John Floyer (1715).

delightfully set off. Then the luxuriant swell of flesh that rose from the small of his back and terminates its double globe at where the thighs are set off, perfectly dazzled one with its watery glistening gloss.

Such titillation had no place in the strict educational literature of the late 17th century, which was moving away from classical influences and taking a rational turn, informed by contemporary advances in medicine, science and educational theory. In *Some Thoughts Concerning Education* (1693), John Locke stated that immersion in cold water makes boys hardy and strong, an idea echoed elsewhere: *Children should daily have their feet bathed in cold water to enable them to better withstand illnesses.*

The first in depth account of the medical and curative effects of immersion, Sir John Floyer's treatise on cold water bathing, draws on history and anecdote for evidence, but also on the author's personal experience as a practising physician, including experiments that he conducted on his patients and on himself.

Floyer prefaces his book with a letter to the Royal College of Physicians advocating the use of bathing in cold water to treat and cure a range of illnesses and conditions including gout, rheumatism, deafness, paralysis, cancer, rickets and mental disorders:

I will next consider the usefulness of Immersion in the contrary temperaments where the natural heat or spirits are but few and the serum does abound, such temperaments make us Dull, Stupid, Foolish and Slow in all our actions; for where the Circulation of humours is slow, there the Animal Spirits act heavily.

The cold water of springs, rivers, ponds, lakes and wells can be used in a variety of ways depending on the disorder. Floyer describes how a course of regular, brief immersions cured a child with drawling speech and swimming up and down a river for two hours relieved indigestion caused by over-indulgence in *fat venison*. A woman with breast cancer so advanced that her death seemed imminent was cured by washing the affected part in well water and bandaging it with a wet cloth, causing the tumour to shrivel and fall away. Some conditions, such as drunkenness or the ague, could be cured by a sudden plunge in cold water (and for this purpose the sea was as good as a river or pond). However, sometimes things went awry with this technique:

I have known a great many Agues cured by a sudden plunge into cold water; but the person to be submerged (for without a duck over head and ears it will not do effectually) should always be told of the design and give their consent. For I knew of a pretty young woman surprised under the notion of gathering some liver-wort, which grew on the Wall by the ponds brink, which was very deep in that place, and as she was stooping her own father (I think) took her by the heels and popped her in. Tis true it cured her Ague but made a worse swop. For she was that moment seized with epileptic fits from the fright, which held her many years after, much to the trouble of her friends and relations. And epilepsies gotten by frights are very stubborn and rarely admit of cure.

As Floyer's work demonstrates, bathing, swimming and diving were starting to attract the attention of the generation of scientists who were emerging in the late 17th century. According to diarist and founder member, John Evelyn, Charles II attended a meeting of the Royal Society in 1667 and discussed swimming and diving with him at some length. The un-named translator who rendered Thevenot's version of *The Art of Swimming* back into English added an eight-page preface of mechanical and scientific observations, which demonstrate a sophisticated understanding of the physics of movement in water. The specific gravity of the body must be matched with the forces required for 'sustentation and motion'. Different movements of the limbs can be refined to make them more efficient. The author also proposes various devices to keep one afloat and to aid propulsion through the water, including attachments 'like fishes' fins'.

In a scientifically-based endeavour also related to swimming, Robert Boyle searched for evidence that would help him establish the length of time a diver could remain under water without taking a breath. This piece of work, discussed in *New Experiments Physico-Mechanicall touching the Spring of Air* (1660) reflects the fact that swimming and diving were essential skills in trades such as ship salvaging and pearl harvesting. They were commonly practised by tradesmen and travellers, as described in Daniel Defoe's *Robinson Crusoe*, published in 1719. In this story, not only is the native Friday an exceptional swimmer, but the hero – Robinson Crusoe – swims from the sinking ship and then back out to the wreck in order to salvage material that will make his island life more comfortable. Crusoe's practical swimming techniques and challenges are closely described, suggesting that Defoe took a modern, technical interest in the skill and probably practised it himself.

Though I swam very well yet I could not deliver myself from the waves to draw breath, half dead with the water I took in. My business was to hold my breath and raise myself upon the water if I could and so by swimming to preserve my breathing and pilot myself towards the shore.

So bathing and swimming played a small but significant part in laying the foundations for the medical, scientific, technical and commercial advances of the Age of Reason.

Early British swimming and magic

But early British swimming was not entirely rational. It concerned more than might, method and medicine. Immersion in water was an act or practice permeated by superstition and myth. Folklore, legend and literature give the story of early British swimming a supernatural cast of heroes, monsters, spirits and shape-shifters. These strange beings allow a glimpse of beliefs and practices, some originating in pre- and early Christian Britain, that were slowly appropriated to fit the new world-views brought by waves of settlers.

Swimming was considered a desirable military skill, the manifestation of a brave and noble spirit. However, in early British sagas and legends, swimming powers are often extended from merely heroic to super-human. One of the earliest mentions of magical heroic swimming can be found in the *Mabinogian*, a set of fantastical tales that were transcribed for the first time in 13th century Wales but which drew on legends and myths from previous generations. One story – *How Culwech Won Olwen* – is a comic tale peopled with giants, hags and a talking salmon which invites two of the protagonists to ride on his shoulders as he swims up the Severn to Gloucester. King Arthur and his knights are comic-heroic figures in five of the Mabinogion tales, including this one. The story ends with Arthur and his men chasing around Wales after a giant boar from Ireland that jumps into the Severn, then swims to Cornwall with the knights following. The Arthurian legends are themselves suffused with watery episodes, from the Lady of the Lake holding up the sword Excalibur, to the three mysterious lake women who bear the dying Arthur away on a boat.

Strange and monstrous water beings were commonplace and even appeared in early Christian stories. St Columba, who was said to have sailed from Ireland to Scotland in AD 563 with twelve companions to share the Christian Gospel, landed on the Isle of Iona which became the hub for his evangelical mission to the Picts and a powerful centre of monasticism. The *Vita Columbae* tells of the saint coming across a group of Picts burying a man who had been killed by a monster while swimming in the River Ness. St Columba admonished the monster, which fled, a feat so impressive that the group converted there and then.

For the Anglo Saxon audience who listened to the poem *Beowulf*, water was not simply an element to be fished or navigated but itself suffused with meaning, populated by grim and voracious beings like the nine monsters that drag the hero to the bottom of the sea. In the poem's second episode of supernatural swimming, Beowulf confronts the mother of Grendel the sea monster, who has been conducting murderous raids upon the Danes and dragging victims down to her lair at the bottom of a dark lake:

> He dived into the Mere – he did not care
> to wait for an answer – and the waves closed over
> the daring man. It was a day's space almost
> before he could glimpse ground at the bottom.
> The grim and greedy guardian of the flood
> keeping her hungry hundred-season watch
> discovered at once that one from above,
> a human, had sounded the home of the monsters.
> She felt for the man and fastened upon him
> her terrible hooks. But no harm came thereby
> to the hale body within -– the harness so ringed him
> that she could not drive her dire fingers through the
> mesh of the mail shirt masking his limbs.

The Scandinavian culture that forms the background to Beowulf was particularly influential on Orkney and Shetland, both under Norwegian rule from the 8th to the mid 15th century. Vestiges of Norwegian mythology are still perceptible in the vibrant folklore of the islands. While some legends concern earth creatures, such as the *trows* or trolls, the constant and powerful impact of the sea on the islander psyche can be traced in stories that depict monstrous beings associated with water. Echoes of Beowulf's enemy Grendel and his mother can be discerned in the legend of the Orcadian *Stoor Worm*, a primordial monster that devours maidens, crunches up towns and dwellings and blights every living thing. Other sea monsters with Scandinavian origins include the *Brigdi*, a finned beast that feeds on boats. The *Sifan* is bright green, one hundred and fifty feet long, with three humps and covered in barnacles as big as herring barrels. The *Nuckaleeve*, a creature given to blighting crops, has a massive head, a single red eye, raw skin with yellow veins and a venomous stink. Folk tales of these monsters per-sisted in Orkney through the nineteenth century and into recent history.

While the folk lore of Orkney and Shetland abounds in watery monsters, there is also a rich proliferation of leg-ends concerning magical beings associated with water elsewhere in the British Isles, which may provide some in-sight into pre-Christian belief systems. These include the ferocious water-bulls that preyed on the coastal fields of the Isle of Man, the sinister *kelpies* or water horses that emerged from lakes in Scotland and Ireland, and the mysterious *Blue Men of the Minch*, who inhabited the stretch of water between the Outer Hebrides and the Scottish mainland. These blue-skinned people posed a threat to sailors who could only save themselves from being dragged underwater by reciting a poem or a riddle.

These myths and legends had their origins in an oral tradition and were never written down in their pure form. So our understanding has to be pieced together from the interpretation of later (Christian) scribes and the bewildered descriptions given by the Romans. Celtic culture was governed by a kaleidoscopic supernatural world, inhabited by an enormous number of ever-changing deities that could take on different animal forms according to the needs of the moment, and regulated by magical spells and curses. Complex rituals were developed to assuage these unpredictable beings. The Romans attempted to establish parallels between the multiple, shifting, native deities and their own more stable godheads, but failed. The Celtic pantheon had little in common with the Roman world view.

It seems likely that the Celts invested water with the power to bestow, or take away, life, health and energy. A number of water-deities were associated with rivers, lakes, pools and wells and many of these were evil in nature, preying on unwary passers-by, causing storms and spreading sickness and death. Such ideas persisted in folk tales that were still current in the 19th century. Some water gods demanded sacrifices of animals and humans. The ritual sacrifice of cattle appeased the deity that ruled over Loch Ness, and Loch Wan in Aberdeen was said to take the first lamb born from the flock that grazed on its banks. The River Dee was the home of the war goddess Aerfen, who needed three human sacrifices each year, a demand so powerful that it was said to precipitate a compulsion to suicide in those who walked nearby. Other great British rivers such as the Dart, the Tay, the Wye, the Ribble and the Trent were also said to demand their own human sacrifice. In certain wind conditions at Huccaby Bridge a wailing cry and fearful shriek could be heard, which were said to be the sound of the Dart claiming a new victim. Sometimes there were physical manifestations of the water's malevolent force, as with the demonic *glastig* – half woman half goat – that was said to live

behind waterfalls in Scotland. The Welsh equivalent – *The Torrent Spectre* – was described by folklorist Elias Owen:

This was an old man, or malignant spirit, who directed and ruled over mountain torrents. He delighted in devastating the lands. His appearance was horrible to behold. He would raise himself half out of the water and ascend like a mist half as high as the near mountain, then dwindle down to the size of a man.

Another evil creature with ancient origins, *Jenny Greentooth* was said to inhabit stagnant pools and ponds in Lancashire, Cheshire and Shropshire. She would rise up and pull children into the water. Frightening stories often had practical functions. Jenny Greentooth probably refers to the duckweed that blankets still water and can entangle the limbs, leading to drowning.

Not all water spirits were malevolent. Some rivers and pools were linked with beings that would protect you from harm and help you achieve your heart's desire. It is still said that if you take a dip in the Fairy Pools, a magical spot on the Isle of Skye beneath the Cuillin mountains, your ailments will be cured and the wish you make while bathing will come true.

Bathing in The Fairy Pools, Skye © Martin Parr/ Magnum.

But the sea, too, was regarded as having healing properties. Well before medical advances made sea-bathing fashionable and the railways made it accessible for industrial city dwellers, country people were turning to the sea for relief from fatigue and illness. Healing rituals, in which diseased people and beasts were dipped in sea water, were documented by Sir John Floyer and others. In the early nineteenth century, prophylactic sea-bathing on a mass scale was recorded in Lancashire: every August, cartloads of artisans and country people would migrate to the coast to bathe naked in the spring tide and to drink sea water for the purposes of healing and purification. In 1825, well before the advent of the railway, Blackpool and Lytham were inundated by these rude and rustic visitors, known as *Padjamers*, who bathed, feasted, drank, cavorted, slept and then disappeared as quickly as they had come. The origins of such ritualistic bathing in spring and neap tides in conjunction with different phases of the moon are unknown, but are possibly pre-Christian.

In his *Description of the Western Islands of Scotland* (1703) minister Martin Martin described a sacrificial ritual that he had observed on the Isle of Lewis:

The inhabitants of this island had an ancient custom to sacrifice to a sea god call'd Shony at Hallow Tide. They came to the church of St Mulvay having each man his provision with him; every family furnished a peck of malt and this was brewed into ale. One of their number was picked out to wade into the sea up to the middle and cried out with a loud voice saying: 'Shony, I give you this cup of ale, hoping you will be so kind as to send us plenty of sea ware (sea weed) for enriching our ground the ensuing year.' And so threw the ale into the sea. This was performed at night time. At his return to the land they all went to the church where there was a candle burning upon the altar. One of them gave a signal and all of them went to the fields and fell to drinking, dancing &c. The ministers of Lewis told me they spent several years before they could persuade the vulgar natives to abandon this ridiculous piece of superstition.

Perhaps St Cuthbert, Bishop of Lindisfarne ten centuries before Martin's experience, was attempting to assuage the pagan sea-god, in an episode described by Bede:

He left the monastery, went down to the sea, which flows beneath, and going into it, until the water reached his neck and arms, spent the night in praising God. When the dawn of day approached, he came out of the water, and, falling on his knees, began to pray again. Whilst he was doing this, two quadrupeds, called otters, came up from the sea, and, lying down before him on the sand, breathed upon his feet, and wiped them with their hair after which, having received his blessing, they returned to their native element. Cuthbert himself returned home in time to join in the accustomed hymns with the other brethren.

The longevity of pagan water gods and deities may partly explain the ambivalence of early British Christians towards water. They may also have been reacting adversely to the hedonism and loose morality associated with Roman-British bathhouses. Whatever the reason, it is known that some early British saints and hermits never washed and that dirt denoted holiness. Saint Godric, for example, walked from England to Jerusalem without washing or changing his clothes and wore a louse-ridden hair shirt in his hermitage near Durham.

Wells and springs seemed to inspire the most intense and sustained forms of reverence amongst the Celts, perhaps because they were seen as a portal into the underworld and the source of life itself. Native rites and rituals evolved with and adapted to the different cultures that settled in Britain. The resident water deities and rituals of worship at wells and springs were slowly integrated with Roman gods and practices. For example, the spring overseen by a triadic Celtic goddess associated with childbirth and healing was incorporated into a shrine to Coventina, found on Hadrian's Wall.

Despite the vigorous efforts of clergy, long standing rituals and customs proved difficult to eradicate and they were gradually absorbed into and integrated with Christian beliefs and practices: ancient sacred springs and wells became *holy* sites where baptisms and healings would take place. Hybrid forms of water worship persisted well into the twentieth century. An important aspect of Celtic faith was the cult of the head, often associated with sacred pools and springs. Celtic warriors venerated the head, decorated skulls with gold and used them as receptacles for offerings to the gods. Within living memory, water from a holy well in Pembrokeshire was known as a cure for whooping cough, as long as it was drunk from a skull (said to be the skull of Saint Teilo).

Celtic and Roman water deity at Coventina's shrine, Hadrian's Wall.

Offerings and ribbons at Saint Nectan's Glen, Cornwall © Martin Parr/Magnum.

Another example of pre-Christian practices concerning wells surviving into the recent past can be found at the Well of the Holy Women, near Teelin in Donegal. Three women grew up near the well and became nuns, whose blessing was sought by fishermen heading out to sea. This group of women seems to be a Christianised version of the gods worshipped by the Celts, which often took triadic forms.

The presence of fish at some Christian holy wells offers another link to the pre-Christian world. Sacred fish were kept at a number of wells. Trout and salmon were sacred to the Celts and may have represented gods of the under-world. A trout with a gold chain around its neck lived in the Golden Well at Peterchurch in Worcester, and it is shown in a painting hanging in the parish church. St Neot's Well in Cornwall contained three fish and at Ffynnon Beris in Gwynedd the appearance or non appearance of fish in the well could be used to predict the future.

In his *Popular Antiquities*, Brand documents the ancient practice of seeking healing at the sacred wells and fountains, bathing in or drinking the water and leaving behind money, bits of rag and other tokens of thanks to the resident spirit. Sir John Floyer, writing in 1701, described how the rise of Puritanism caused the practice of bathing in holy wells to go somewhat into decline:

Immersion was generally practised by the ancients and it continued in use until the beginning of the last age. It is very probable that the change of religious opinions had no small influence in the use of Cold baths; for anciently the virtues of the holy wells were imputed to some saint, which the last age did not credit and therefore rejected the use of Cold Baths with the opinion of the Virtue of the saint, after which came the disuse of the Baptismal immersion also.

When today's tourists drop a penny into a wishing well they are probably unaware that their action links back to the ancient practice of leaving an offering to assuage or thank the spirit of the well. Offerings could include pins, money, rags tied to trees, pine cones, corks, pebbles, keys, food, flowers, religious effigies, crutches and even animal sacrifices. Yet again, the Christian church was pragmatic in appropriating the tradition: collection boxes can be seen near many holy wells today. Some sacred sites, such as St Nectan's Glen near Tintagel still inspire visitors to leave offerings and tokens. Twigs and branches around the

Mary Sutton, a suspected witch, being 'swum' in 1612.

holy pool are festooned with ribbons, coins are pressed into the bark of nearby trees, and people leave photographs of loved ones who are sick or who have died, together with messages and blessings scratched on to slate.

While many wells had the power to heal and foretell the future, others had more malign powers. They were known as *cursing wells*. Excavations at Aquae Sulis revealed around 40 curses inscribed on lead sheets near the sacred warm spring:

May he who carried off Vilbia from me become as liquid as water.

Most rituals began at sunrise often on a particular day, which then became a saint's day once the Christians had appropriated the wells. Documented rituals include walking sunwise or clockwise round the well, either three, seven or nine times, drinking the water, praying, bathing parts of the body, leaving an offering and perhaps walking around adjacent stones, buildings and trees. Anticlockwise perambulation was considered unlucky or even evil.

Early in the seventeenth century, an old woman living alone in Kircudbrightshire was accused of witchcraft because she had walked the wrong way round a well. She was convicted and punished by being rolled down hill in a blazing tar barrel. This episode suggests the sinister power of water, a power that was exercised in the witch-hunts that flourished in Britain in the 16th and 17th centuries. People – usually women – thought to be witches were often tried by being thrown into water, an ordeal called *swimming*.

The custom of trial by water or *indicium aquae* was first formally recorded during the rule of King Athelstan (928-930) although it probably has pre-Christian roots. For Christians, water had sacred power and as well as being used in baptism it could reveal and repel servants of the devil. James I legitimised the practice of swimming suspected witches by stating in *Daemonologie* (1597) that *God hath appointed that the water shall refuse to receive them in her bosome, that have shaken off the sacred water of Baptism and wilfully refused the benefit thereof.* The suspect had her right thumb tied to her left big toe and vice versa, then was secured by ropes and thrown into a deep river or pond three times. If she sank below the surface, she was innocent. If she floated, she was guilty, fished out and put to death. The last execution of a witch in England took place in 1685 although there are accounts of suspects being swum in rural areas as late as 1864.

Other than their reaction to water, witches could also be identified by a number of other features, for example the inability to shed tears, or having a teat in the armpit or groin from which an imp could suckle milk or blood. Another sign of witchery was association with animals as familiars, and some witches reputedly had the power to transform themselves into a hare or a cat. This power has resonances with the shape-shifting abilities of Celtic deities

One of the first accounts of shape-shifting can be found in the Irish *Book of Invasions*, a set of fantastical stories written down by medieval Christian monks but referring back to the belief structures of the Celts and even the pre-Celts. One of the key protagonists is Fintan, who is said to have established the five great provinces of Ireland. He survived the Great Flood by changing himself at will to fish, falcon or eagle. A fragment from *The Song of Amheirigin*, said to originate in oral traditions from around 1000 BC, shows how moving between human, animal and inanimate forms was embedded in the earliest culture:

> *I am a stag of seven tines*
> *I am a flood across a plain*
> *I am a wind on a deep lake*
> *I am a tear the sun lets fall*
> *I am a hawk above the cliff*
> *I am a thorn beneath the nail*
> *I am a wonder among the flowers*
> *I am a spear that rears for blood*
> *I am a salmon in a pool*
> *I am a lure from paradise*
> *I am a hill where poets walk*
> *I am a boar ruthless and red*
> *I am a breaker threatening doom*
> *I am a tide that drags to death…*

More shape-shifting occurs in the *Mabinogion*, when a baby boy is born: *There and then, as soon as he was baptised he made for the sea. As soon as he came to the sea he received the sea's nature and swam as well as the best fish in the sea. And for that reason he was called Dylan Eil Ton – Sea Son of Wave.*

Some beings in early British culture did not shape shift, but combined two forms in one. The mermaid has become familiar to us thanks to fairy tales and Disneyfication: half woman, half fish, she can survive in both water and air. Such an ambiguous creature was celebrated by the Romans in the form of the merman Triton, a sea god who could calm or whip up the sea by blowing on his conch-shell. A beautiful mosaic showing a bi-tailed

merman can be seen on the floor of Brading Villa on the Isle of Wight.

Once again, the image of the mermaid was appropriated by early Christians, who judged her habit of looking in a mirror to be a symbol of temptation and vanity. Some suggest a more elevated significance: the mermaid symbolises Christ's dual identity – half human half god – and is therefore a profoundly holy image. However they were interpreted, mermaids were undoubtedly an important symbol within Christian culture. Images of mermaids can be found in numerous medieval ecclesiastical buildings (for example carved on a wooden chair in Zennor parish church in Cornwall and on the misericords in Bristol Cathedral).

Brand writes of an invasion of mer-people on the Isle of Man during the rule of Oliver Cromwell, putting this down to the fact that so few ships took to the sea at that time and the mermaids could come to shore and sit combing their hair, undisturbed. Mermaids were not just sea-creatures; several legends had them populating rivers and deep inland pools. One was said to appear at Mermaid's Pool below Kinder Downfall in Derbyshire every Easter eve. Black Mere, near Leek in Staffordshire was also thought to have a mermaid in residence.

Mer-people have ancient origins. In early Irish and Scottish stories, a fisherman meets a mermaid and steals her salmon skin cap. The mermaid marries the fisherman and they have children together, then she finds her cap one day and returns to the waves. The children of these mermaids have particular characteristics such as red hair,

Triton mosaic, Brading Roman Villa, Isle of Wight.

Mermaid, Zennor parish church, Cornwall © Martin Parr/Magnum.

a talent for fishing, and difficulty sleeping or speaking.

This tale has clear parallels with the legend of the *selkies*, or seal people, which is still commonly told around the northern and western coasts of Scotland and Ireland. The story goes like this: A man is walking along a beach and comes across a beautiful maiden dancing on the sand. She is a seal woman who has removed her skin and taken human form. The man sees the soft grey skin lying on a rock, steals it and hides it in his barn. The maiden marries him and bears him children. The marriage is a happy one, although the wife constantly pines for the cool sea. One of her children finds the soft grey skin and shows it to her. She puts it on and returns to the sea, bidding farewell to her husband and children and telling them to watch for her in a certain place at a certain time each day and she will make sure they have enough fresh fish to eat.

It is said that the selkie children have particularly seal-like qualities: round faces, big eyes, leathery skin on their hands and webbed fingers. Some even smell of fish. It is still the case in some north western coastal communities that people are regarded as being *'from the selkie'*.

Other stories tell of seals repaying acts of kindness, such as sparing their pups from slaughter, with dramatic rescues. The benevolent selkies form a sharp contrast with the scary Orcadian *Finfolk*. These are creatures that live during the winter in a fantastic palace beneath the sea (Finfolkaheem) and on a beautiful island (Hildaland) in the summer. This island only appears occasionally to human eyes and has rich cornfields, white horses and lush pastures.

Finfolk probably have roots in Norse mythology. They share a common trait with hill folk and trows: they like kidnapping mortals and getting hold of their silver. The Finman appears to humans as a dark-featured man wearing long draped clothing to hide his fins hanging down. He has magical powers that are reminiscent of Beowulf's superhuman abilities. For example, he can row from Orkney to Norway with only seven strokes of the oar.

As a child of the Finfolk, the Finwife is said to begin her life as a mermaid – always beautiful with a long, glistening fish tail. If lucky enough to find a human husband, she loses her tail and becomes a lovely woman. If, however, the young mermaid marries a Finman – a fate that awaits her if she cannot find a human mate – she is doomed to become increasingly ugly, eventually turning into a haggard Finwife. The Finwife is often sent to shore to earn precious silver for her husband. Once settled on land, she will earn a living by spinning and knitting, but also using witch-like skills, for example curing sick men and cattle. She is said to keep a black cat that has the ability to change into a fish so it can carry messages between its mistress and her relatives in Finfolkaheem.

The legend of the Finfolk may seem ancient, but there is evidence that it still has a place in the modern Orcadian mindset. On July 14th, 1990, a ferry commissioned by the Orkney Heritage Society and the Royal Society for the Protection of Birds, landed a number of passengers on the uninhabited island of Eynhallow for a day visit. When the boat reached the island, eighty-eight visitors were counted off. At the end of the day, only eighty six returned. This sparked off a massive air and sea search. Local police scoured the area. A helicopter with heat-sensing equipment was dispatched by the Shetland Coastguard, but nothing was found.

Oddly, no-one was reported missing. No-one knew who the two missing passengers were. The island of Eynhallow was once thought to be Hildaland, the ancestral summer home of the Finfolk. Following the incident, rumours

Mermaid scarecrow, Sanday, Orkney © Martin Parr/Magnum.

started to circulate that the two missing passengers were Finfolk returning to their summer home. Or they may have perhaps been stolen away by the sea dwellers, on the prowl for human partners. The mystery was never solved.

Orkney, August

The sky is huge. The islands, mostly flat and treeless, look like low cloud on the horizon, each one a narrow grey brushstroke that briefly widens then tapers back down to the sea. When the sun manages to break through, brief patches of startling green suggest the richness of the pastureland.

I have been reading about the selkies and am looking forward to swimming here, because seals are plentiful. When I find an isolated sandy beach at the Ayre of Myers on Stronsay, sheltered from the wind, with clear turquoise water lapping at the stones, I sit down to wait. Sure enough within a few minutes a head emerges from the water. It is a grey seal (you can tell this by the elongated snout) and it seems curious. It looks around for a while, then dives and emerges even closer to shore, so close I can see its thick whiskers and hear its snuffling, sighing breath. I get up and start to change into my swimsuit, which is grey and soft, and the seal moves further out, still watching. I'm not alarmed, as the creature seems gentle and shy, so I walk calmly into the water and bathe. The seal disappears.

Next day, I take the ferry through the rain to Sanday, an island lying fifteen miles north of the Orkney mainland. It is the day of the agricultural show and the Sanday farmers are eyeing up each others' sheep, goats, poultry and cattle. One man carefully washes the splattered rump of a bullock and slowly combs its tail in preparation for the show ring. The show is a serious business. People here seem reserved, industrious, not much inclined to chatter or fun.

This makes it all the more startling to come across the scarecrow competition, put on as part of Sanday's summer festivities. There are scarecrows everywhere across the island. Scarecrows are busy at work in potato patches, leaning against tumbling stone walls, peering at passers

by. I see two scarecrows fishing in a garden pond, another crouched over the handlebars of a bicycle that is propped against a wall. One, wearing sunglasses and brandishing a cocktail glass relaxes in an easy chair by the roadside and another sits astride a motorbike, its helmeted head lowered, giving the impression it is travelling at great speed. Outside the Post Office, a woman scarecrow is poised in the act of posting a letter. And by a bleak, isolated farm, a mother scarecrow with long straw hair pushes a baby scarecrow in a buggy and waves at by-passers, her raised hand buffeted by the wind.

The morning's rain has given way to a thick white sea fog that covers everything and makes it hard to tell where the fields end and the sea begins. I want to find Otters Wick beach on the Bay of Lopness, a place renowned for seals, and to swim there if possible. I drive slowly, struggling to follow the map and feeling unnerved as the road just ahead disappears into whiteness. I get to the end of the road and park. Just there, lashed to a fence post with blue fishing net, stands a mermaid scarecrow. Her head and upper body are made of plastic shopping bags, stuffed and painted pink. Her tail is of grey, sequinned material. Her hair is made of yellow wool, her eyes and lips of felt, her ears of mussel shells. A sheet of paper in a plastic cover is fixed to her tail. It tells the story of the Finfolk.

The fog is thickening, despite the wind. Surprisingly for such an isolated beach and such vile weather, I can just make out a figure, wearing a long coat, walking away along the curve of water in the distance.

The sand is smooth and creamy as paper, and seaweed loops like fine handwriting on its surface. The sea roars and breakers push against an outcrop of large stones. A cream boulder moves and I realise it is a young, fat seal that has turned its head to watch me. The walking figure has disappeared into the fog. I wonder about the safety of bathing here. There is a place where the water is protected from the wind and is fairly calm, and the rising tide means I would have just enough depth. I could swim. But thinking about the Finwoman scarecrow, the watching seal and the dark, disappearing figure, I wrap my costume in my towel and walk back to the car.

The match for every disorder: sea bathing for health

And all, impatient of dry land, agree
With one consent to rush into the sea.
William Cowper

Scarborough, August Bank Holiday, 2009, 11.30 am. A cool, cloudy day. The sun is faintly visible behind pale cloud that spreads across the sky to the horizon. I sit in front of the Pump Room and look back across the wide, flat beach to where the sea slowly creeps up the sand with the rising tide. The sand gleams in the pale light. Here and there, the creamy expanse is dotted with family groups. A father and two boys play cricket with pink plastic bat, ball and wickets.

By the dark green sea wall two women, perhaps mother and daughter, are sitting on deckchairs, a picnic basket at their feet. The younger is engrossed in a newspaper. The other has a plaid blanket covering her knees and tucked up under her chin. Her head to one side, she watches a little girl who is rhythmically throwing a yellow beach ball against the wall, almost in slow motion, catching it as it bounces back, then throwing it again.

A little way away is the only person on the beach that I can see who is in swimwear: a boy of about 12, plump and fair, in red sandy trunks that flap damply round his legs. He uses his spade meticulously and is busily constructing an elaborate edifice edged with moats and criss-crossed with inlets and channels. He works by himself, absorbed and concentrated as the water trickles towards him. He seems oblivious to the cold but the breeze has an edge to it that makes me glad of my coat. A family walks along the beach: two boys, both in red and white strip, are arguing and tussling over a football. Their father walks silently along behind them, bearing a coolbag. He tugs the zip on his fleece, pulling the two syllables 'Eng' and 'land' together across his chest. The boys' mother talks into a mobile phone and carries a plastic bag full of fluorescent pink candy floss.

I make up my mind: this is the time. I walk down to the beach, towards the rising water, which looks uninvitingly brown and almost menacing as it creeps upwards, sliding and trickling across the sand. I find a flat rock where my clothes will be dry. I start to change, shivering as I pull off my coat. Nearby, a young family is encamped on a waterproof-backed tartan rug on the sand. The toddler clumsily wields a small plastic spade, pats sand into a bucket, half empties it then fills it again. The mother lies on her back on the blanket, dead asleep, her arms thrown back across her face, her mouth open. The father, with green waxed jacket zipped up and green waxed hat pulled firmly down, lies on his side with his head propped on his hand. He's

Beach scene, Scarborough, August Bank Holiday © Martin Parr/Magnum.

watching the child but also seems to be keeping an amused eye on me as I struggle into my costume under the flapping towel.

Just at the water's edge two children dressed in wetsuits, collect buckets of seawater to fill a channel running up to a crudely built barrier of sand. Occasionally they lie down on the sand and shriek as the waves gently roll over them. Their mother stands close by, silent and immobile, lilac trousers rolled above her pale knees, white legs, bare feet, arms folded, cardigan buttoned, lost in thought, watching.

I walk into the sea. It's not dirty, just sandy. I move in, and make tentative progress into deeper water. I can't see my feet, so slide them cautiously forward, mindful of flatfish and weaverfish. A soft drift of weed. The edge of a stone. A creature, perhaps a tiny crab, scurries over my foot. I keep going. The water edges up my calves, over my knees, up my thighs, to my waist. It feels warm in comparison with the air, so I bend forward to get out of the breeze which then provokes tiny teasing waves to splash into my face. At last I am floating and can move out of my depth. Further out in the bay, a speed boat crammed with people cuts through the grey, trailing laughter and shrieks.

I swim out. The water is a deep bottle green now, and clearer. It feels cold. I float for a bit and turn round to look up at the elegant façade of the spa building with its glassed enclosure, where the last resident seaside orchestra in England – a five-piece – still plays. I can see the elaborate Valley Bridge that runs across the river gorge, the green domes of the Grand Hotel, and the cliff lifts linking the beaches with the upper town. The aristocratic Georgian terraces contrast with the semi-circle of cheery wooden beach huts with red tiled roofs and verandas, that sit near the remains of the great South Bay seawater pool.

It's extraordinary to think that, four hundred years ago, Scarborough was an undistinguished town that was about to be transformed by bathing. This is where the vogue for sea-bathing began, and yet in 2009, in August, at the height of the summer season, at mid-day, I am the only person in the water.

* * * * *

By the middle of the twelfth century Scarborough was well established as a port and trading centre selling fish – mostly herring – metal, salt, pottery, and goods imported from the Low Countries. Scarborough-built vessels carried butter and linen, imported timber, tow and tar and later transported coal from the Durham and Northumberland fields along the coast of the UK and out across the North Sea to the Russian and Baltic states. But the town's early prosperity fluctuated, affected by wars, rebellions and epidemics, particularly the Black Death. During the seventeenth century, nearby Hull was growing in importance as a port, managing increased trade on the back of the agricultural and industrial developments in Yorkshire and the East Midlands. As Hull grew and prospered, Scarborough started to decline. But, in the middle of the seventeenth century, the town's luck suddenly changed.

In 1626, a source of mineral-rich water was discovered at the base of the cliffs overlooking the expanse of sand south of the harbour. The water's healing properties soon attracted local invalids and the wealthy infirm from further afield. Under the cliffs, a basic spa house was erected, providing shelter and rudimentary facilities. Here, Dicky Dickinson, the Governor of the *Spaw* extracted funds and supervised the health-seekers as they sipped the healing liquid from drinking horns. In 1637, Dr Robert Wittie, a physician from Hull, tried the waters of the Scarborough springs for himself and then took samples of the water to analyse in his laboratory, where he found traces of vitriol, nitre, alum, salt, and iron. *Scarborough water*, he declared, *cleanses the stomach, opens the lungs, cures asthma and scurvy, purifies the blood, cures jaunders both yellow and black and the leprosie and is a most sovereign remedy against Hypochondriack Melancholly and Windiness.*

Dr Wittie recommended drinking five to eight pints of spa water, early in the morning, followed by exercise on the sands. Taking the waters would be most advisable during the period from May to September, as there would be less chance of proceedings being disrupted by stormy or inclement weather. One day, perhaps as he was gazing out over Scarborough's sandy waters rising across the fine beach towards the spa house, Wittie made a conceptual leap. The idea he came up with was to have an extraordinary impact. It would transform the relationship between man and sea, sow the seeds of a massive industry and change the fortunes of Britain's coastal town and villages.

If mineral-rich water had such healing properties, why shouldn't sea water, arguably the most mineral-laden of all, offer even more health benefits?

Dr Wittie didn't stop at the idea of drinking sea water. Reflecting on the success of inland spas such as Bath and Harrogate, where people bathed in mineral-rich water as well as ingesting it, he suggested that immersion in sea water could promote health and wellbeing. Bathing in and drinking sea water – followed by vigorous exercise – were declared to be excellent remedies for the gout, headaches, tumours and numerous other physical and mental ailments.

Wittie's ideas were in tune with contemporary advances in scientific and medical thinking. He might have speculated that benefits from bathing in seawater would not derive simply from the high mineral content but from *the cold*. The most eminent advocate of cold bathing, Sir John Floyer (1649-1734), a Lichfield-based physician who was said to have attended the royal family, wrote a number of medical and theological texts on the subject, the most comprehensive of which was his *Psychrolousia or History of Cold Bathing Both Ancient and Modern*, published in 1715. He followed this in 1722 with *An Essay to Restore the Dipping of Infants in their Baptism*.

Like Newton and Locke, Floyer was a child of the Scientific Revolution and himself contributed to advances in empirical thinking and experimental methods in science and medicine. He was the first physician to time the pulse accurately. In true empirical style, he observed and documented his own ailments, most notably his asthma, and tried out remedies and treatments before prescribing them for his patients.

Despite being at the cutting edge of some aspects of the new medicine, Floyer adhered to Galen's theory that human physiology comprised four *humours* or bodily fluids (blood, phlegm, black bile and yellow bile). Sickness and infirmity, both physical and mental, were considered to be caused by imbalance of the humours, or by an insufficiency of one of them. Health could be restored by bleeding the patient, by administering emetic or laxative medications, derived from herbs and plants, and, in his view, by immersion or bathing the affected part in cold water.

Floyer's scientific enquires extended to documenting historical and traditional health remedies and practices.

A true scientist, he studied and catalogued medicinal plants that were used in local folk remedies. He also travelled round the country visiting springs and wells, watching closely how they were used by local people. Floyer commented that the Civil War had caused the neglect of natural springs and wells because of their associations with saints, resulting in the occurrence of many diseases that would otherwise have been prevented. Nevertheless, he found much evidence of their continued use:

They go into the water in their shirts, and when they come out, they dress themselves in their wet linen, which they wear all day, and much commend that for closing the pores and keeping themselves cool; and that they do not commonly receive any injury or catch any cold thereby, I am fully convinced from the experiments I have seen made of it.

An Enquiry into the Right Use and Abuses of the Hot, Cold and Temperate Baths in England (first published in 1697) pioneered the practice of hydrotherapy. And, in his history of cold bathing, Floyer drew on the work of physicians of the ancient world, as well as contemporary scholars and practitioners. His treatise was addressed to the Royal College of Physicians in London and represented an attempt to provide convincing evidence of a scientific basis for the curative powers of cold water. The treatise comprises numerous descriptions of miraculous cures that Floyer had either witnessed with his own eyes or heard about, together with accounts written by fellow physicians and testimonials from patients restored to health thanks to bathing in cold water.

Extracts from the history give an insight into the lives and struggles of ordinary people who became ill and sought medical treatment at the beginning of the 18th century:

The case of Mrs Wats of Leicester is most remarkable who from a Skeleton from an ill habit, decayed Stomach, Hysterick &c and so tender that she could not bear the Wind to blow upon her; by the use of cold Immersion she is become Strong, Vigorous and Healthful. And I am told that she is hardened to that degree that she walks anywhere in the Weather without wrapping or catching Cold.

I was formerly much troubled by a sort of little flat Worms that I should often void in my Excrement; but on certain time going to Swim in a very cold deep pond that was fed by many Springs when I came out I found in my Stool a great cluster of the Worms and from that time was never more troubled with them. I only tell you this as the Fact. The Philosophy I must leave to you and your Brethren to determine the why and how this Cure was wrought. So expecting your advice by the next Post I am, dear Sir, your humble servant, Jo. Eldred.

And here note I have observed in several persons afflicted with old inveterate Pains of the Stomach, when neither Bitters, Aromaticks, Burnt Wine or Strong Waters nor anodyns as Opium &c nor external Applications such as Sponges, Fomentation, Embrocations &c has all failed, Cold water by continual application to the part, for an hour or two, has not only given ease but made a compleat and perfect Cure.

Floyer's book provides abundant evidence that application of, or immersion in, cold water from wells, springs, pools and rivers played an important part in the folk medicine of his time. Interestingly, sea water is barely mentioned, other than as a cure for drunken sailors. The drunk is thrown into the sea, *which excites their stupid senses and makes them very sober.* However, Floyer makes a case for using seawater *since we live on an Island and have the Sea about us we cannot want an excellent Cold Bath*, backing this up with a dramatic story related by Mr Edward Boswell:

I being on board the Elizabeth, a merchant man in the year 93 I had got a terrible Ague which held me about five weeks. We lay at anchor in Torbay and had extream bad weather, insomuch that I was perpetually wet, during the storm, the ship being very leaky and I forcd to be on deck. It was extream frosty weather and sharp hard gales of wind, our ship was forcd on shoar on the rocks, beating herself to pieces. I was resolved to commit myself to the seas and the mercies of almighty God and being a pretty good swimmer I leapt overboard, being weak and feeble I could not reach the shore and my strength being gone I resignd myself up for another world. But being

near the Shoar a Black leap'd in and caught hold of me and pluckd me out. I was speechless. The people got me into a house and laid me in Bed and the next day I was as well as ever I was in my life. In a few days I set forwards towards London having nothing but a thin Waist Coat and Calamanco breeches. So I travelled 80 miles in the Snow without either Shoes or stockings. But not withstanding these severe hardships, I never catch'd Cold.

Although a less renowned scientist than Floyer, Wittie proved a remarkably effective businessman and made a convincing case for the health-promoting properties of immersion in sea water. This seemed to him a natural extension of the exercise on the sands recommended for those taking the waters. He suggested that men should dip for five minutes daily before breakfast. Invalids, women and children were advised to take dips of two minutes' duration, three hours after breakfast, three times a week. Imbibing sea water, with its purging and emetic effects, would cleanse the body, rebalance the humours and restore health.

Wittie's ideas had an almost miraculous impact on Scarborough's wavering reputation and fortunes. The town's fortuitous combination of desirable features – a mineral spring and a wide flat sandy beach, ideal for exercise, gradually shelving into sea water – made it very attractive to wealthy invalids, who could afford to stay for a few weeks during the summer months. Attitudes towards the sea were transformed. Previously viewed as inhospitable and threatening, the sea and the sea-shore became places that invited recreation and the pursuit of well being. As early as 1662, Sir John Reresby was noting that *many people of quality came that Summer for their health or diversion*. By the summer of 1733 over 1,000 visitors were recorded at Scarborough, many of them members of the northern aristocracy.

Pleasure certainly seems much in evidence in John Setterington's print of Scarborough in 1725, which is kept in the town's public library. The print shows the castle walls above the built-up harbour area and the sea thick with sailing ships. At some distance south of this activity there is an open beach landscape, backed by cliffs. The spa building sits at the foot of the cliffs, looking out across the sweep of South Bay. The sands are dotted with men and women, some on horseback, some walking, some being carried from the sea to the spa building in sedan chairs. A little way out from the shore there are some

Sea-bathing at Scarborough by John Setterington (1725).

rowing boats with partially covered areas from which men are diving. Other figures can be seen frolicking in the waves. At the water's edge there is a kind of tent on a wheeled framework from which a figure emerges and moves towards the water.

This looks like a prototype bathing machine, a device that offered bathers both protection from the elements and a degree of modesty as they prepared for their dip. Bathers entered the machine to remove their clothing, while the machine was pulled down into the water by horses. Later

bathing machines were equipped with *modesty hoods*, a kind of tunnel of cloth on an extending framework that could be pulled down to the water over the ladder and ensure the bather remained unseen.

Bearing in mind the fact that not everyone could swim and many were both fearful of the sea and shocked by the cold, bathers often required assistance from a *dipper*. Dippers were usually women, dressed in rough flannel, who would help bathers into the water then push them under the surface, while keeping a firm grip to ensure

they did not drown. Occasionally, dippers were required to effect a rescue as when, some decades later, the Prince Regent nearly succumbed to a heavy sea in Brighton and had to be pulled out by his dipper, Old Smoker.

In 1733, a visitor to Scarborough wrote a letter home describing the new trend: *It is the custom for not only gentlemen but the ladies also to bathe in the seas; the gentlemen go out a little way to sea in boats (called here 'cobbles') and jump in naked directly: tis usual for gentlemen to hire one of these boats and put out a little way to sea a-fishing.*

The ladies have the conveniency of gowns and guides. There are two little houses on the shore to retire for dressing in. What virtues our physicians ascribe to cold baths in general are much more effectual by the additional weight of salt in sea water: an advantage which no Spaw in England can boast of but Scarborough.

It isn't hard to see the attraction of Scarborough's open landscape, with the wide sweep of sand, the magnificent cliffs and the bracing air. Health-seekers had previously had to endure the crowds at inland spas, where increasing

Bookshop, Scarborough (1812).

numbers gathered to enjoy the benefits of drinking and bathing in warm, mineral-rich water. In *Humphrey Clinker*, through the character of Squire Bramble, Tobias Smollett vividly describes the less pleasant aspects of such close encounters:

The first object that saluted my eyes was a child, full of scrofulous ulcers, carried in the arms of one of the guides, under the very noses of the bathers. I was so shocked at the sight that I retired immediately with indignation and disgust. Suppose the matter of those ulcers, floating in the water, comes in contact with my skin, when the pores are all open. I would ask you what must be the consequence? We know not what sores may be running into the waters while we are bathing and what sort of matter we may thus imbibe: the King's evil,

the scurvy, and the cancer. No doubt the heat will render the virus more volatile and penetrating.

In prose as dense and saturated as the element he describes, Bramble speculates that the bathing water might also be drunk by the invalids, along with the *scourings of the bathers, medicated with sweat, dirt and dandruff and abominable discharges of various kinds from twenty different diseased bodies, parboiling in the kettle below.* No wonder the alternative of Scarborough, with its lively air and open vistas, seemed so attractive. Sea-bathing caught on and Scarborough attracted increasing numbers of noble visitors for the summer season, including the Duke of York, the Duke of Rutland and the Marquis of Granby, together with their families and retinues of attendants.

How did Scarborough manage to accommodate the sudden influx of fashionable and aristocratic sea water enthusiasts? The earliest visitors lodged in the houses of merchants and mariners, humble dwellings that clustered around the harbour area. Meals were sent out to lodgings, or the visitors could dine at inns, coffee houses or the spa house. But, as the fashion for sea-bathing escalated, such cramped facilities soon proved inadequate for the visitors in terms of size, comfort and elegance. Local houses had been designed to provide the maximum shelter and protection from the sea, whereas the visitors, keenly appreciative of the picturesque, wanted to gaze upon and admire it. In St Nicholas Cliff, Newborough Street and Queen Street, *superior lodgings* were built and existing dwellings adapted so that they could be rented by visitors in the summer season and used by the owners through the winter.

By 1733, the area above the Scarborough Spa had a new assembly room built to accommodate the bathers' other pursuits: dining, drinking, dancing, flirting, gambling and gossiping. Just as in the inland spas, Scarborough's bathing season saw the growth of complex social rituals, intrigues and liaisons. It was as if Bath, Matlock and Harrogate had been plucked from their inland settings and re-positioned with a sea view.

Along the scrubby cliff top, previously grazed by sheep, a genteel *upper town* developed, providing many facilities for well-heeled incomers to fill the hours after bathing with refined activity. Here there were fine houses with big windows affording splendid sea views, paved roads and walkways, coffee houses, Ward's circulating library, a bowling green, portrait painting studios, ballrooms, billiard rooms, and a playhouse. A public garden was laid out near Huntriss Row, where visitors could recover from their morning exertions with a gentle promenade.

And there were the shops. The bathers could buy whatever took their fancy, from a wig to a sedan chair. Bland's mercery, Lease's clocks, Deard's toys, Dalrymple's cottons and Thompson's hosiery awaited their custom. Seaside memorabilia – pebble and jet ornaments, pieces of coral and ornate shells – sold well. Traders capitalised on the market for fancy goods, a trend that resulted in the establishment of huge emporia such as Longbottom's in St Nicholas Cliff. Schofield's bookshop and library advertised 4,000 volumes ranging from *light summer reading to more serious works of learned and elegant writers*.

The print opposite (which is dated 1812 – five years after the Slave Trade was abolished) shows a number of elegant browsers in a Scarborough bookshop, including one older woman attended by a black servant in full livery. The imagery suggests the affluence of Scarborough's clientele.

In later years, as the prosperous middle classes flocked to Scarborough from the industrial and commercial areas of the North, the town further increased its stock of attractions providing more bookshops, a subscription newsroom, museums, and no less than three camera obscura. And as its fortunes boomed, Scarborough established a number of local industries to manufacture or supply whatever was needed to bolster the tourist infrastructure: bricks, tiles and ironwork, carriages and upholstery, ales and porters.

Scarborough's rapid development as a resort was mirrored in seaside towns across the UK, from Skegness to Tenby, Brighton to Blackpool, as sea-bathing caught on with the nobility, the rich and the fashionable. Problematic relations with France had forced many to abandon the aristocratic tradition of the European Grand Tour and seek their summer recreation closer to home. Royal bathers consolidated the trend. George III, recovering from his first attack of porphyria, tried sea-bathing and drinking sea water. Weymouth was his favourite watering hole. The town was within reasonable striking distance, by carriage, of London. Like Scarborough, Weymouth combined the attractions of natural mineral springs, a curving shoreline that was relatively protected from the worst of the elements, gentle access into sea water and fine, firm sandy beaches ideal for bathing machines and exercise.

The King's brother, the Duke of Gloucester, had already built a comfortable mansion fronting onto the sea at Weymouth, used by the king in 1789 on his first visit to the town with Queen Caroline, three of their daughters, and a large retinue of courtiers. The King bathed daily before breakfast, emerging from his bathing machine and entering the water with the aid of a dipper. An orchestra was hastily assembled on the beach and this would strike up with the national anthem as he bobbed up and down. The King was to visit Weymouth fourteen more times until 1805, when failing health confined him to London. In the years between 1789 and 1805, under such dedicated royal patronage, Weymouth flourished. Buildings and facilities sprang up and everyone seemed to take to the water, as *The Times* noted:

George III's bathing machine at Weymouth © Martin Parr/Magnum.

The Weymouth belles, following the example set by
Royal beauties
Bathe now, who never bathed before
And those who always bathed, now bathe the more.

Sea-bathing attracted property developers, investors, businessmen, builders, speculators and medical men galore to hitherto undistinguished seaside towns and hamlets. Entrepreneurs furnished the bathers with everything they needed, from bathing machines and the services of a dipper to a warming dish of chocolate. Dank seaside towns and villages, that had previously struggled to survive through fishing and trade, were rapidly transformed into centres of luxury and ostentation.

Brighton in particular, patronised by the Prince Regent from 1783 onward, capitalised on the pleasure principle. Here, the seaside was barely 50 miles from London. Brighton became a site, not so much for the pursuit of health and exercise, but for ostentatious displays of opulence and indulgence. This was epitomised in the flamboyant Pavilion, designed by the Prince Regent, whose patronage was driven more by his fleshly appetites than his quest for health. The Prince's excesses and foibles were remorselessly satirised by the cartoonists of the day.

The Prince Regent in Brighton, by George Cruikshank (1816).

Patronised at first by aristocracy and gentlefolk, who could assert and demonstrate their nobility by stepping fearlessly into the waves, and who relished their escape from the social stew of the inland spas, the seaside began to attract increasing numbers of wealthy middle classes as the eighteenth century ended. Though far from aristocratic, Jane Austen was an enthusiastic practitioner of sea-bathing. In a letter to her sister Cassandra sent from Lyme Regis, where she spent a few weeks in the summer of 1803, she wrote:

The Bathing was so delightful this morning and Molly so pressing with me to enjoy myself that I believe I staid in rather too long, as since the middle of the day I have felt unreasonably tired. I shall be more careful another time and shall not bathe tomorrow as I had before intended.

The beach was open to all comers, and, itself the most liminal of environments, was spacious enough to accommodate people from different parts of the social spectrum: people whose paths would never ordinarily cross in the course of life back home.

Indeed, all kinds of boundaries were breached by bathing. One of the by-products of the bathing phenomenon was the chance for strollers on the shore to contemplate male and female bathers in various states of undress, or even totally naked. Different customs and dress codes applied in different places. In Scarborough, as we have seen, the ladies bathed in gowns, but these, when dripping wet and clinging, or floating upward on a wave, might well have exposed more of the female form than was commonly on view. One Scarborough wag described how spectators, using their seeing glasses (telescopes) ostensibly to scrutinise the collier fleets in fact trained them steadily on *the nymphs emerging from the sea.*

Thomas Rowlandson's etching, *Venus's Bathing (Margate): A fashionable dip* (1790), suggests that, in other resorts, persistent spectators like those standing on the cliffs, might have been rewarded with glimpses of women entering the water completely unhampered by clothing.

The state of undress demanded for a dip was a potential source of embarrassment not only to female bathers. Matt Bramble tells how he was bathing at six in the morning at Scarborough. *The wind blowing from the North and the weather being so hazy, the water proved so chill* that it caused him to shout out and sob while bathing, and his servant Humphrey Clinker, thinking he was drowning or under attack, rushed into the sea to rescue him and pulled him by his ear out onto the beach where he lay without a stitch *to the astonishment of all the people, men women and children there assembled.* Bramble continues: *I have received benefit both from the chalybeate (mineral water) and the sea, and would have used them longer had not this most ridiculous adventure, by making me the town talk, obliged me to leave the place. I can't bear the thought of affording a spectacle to the multitude.*

The cold water bathing phenomenon was not just confined to the coast. Inland, entrepreneurs explored the commercial potential of river and spring water. A spring-fed pond near Old Street in London, previously used for duck hunting, was the first body of natural water to be transformed in this way. In 1743, a jeweller named William Kemp converted it into London's first outdoor public swimming bath, changing its name from Perilous Pond to The Peerless Pool. The pool was 170 feet long, 108 feet wide and between 3-5 feet deep. Its sides were built up and the bottom coated with fine gravel. Bathers changed in marble-clad dressing rooms, and descended into the water via marble steps. They were shielded from the sun and from prying eyes by trees and an arcade. In keeping with bathing resort traditions, Kemp provided a range of facilities for the entertainment of his bathing customers. These

included a canal stocked with carp and tench, a lending library and bowling green. He also offered ice skating in winter, when the weather permitted.

William Hone visited the Peerless Pool in 1826 and described a lively scene, suggesting that the bathers could be divided into two groups – those who reluctantly immersed themselves, presumably for medicinal purposes, and those for whom playing in the water was pure fun:

Trees enough remain to shade the visitor from the heat of the sun on the brink. On a summer evening it is amusing to survey the conduct of the bathers; some boldly dive, others timorous stand and then descend step by step, unwilling and slow; choice swimmers attract attention by divings and somersets, and the whole sheet of water sometimes rings with merriment. Every fine Thursday and Saturday afternoon in the summer columns of Bluecoat boys, more than a score in each, headed by their respective beadles, arrive and some half strip themselves 'ere they reach their destination. The rapid plunges they make into the Pool and their hilarity in the bath testify their enjoyment of the tepid fluid.

Not to be outdone, John Pinch designed and built the Cleveland Pools in Bath in 1814. These were filled with water diverted from the River Avon that flows nearby, and bordered on one side with an elegant semi-circular terrace comprising the bath house and dressing rooms. Cleveland Pools still stand today, the oldest swimming baths in Britain, although they are no longer open to the public.

Were these early bathers and their physicians justified in their belief that immersion in cold water can bring health benefits?

A study in Germany has found that regular winter swimmers show an adaptive response to cold water through enhanced anti-oxidative defence, as measured by several blood markers. Other research exploring the effect of regular immersion in cold water on immunity shows an increase in both the number and activity of cytotoxic lymphocytes. Full body cold water immersion and cryotherapy (entering a cold air chamber) have also been shown to result in a sustained increase in norepinephrine, which can help to relieve pain. Exposure to cold also increases metabolic rate. Cold water therapy has been shown to have potential benefits for people with chronic fatigue syndrome, some (non-lymphoid) types of cancers and chronic heart failure.

Some ladies bathed naked. *Venus's Bathing (Margate). A fashionable dip by* Thomas Rowlandson (c.1800).

Cleveland Pools, Bath © Susie Parr.

In his book *Waterlog* (1999) Roger Deakin cites – but does not reference – research undertaken by NASA scientists and by the British Heart Foundation, which suggests that regular cold bathing has some significant positive effects. Volunteers took cold baths daily for a period of twelve weeks. Their blood was tested and their heart rates and blood pressure monitored on a regular basis. In every case, blood pressure and cholesterol levels decreased and volunteers lost weight. Clotting rates were reduced and there was an increase in white cells, strengthening the immune system. Cold baths boosted the production of plasmin, which can prevent the formation of blood clots before they can cause strokes or heart attacks. Male volunteers produced more testosterone and women more oestrogen and progesterone, stimulating fertility and boosting libido. Perhaps the tale that appears in Sir John Floyer's history of cold water bathing is rooted in scientific fact:

Dr Savory told me that Fellow which he mentioned in his Letter that used to fish up to the Chin in Cold Water found that it did ad venerem stimulare &c and several of our Winter Bathers (nay even in Frost and Snow) have complained that all the injury they found by Cold Bathing was that it did 'famem ad venerem nimis augere' which made one say:

> Cold bathing has this Good alone,
> It makes Old John to hug Old Joan.
> And gives a sort of resurrection
> To buried Joys through lost erection.

And does fresh kindnesses entail
On a Wife Tasteless, Old and Stale.

Many of the regular bathers interviewed for this book comment on the health benefits brought by cold water bathing. Since she started bathing every morning before work, Martina Watts, one of the Brighton sea swimmers, feels her psoriasis has eased and her chronic fatigue syndrome is more under control. Pete Roberts of Runcorn feels that regular immersion in cold water has kept him going since the advent of congestive heart failure, ten years ago:

'I'm actually five years past my die-by date. Once a week is enough for the medical benefits, the internal changes that came with the training. I get ticked off by my doctor if I stop doing it. He says it's what's keeping me alive.'

David Sawyers, who bathes daily in the sea at Brighton, reflects on how his regular dips have helped him manage his severe and chronic arthritis and deal with the resulting depression:

'Arthritis first showed up in my toes, then it caught me in the neck and the spine. I found movement became very painful indeed and I couldn't do what I wanted. I lost myself. And it was literally in the water I managed to find myself again. There is a suggestion that the cold can dampen inflammation and I do have a greater freedom of movement in the water than on the land without irritating damaged joints. But in learning to manage my disabilities in the context of the ever changing conditions of the sea, developing that sort of responsiveness, becoming no longer frightened but at home amid the forces of the waters around me, I had regained myself. I could feel once more that I was the person I had always been and I was able to lift the depression. I'm using the sea to bolster my self esteem and also the grip I have on reality. That's why – come rain, shine, sleet or snow – I will battle my way down to the beach and get into that water.'

For David, the gains of cold water sea-bathing are both physical and psychological and far outweigh any discomfort. Swimming in 2011, he is quite in tune with the bathers of the eighteenth and nineteenth centuries.

Although she loved to bathe, Jane Austen was quick to satirise the quasi-medical propaganda of seaside speculators who were trying to persuade potential bathers that sea water was the panacea for all ills. In her final, sadly

David Sawyers emerging from the sea at Brighton © Martin Parr/Magnum.

unfinished novel, *Sanditon*, she delicately lampoons the pretensions of an enthusiastic speculator. Mr Parker is seeking to establish an undistinguished seaside village, Sanditon, on the resort map. Having invested in building a number of properties for renting out during the season, Mr Parker is keen to encourage any interest from potential visitors, particularly those who are frail or infirm:

The finest, purest sea breeze on the coast – acknowledged to be so – excellent bathing – fine hard sand – deep water ten yards from the shore – no mud – no weeds – no slimy rocks. Never was there a place more palpably designed by nature for the resort of the invalid – the very spot which thousands seemed in need of! The most desirable distance from London! The sea air and sea-bathing together were nearly infallible, one or the other of them being a match for every disorder of the stomach the lungs or the blood. They were anti-spasmodic, anti-pulmonary, anti-septic, anti-bilious and anti-rheumatic. Nobody could catch cold by the sea; nobody wanted appetite by the sea; nobody wanted spirits; nobody wanted strength. If the sea breeze failed, the sea bath was the certain corrective.

Mr Parker's eulogies about Sanditon are conveyed with such acidic precision that it makes one think that Jane Austen must have endured a number of monologues on the topic of resort development:

Sanditon was a second wife and four children to him, hardly less dear and certainly more engrossing. He could talk of it forever. It had indeed the highest claims; not only of birthplace, property and home. It was his mine, his lottery, his speculation and his hobby horse; his occupation, his hope and his futurity.

The aspirations and obsessions of commercial developers were fair game for Jane Austen. But her attention was also caught by a new trend, the Romanticism that was at the time sweeping through European philosophy, literature and art. Her own love of simple, natural beauty was probably in keeping with this movement, but, in *Sanditon*, she could not help mocking the Romantic sensibility:

He began, in a tone of great taste and feeling, to talk of the sea and the sea shore; and ran with energy through all the usual phrases employed in praise of their sublimity and descriptive of the undescribable emotions they excite in the mind of sensibility. The terrific grandeur of the ocean in a storm, its glass surface in a calm, its gulls and its samphire and the deep fathoms of its abysses, its quick vicissitudes, its direful deceptions, its mariners tempting it in sunshine and overwhelmed by sudden tempest – all were eagerly and fluently touched.

Jane Austen was a contemporary of early Romantic poets Wordsworth, Byron and Shelley and clearly alive to the relationship with nature and the landscape that they were exploring. These poets, and the later Romantic writers and artists, were transforming contemporary attitudes to the landscape and to river, lake and sea. The site of spiritual, functional, experimental, medical and social practices was becoming imbued with emotional and metaphorical significance. This change was to be reflected in how people bathed, and how they wrote about bathing.

Silent with swimming sense: Romantic bathing

Eskdale, late July, my first visit since a family holiday here 48 years ago. After supper, I take a walk from the pub down to King George's Pool. The air is cool and clear. The low sun makes the high slopes of Scafell Pike gleam pink and the postbox glow from the hedge. As I walk down the road, the air is so still that every sound is intensified: I can hear every baa and caw, and the river rushing. A faintly rotten scent rises from fresh silage, plastic-bound in the fields. A tang of bracken. It has been a hot day, but now the air feels soft. A cloud of midges bulges over the river bank. The beige and pink stone of the bridge still feels warm to the touch.

Access to the pool from the bank is difficult because sharp stones and knobbly pebbles lie underfoot. Earlier today I tried swimming from the exact place where I posed for a photo, aged six, paddling myself around on a lilo. I found it awkward getting into the water, and when I finally plunged it was shockingly cold.

Now, as dusk starts to fall, standing on the bridge and looking down at the pool where the long weed trails, I see the perfect place to sit and dangle my feet or indeed to enter easily into water deep enough to swim. If you climb over the wall by the bridge there are foot and hand holds that allow an easy descent the eight or so feet to a little grassy embankment. From there, slabs of rock lead, step-like, straight into the pool. This must be the spot where, for centuries, people have entered the brown water, slipping in with ease rather than struggling over the pebbles and stones. I climb down to the patch of grass, kick off my shoes, sit amongst bracken and beech, and trail my feet. The wall is exquisite: tiny sedums grow in every crevice. Blackberries are ripening, but not yet ripe.

I think about our family holidays and swimming here and how the scents and sounds of this place feel so sharp, so familiar. And I think of all the things that have happened to my family as the years have rushed past. My mother and aunt dead, my father frail, my brother emigrated, my sister overcoming serious illness. I feel a rush of memory and a sense of things changing and moving on around me and through me. I must bathe. Quickly I take off my clothes and enter the water in the dim light. It feels sublime: sad, sensuous, daring, mystical, nostalgic, intimate. Romantic in every sense.

* * * * *

Susie Parr in the river at Eskdale, Cumbria, as a child and in 2007.

Coniston by Joseph Arthur Palliser Severn.

This is the perfect place to have a Romantic swim. Two hundred years ago, this landscape of mountains, lakes and rivers helped to inspire a profound and radical shift in philosophy that still shapes our perception of the natural world today. The poet William Wordsworth was born in Cockermouth, only ten miles away from Eskdale, and lived for many years in Grasmere with his sister Dorothy, wife Mary and children. In November 1799, Wordsworth took Samuel Coleridge, another poet, on a walking tour of the area that formed the backdrop to his childhood. Accompanied by Wordsworth's brother John, the poets set out on a journey lasting several days. Their route covered Hawkshead, Ambleside, Windermere, Bowness, Grasmere, Keswick, and Grisedale Tarn, high in the northern mountains.

Coleridge was enraptured by what he saw: *a world of scenery absolutely new to me*. In a letter to Dorothy, Wordsworth's sister, he praised the *diversity of harmonious features, in the majesty of its beauties – O my God – and the Black Crags close under the snowy mountains, whose snows were pinkish from the setting sun.*

Wordsworth and Coleridge were key figures in the Romantic movement – an artistic and philosophical phenomenon that swept through mid/late eighteenth century Europe. In part, Romanticism was a reaction to the prevailing Enlightenment view that progress could only be effected through the application of reason and dedication to scientific method.

In an increasingly rational age, Romantic writers such as Wordsworth and Coleridge broke the mould by celebrating the power of the imagination. Rejecting a rule-bound, conventional society, they asserted the value of the self, of individual experience and subjectivity. The core of Romanticism was a sense of wonder at the infinite and unknowable aspects of human experience. Innocence and simplicity were valued above sophistication, artifice and satire. The poets explored the perspectives of children (for example in William Blake's *Songs of Innocence and Experience*) and of simple country folk like the shepherd Michael in *Lyrical Ballads*. Instead of elaborate conceits and classical forms of expression, popular amongst Enlightenment poets, they used day-to-day idioms and simple, straight-forward language.

Despite their emphasis on personal experience, subjectivity and the internal world, Romantic thinkers, writers and artists did not operate in a political vacuum. They were much influenced by international events. The American and French Revolutions had a profound impact, particularly on the early Romantic poets, inspiring anti-establishment thinking and aspirations for a society based on principles of equality and liberty. Witnessing the degradations of poor and disadvantaged people (as Wordsworth describes in *The Prelude*) prompted the poets to dream of building a better, fairer society. Coleridge was known as a political agitator, preacher and orator as well as a poet. For a while, he harboured an ambition to establish a radical alternative community (a *Pantisocracy*) in America, in which all members would have equal status. Blake's seemingly naïve poetry and painting were, amongst other things, vehicles for his profoundly radical views. Through them, he protested against the slave trade and other abuses.

The second generation British Romantic poets (Byron, Keats and Shelley) were equally politically engaged, despite more privileged backgrounds and exotic lifestyles, ways of living that contrasted with Wordsworth's sober existence in his Lakeland homestead. The repressive Tory government of the time, alarmed by the possibility of revolution being triggered on British soil, was on the look out for trouble. Shelley, the son of a Whig peer, was sent down from Oxford because of his atheistic and political views. He joined a rebellion in Ireland, wrote a satirical protest against the Peterloo Massacre, depicted a state without monarchy in *Prometheus Unbound* and ended his days exiled in Italy.

The dashing Lord Byron made his maiden speech in the House of Lords in 1812 – a passionate defence of the Nottinghamshire Frame Breakers. Despite the dissolute celebrity lifestyle that accompanied the publication of his epic poem *Childe Harold*, Byron maintained a political vision throughout his life. Indeed, his political engagement led him to his death. In 1823 he joined the Greek forces in their struggle for independence from Ottoman Turkey, spending £4,000 of his own money to re-equip the Greek fleet. He died of marsh fever at Missolonghi, Greece, in 1824, a hero of almost mythical proportions across Europe.

In contrast to the immediacy of their political engagement, Romantic writers were also drawn to ancient and exotic cultures, distant in time or place from the challenging and changing world in which they lived. Inspired by classical and medieval legends and supernatural tales, their taste for the extreme and different also led them to push the boundaries of the emotions, passions and senses. For some, like Coleridge and de Quincey, this manifested itself in addiction to opium through which they could explore the potential of chemically-enhanced imagination. Others, like Byron and Shelley (whose first wife drowned herself in the Serpentine) indulged in a series of scandalous relationships. As well as his numerous encounters with lovers of both sexes, Byron had an incestuous relationship with his half sister and fathered her child. He was described by one of his lovers, Lady Caroline Lamb, as *mad, bad and dangerous to know.*

If not mad, Byron was certainly eccentric – he kept a tame bear while he was at Cambridge because dogs were not allowed. His pastimes included drinking, fencing, pistol shooting, riding, politics, and, of course, sexual adventures. He spent many years away from England, travelling in Europe, Greece and Turkey. The success of *Childe Harold* made him a household name, the focus of adoring attention amongst women readers. He was perceived as an exotic figure: remote, ironical, adventurous, outrageous. Byron was one of the Britain's first celebrities, his status enhanced by his extraordinary good looks.

Despite his urbane lifestyle, Byron was stirred by nature and the landscape, particularly by the sea. Appreciation of the natural world was perhaps one of the most predominant features of Romanticism. Particularly in Britain, Romantic thinkers and artists were responding to rapid

George Gordon, 6th Lord Byron by Charles Turner.

transformations in agricultural practice and the escalation of urban life as the Industrial Revolution took hold. To be alone, contemplating wild, lonely places, freed the spirit to rise above the degradations of the new industries and the grim mill towns thronged with workers. Romantic thinkers were also, in part, reacting against the neoclassical view that sophisticated urban life, as played out in cities like London and Edinburgh, was the ultimate cultural experience.

But they were also starting to look at and think about the living British landscape. The war with France had made the customary European Grand Tour inadvisable, with the result that British poets and artists, such as Wordsworth and Constable, had to be content with depicting *homely and familiar scenes*, as Walpole put it, rather than idealised vistas in classical settings. As they gazed on their native fields, hills, hedgerows, rivers, lakes and seas, the poets started to gain new insights into human identity and imagination. This set the scene for an intense focus on enduring and changing aspects of the landscape, and an exploration of the relationship between Nature and the human mind.

Bathing plays a part in this unfolding relationship between man and Nature, perhaps because immersion in cold water is a particularly intimate and intense experience. British poets and artists of the period related to natural water in extraordinarily distinctive and diverse ways, each demonstrating a particular aspect of Romanticism. How they behaved in and near water, and how they experienced seas, rivers and lakes, changed popular perception and conceptualisation of these bodies of water. Rather than being seen simply as functional resources that could be fished, sailed, controlled, harnessed and used, Britain's waters were considered by the Romantics to possess their own un-tameable, awe-inspiring power, and to be capable of shaping and interacting with human identity. Romanticism transformed bathing from a medical treatment into an essentially Romantic experience: intimate, mystical, sublime, daring, and sensuous.

Many of the key Romantic figures bathed. Coleridge, for example, endeavoured to improve his fragile health through sea-bathing. Yet his poetic account of bathing in Scarborough in 1801, when he was 29 years old, expresses the rapturous nature of his experience, different indeed from the fearful and grim ordeal described by Smollett in *Humphrey Clinker*:

On Revisiting the Sea Shore
(after long absence under strong medical recommendation not to bathe)

God be with thee, gladsome Ocean!
How gladly greet I thee once more!
Ships and waves and ceaseless motion,
And men rejoicing on thy shore.

Dissuading spake the mild Physician,
'Those briny waves for thee are Death!'
But my soul fulfilled her mission,
And lo! I breathe untroubled breath!

Fashion's pining sons and daughters,
That seek the crowd they seem to fly,
Trembling, they approach thy waters;
And what cares Nature, if they die?

Me a thousand hopes and pleasures,
A thousand recollections bland,
Thoughts sublime and stately measures,
Revisit on thy echoing strand.

Dreams, (the Soul herself forsaking),
Tearful raptures, boyish mirth;
Silent adorations making
A blessed shadow of this Earth!

O ye hopes that stir within me,
Health comes with you from above!
God is with me, God is in me!
I cannot die, if Life be Love!

These lines feel conventional and hymn-like, but they bear some of the hallmarks of Romanticism: a rejection of orthodoxy, a rapturous sense of the sublime and an intense focus on the relationship between the spiritual, the subjective and Nature. For the young Coleridge, the *lovely shapes* of mountains, lakes and sea-shore articulated God's *eternal language*.

Coleridge used a bathing metaphor in a poem *This Lime-tree Bower my Prison*, written when an injury to his foot prevented him from walking with some friends. In the poem, he imagines his visitors entranced by the landscape that they are passing through on their walk, an experience he cannot share as he is marooned in his garden. His choice of the word *'swimming'* conveys an image of him immersed in the sights, sounds and scents of nature:

And kindle thou blue Ocean! So my friend
Struck with deep joy may stand,
As I have stood,
Silent with swimming sense; yea gazing round
On the wide landscape.

For Wordsworth, too, bathing was important. It was part of childhood experience, an expression of his intimate relationship with local rivers and lakes. In *The Prelude,* or *Growth of a Poet's Mind*, he charts his intellectual, spiritual and poetic development, describing how the dramatic landscape of the Lake District influenced his youthful imagination, and shaped what we would now call his identity. For the young Wordsworth, the River Derwent, that ran behind his parents' house in Cockermouth and personified as *a tempting playmate whom we dearly loved*, was always there in the background, a constant companion *that loved to blend his murmurs with my nurse's song and sent a voice that flowed along my dreams*. Wordsworth's perception of the river as a nurturing presence in his childhood is poignant: his mother died when he was seven and his father when he was eleven.

Wordsworth describes how his imagination became interconnected with nature. He *held unconscious intercourse with beauty, drinking in pure, organic pleasure*. This intimate, innocent relationship with his local landscape is perfectly conveyed in his description of bathing in the river as a child:

Oh many a time have I, a five year's child,
In a small mill-race severed from his stream,
Made one long bathing of a summer's day;
Basked in the sun and plunged and basked again.

The young Wordsworth was simultaneously immersing himself in the natural world and internalising it. His plunges in the river symbolised this interfusion. Throughout his adult life, too, he embedded himself in the landscape of the Lake District, particularly during the period he lived at Dove Cottage in Grasmere with his sister Dorothy, and later his wife Mary. Wordsworth's relationship with the landscape was mediated through homesteading activities: setting peas and weeding turnips in the cottage garden and fishing for pike in the lake. But above all, he would walk – with Dorothy, with his brothers, with the Coleridges and the many visitors who called. Although not a poet, Dorothy's journals express her exquisitely sensitive appreciation of the natural beauties around her –

SAMUEL TAYLOR COLERIDGE,

Portrait of Samuel Taylor Coleridge as a Young Man by Robert Hancock.

both great and small – and demonstrate the central role that walking played in the siblings' lives, a continuous counterpoint to the rhythm of their domestic rituals:

23rd March 1798
Coleridge dined with us. He brought his ballad finished. We walked with him to the miner's house. A beautiful evening, very starry, the horned moon.

24th March
Coleridge, the Chesters and Ellen Cruikshank called. We walked with them through the wood. Went in the evening to get eggs, returned through the wood. A duller night than last night: a sort of white shade over the blue sky. The spring continues to advance very slowly. Some brambles I observed today budding afresh and those have shed their old leaves. The crooked arm of the old oak points upwards to the moon.

28th March
Hung out the linen.

29th March
Coleridge dined with us.

30th March
Walked I know not where.

31st March
Walked.

Dorothy's journal entries take the reader through the changing seasons in Grasmere. The siblings walked no matter what the conditions – rain, ice, snow, and sweltering heat:

We almost melted before we were at the top of the hill. We saw Coleridge on the side of the water, he crossed the Beck to us. We climbed the hill but looked in vain for shade except at the foot of a great waterfall and there we did not like to stay on account of the loose stones above our heads. We came down and rested upon a moss covered rock rising out of the river. There we lay, ate our dinner and stayed until about 4 o'clock or later. William and C repeated and read verses. I drank a little Brandy and water and was in Heaven.

Hot weather did not agree with Dorothy *(I was obliged to lie down after dinner from excessive heat and headache)*. She describes how the men found relief:

Thursday 31st July 1800
All the morning I was busy copying poems. Gathered peas and in the afternoon Coleridge came, very hot, and he brought the 2nd volume of the anthology. The men went to bathe and we afterwards sailed down to Loughrigg. Read poems on the water and let the boat take its own course. We walked a long time upon Loughrigg and returned in the grey twilight. The moon was just setting as we reached home.

Dorothy's observations helped to make William alive to the smallest details of the landscape in which they were both immersed, to *the violet by the mossy stone*. His work accommodates massive changes in scale, juxtaposing observations of grand mountain and cloudscapes with minute descriptions of plants and pebbles.

One visual equivalent can be found in Constable's *Hampstead Heath with Pond and Bathers*, painted in 1821. Constable places the tiny figures of the bathers within an immense land, sky and cloudscape. Like Wordsworth, he creates a kind of psycho-geography, where day-to-day practices within a recognisable, precisely observed landscape link the ordinary with the sublime.

The Romantic appreciation of the overwhelming power of real, living landscapes contrasted starkly with earlier, neo-classical representations of Britain's natural waters. In his *Epistle to Lord Burlington on the Use of Riches*, Alexander Pope's idealised waterscapes are tamed and controlled – a testimony to rational and technical advancement:

Bid the broad Arch the dangerous flood contain,
The Mole projected break the roaring Main;
Back to his bounds their subject Sea command,
And roll obedient Rivers through the Land;

In contrast, his *Spring Pastoral*, written some 70 years before *The Prologue*, turns London's great working river into a classical tableau, stylised, sterile and artificial:

Hampstead Heath with Pond and Bathers by John Constable (1821).

Fair Thames flow sweetly from thy sacred Spring,
While on thy banks Sicilian Muses sing;
Let Vernal Airs through trembling Osiers play,
And Albion's cliffs resound the Rural Lay.

The Thames is represented in a very different light in Pope's poem *The Dunciad* (a satirical take on *The Aeniad*), first published in 1728, in which he lampoons the poets, writers, critics and booksellers who were his contemporaries. He depicts his victims as unscrupulous, dull, untalented and ferociously competitive, scrabbling for financial gain and taking part in 'heroic' games, which include bathing in the Thames. By describing the urban river setting for the games in harshly realistic detail, Pope undermines the posturing and pretensions of the competitors:

This labour past, by Bridewell all descend,
(As morning prayer, and flagellation end)
To where Fleet-ditch with disemboguing streams
Rolls the large tribute of dead dogs to Thames,
The king of dikes! than whom no sluice of mud
With deeper sable blots the silver flood.
Here strip, my children! here at once leap in,
Here prove who best can dash through thick and thin,
And who the most in love of dirt excel,
Or dark dexterity of groping well.
Who flings most filth, and wide pollutes around
The stream, be his the weekly journals bound;
A pig of lead to him who dives the best;
A peck of coals a-piece shall glad the rest.

Degraded, foul-smelling sludge, pastoral artefact, controlled routes for trade and transport: Pope's contrasting visions of the river could not be more at odds with the Romantic response to natural water:

With what ineffable pleasure have I not gazed, and gazed again, losing my breath through my eyes – my very soul diffused through my eyes – my very soul diffused itself in the scene – and seeming to become all the sense, glided in the scarcely-agitated waves, melting in the freshening breeze – imperceptibly recalling the reveries of childhood.
(Mary Wollstonecraft on a visit to Norway, Letter 8.)

Nature was overwhelming to the Romantic sensibility. Charlotte Bronte, who lived in one of the most land-locked locations in Britain, had her first sight of the sea on a visit to Bridlington in 1839. Her friend Ellen Nussey reported: *She was quite overpowered, she could not speak till she had shed some tears… her eyes were red and swollen, she was still trembling… for the remainder of the day she was* very quiet, subdued and exhausted. Eulogies on the topic of the sea and nature, having originated in high literature, quickly became increasingly commonplace in the discourse of ordinary people. Jane Austen satirises the tendency in *Sanditon*:

She could not but think him a Man of feeling till he began to stagger her by the number of his Quotations and the Bewilderment of some of his sentences.

Jane's amusement at Romantic excesses was probably fuelled by reports of the antics of her young contemporaries, Byron and Shelley, and, like many readers in Britain, she must have followed news of them with interest. Shelley, for example, displayed much of his notorious eccentricity when around water. He was transfixed by reflections and could often be found staring into pools, ponds and puddles, deep in thought. As a boy at Eton he would escape the bullies who were attracted by his odd behaviour and go to a little wood by a bubbling spring. Mary Shelley writes:

His happiest hours were spent here. He sat on the rough hewn steps that led to the spring, now reading a favourite book, now musing with speculation beyond his years on the still unravelled skein of morals or metaphysics.

At the age of 19, Shelley walked from Sussex to his uncle's estate in the Elan Valley in Wales. According to an account given in 1878 by the woman who delivered post to his uncle, Shelley behaved very oddly during his stay, dipping in and out of the mountain streams and sailing toy boats down the rivulets, on one occasion putting a cat on board.

In his memoirs of the poets, Edward Trelawney (an admirer who spent a lot of time with Shelley and Byron in the last years of their lives) described how living in Italy seemed to intensify Shelley's obsession: *Shelley never flourished far from water. When compelled to take up his quarters in a town, he every morning, with the instinct that guides the water-birds, fled to the nearest lake, river or sea-shore, only returning to roost at night.* A truly elemental poet, he often sat by lakes, ponds or rivers to write poetry or translate classical texts. But the attraction of water had a darker side for the poet. His fascination became increasingly perplexed, melancholic and sinister.

Trelawney noted that Shelley was given to disappearing for long periods and often his long-suffering second wife Mary (the daughter of Mary Wollstonecraft) would search for him, fearing that he had drowned himself. On one occasion Trelawney found him in a pine forest, by a deep pool *gazing on the dark mirror beneath, so lost in his bardish reverie that he did not hear my approach.* Shelley said:

'The river flows by like Time and all the sounds of Nature harmonise; they soothe: it is only the human animal that is discordant with Nature, and that disturbs me. It is difficult to perceive why and for what purpose we are here, a perpetual torment to ourselves and every living thing.'

Although he was so drawn to water, Shelley could not swim, a deficiency he much regretted. Ruefully, he watched Trelawney, who was an accomplished swimmer, showing off some tricks he had learned on his trips to the South Seas. As Trelawney dressed, Shelley asked: *'Why can't I swim? It seems so very easy.'*

Trelawney told him that he would be able to swim if he would only think positively about it. He gave Shelley some tips about how to float, whereupon Shelley stripped and plunged headlong into the water. He went straight to the bottom and lay there *not making the least struggle or effort to save himself.* Trelawney was forced to rescue him.

While Shelley never learned to swim properly, he regularly bathed in shallow water, rivulets, waterfalls and ponds. He also found another way of getting as close as possible to water without actually being in it… he had his own sailing boat built and brought to La Spezia, where he tried to learn how to handle it. But *he was so uncommonly awkward* that he could not get to grips with the skills required. Because he struggled to control the boat, which was large and awkward to manoeuvre close to shore, a friend built him a small dinghy, a bit like a coracle. This delighted him, even though he was constantly capsizing it.

Gradually, Shelley learned how to control the fragile craft and started to venture out onto the open sea, even in bad weather. He got into the habit of paddling the dinghy out and then letting it drift back in to shore. On one occasion, Trelawney had to rescue his friend again. The boat had capsized and, as Trelawney dragged him to shore, Shelley was spluttering and *shrieking with delight as the crisp waves curled up and over him.* One very hot day, Shelley even took a visitor and her two infant children out in his boat in order to catch some cooler air. To her alarm, having sculled out a long way into deep water, Shelley rested on his oars and fell into a reverie, *probably reviewing all*

he had gone through of suffering and of wrong, with no present or future. He suggested that together they should *solve the great mystery* – a proposal that understandably struck fear into her heart. She managed to persuade him to row her little family back to shore. She said to Trelawney: *'He is seeking after what we all avoid: death. You won't catch me in a boat with Shelley alone.'*

Shelley's eccentric behaviour around water sometimes caused consternation. On one very warm evening he went out just before important visitors were expected for dinner, to dip and bathe in the shallows. He stripped off his clothes and placed them in his boat, which then capsized, sending them into the water. Trelawney describes how the party, which included a number of ladies sitting around the dining table, was astounded by the spectacle of Shelley, naked, creeping around the edges of the room towards his bed chamber:

The brine from his shock of hair trickling down his innocent nose; if he were girt with a feathered cincture or anything else, it was not visible; small fragments of seaweed clung to his hair, and he was odorous of the salt brine. He was gliding noiselessly round the two sides of the saloon to his room and might possibly have succeeded unnoticed but for the refined and excitable lady calling attention to such an unprecedented license, even in a poet.

Shelley's relationship with water reached its grim climax when he drowned in the Bay of Spezia, his boat (the *Don Juan*) going down in a storm. It was rumoured that he refused help from an Italian captain who tried to assist the struggling crew and restrained his shipmates from lowering the sails, an act that might have saved them from the mountainous waves. His body was washed ashore, a copy of Keats' poems marked and folded back in his pocket. His manner of death became in itself a Romantic symbol, commemorated in the statue by Edward Onslow Ford (finished in 1892) that now stands in University College, Oxford.

Shelley's remains were cremated on the beach in a ceremony organised by Trelawney and attended by Byron, who had spent a good deal of time with the poet and his wife in the months before he died. As Shelley's pyre blazed, Byron became agitated and overcome with emotion. He plunged into the sea to swim, saying: *'Let us try the strength of these waters that drowned our friends. How far do you think they were out when their*

The Funeral of Shelley by Louis Edouard Paul Fournier (1889).

boat sank?' Trelawney accompanied Byron and the pair swam out about a mile before Byron became sea sick and was prevailed upon to return to shore.

This act was typical of Byron's approach to swimming: spontaneous, competitive, flamboyant, and daring. There is some speculation that Byron suffered from bi-polar syndrome, swinging between paralysing depression and agitated overdrive. Swimming could both cheer him when he was low and calm him when he was in the throes of mania. He described to his friend Thomas Medwin how sea swimming particularly affected him: *'I delight in the sea and come out with a buoyancy of spirits'*.

Other theories suggest that Byron undertook challenging and extreme swims in order to prove his physical prowess

in spite of his lameness (caused by a contracted Achilles' tendon). Certainly, he was highly competitive and constantly boasted about his riding, boxing and fencing. But it was in swimming that he excelled, as Trelawney noted: *He was built for floating – with a flexible body, open chest, broad beam and round limbs. If the sea were warm and smooth he would stay in it for hours.*

Byron had learned to swim as a child in Scotland and bathed in the river at Harrow, where he went to school (always wearing trousers to conceal his wasted lower limb and often swimming at a distance from the other boys, to avoid ridicule). When he was at Cambridge, Byron swam with his friend Edward Long in the River Cam, near Grantchester, diving for plates and shillings in the pool that now bears his name. In 1806, Byron was struggling to control his weight (at five foot eight inches he weighed over fourteen stone). Apparently in the grip of mania, he went to extraordinary lengths to slim down, taking nothing but a quarter pound of meat a day, washed down with wine, and running and playing cricket whilst wearing seven waistcoats and a greatcoat to induce a sweat. It was during this phase that Byron swam three miles down the River Thames. This was his first marathon swim.

Byron's life was punctuated by daring swimming adventures, particularly during the period of his Grand Tour, when he travelled through Greece, Turkey, Portugal, Spain and Malta. In 1809 he wrote from Lisbon: *I am very happy here because I loves oranges, talk bad Latin to the monks,*

I goes into society (with my pocket pistols) and I swims the Tagus all at once. This referred to the considerable feat of swimming up river from old Lisbon to Belem Castle, despite treacherous winds and currents.

In 1810, Byron travelled to Constantinople (now Istanbul). On May 3rd, with his friend Richard Ekenhead, he re-enacted the feat achieved by the mythical Leander for the love of Hero, swimming across the Hellespont from Asia to Europe, a distance of more than four miles. Byron completed the swim in one hour and ten minutes. He was extremely proud of this and his other swimming exploits: *The current was very strong and cold, some large fish near us when we were half way across, we were not fatigued*

Shelley Memorial, University College, Oxford © Martin Parr/Magnum.

Lord Byron reposing in the house of a fisherman having swum the Hellespont by Sir William Allan (1831).

but a little chilled. I plume myself on this achievement more than I could possibly do on any kind of glory, political, poetical, or rhetorical.

In the rhyming account of his feat, Byron struck a more ironic tone:

> *For me, degenerate modern wretch*
> *Though in the genial month of May*
> *My dripping limbs I faintly stretch*
> *And think I've done a feat today*

Byron lived in Venice from 1816-1819, lodging in the Palazzo Mocenigo where he established a menagerie of cats, a mastiff, a fox, a wolf, a crow, two monkeys and a pair of cranes. It was estimated that he seduced upwards of two hundred people in Venice, commenting: *'It is a very good place for women'*. His letters describe an intemperate lifestyle, in which swimming played a major part. He was said to have plunged into the canals on many occasions, often in order to escape from compromising situations. He was also in the habit of swimming home to his Palazzo, pushing a candle in front of him on a little wooden board and looking up at the lighted windows to see if he could spy any young women undressing.

In Venice, Byron met Cavalier Angelo Mengaldo, who had served in Napolean's army and who boasted of swimming across the Berezina under enemy fire. In his usual competitive style, Byron challenged Mengaldo to a race – a swim from Lido, across the Venetian lagoon, and up the Grand Canal – a distance of four and a half miles. Mengaldo accepted the challenge and the pair were joined by a young Englishman, Alexander Scott. Byron quickly outdistanced the others. Mengaldo gave up halfway across the lagoon and Scott quit at the Rialto Bridge. Byron was elated at his victory and his fame as a swimmer came to eclipse his renown as a poet, at least in Italy. On the shore of the Bay of Spezia, where Shelley drowned, a plinth commemorates *Lord Byron, Noted English Swimmer and Poet.*

But, for Byron, swimming was more than a means of demonstrating his power and superiority. In 1813 he wrote:

The great object of life is Sensation. To feel that we exist, even though in pain. It is the 'craving void' that drives us to Gaming, to Battle, to Travel – to intemperate but keenly felt pursuits of every description whose principal attraction is the agitation inseparable from their accomplishment.

Swimming can be added to the list of Byron's intemperate but keenly felt pursuits. In *Childe Harold* (which is in part autobiographical) he describes the complex sensations triggered by immersion in the sea. The experience was clearly a pleasurable and sensuous one, made more thrilling by an undercurrent of fear:

> *And I have loved thee Ocean! And my joy*
> *Of youthful sports was on thy breast to be*
> *Borne like thy bubbles, onward: from a boy*
> *I wanton'd with thy breakers – they to me*
> *Were a delight; and if the freshening sea*
> *Made them a terror – 'twas a pleasing fear;*
> *For I was as it were a child of thee*
> *And trusted to thy billows far and near,*
> *And laid my hand upon thy mane – as I do here.*

Some of the most important British Romantic poets had strong and distinctive relationships with water. Wordsworth's experience of the living landscape and the interfusion of nature and imagination was symbolised by his childhood dips in the Derwent and bathing as an adult with family and friends in the lakes near Dove Cottage. For Shelley, water was a mystical element, seeming to hold the unfathomable secrets of life and death. And for Byron, water was a source of sensuous gratification and a theatre for daring and extreme acts.

The distinctive Romantic relationship with water and the natural world changed the popular view of swimming and bathing. It underpinned the work of later, post-Romantic poets, who developed the idea of synergy between man and element, albeit taking the concept in different directions. For example, Algernon Swinburne (1837-1909), Tennyson's outrageous contemporary, was much influenced by Byron's lifestyle, and his quest for Sensation. Throughout his childhood, spent in Northumberland and on the Isle of Wight, Swinburne was transfixed by the sea. Somewhat surprisingly for such a slight, nervous-looking figure with pale skin and flaming red hair, he developed a life-long passion for bathing, particularly in rough waters. An extract from his novel *Lesbia Brandon*, whose hero Herbert is modelled on the young Swinburne, suggests why this might be:

He wanted no teaching to make him face a heavy sea: he panted and shouted with pleasure among breakers where he could not stand two minutes; the blow of the roller that

Portrait of Algernon Charles Swinburne by William Bell Scott.

beat him off his feet made him laugh and cry out in ecstasy; he rioted in the roaring water like a young sea-beast, sprang at the throat of waves that threw him flat, pressed up against their soft fierce bosoms and fought for their sharp embraces; grappled with them as lover with lover; flung himself upon them with limbs that laboured and yielded deliciously, till the scourging of the surf made him red from shoulders to the knees and sent him on shore whipped by the sea into a single blush of the whole skin, breathless and untried.

Swinburne led an unorthodox life, and his work often caused outrage amongst readers for its explicitly sexual

Sketch of a Seated Boy by Henry Scott Tuke (1917).

content and emphasis on the pleasures of sado-masochism. His descriptions of bathing in the sea combine these two elements. The sea becomes his lover, both sensuous and cruel:

I will go down to her, I and none other
Close with her, kiss her and mix her with me;
Cling to her, strive with her, hold her fast...

Sea that are clothed with the sun and the rain
Thy sweet hard kisses are strong like wine
Thy large embraces are keen like pain...

My lips will feast on the foam of thy lips
I shall rise with thy rising, with thee subside.

Unsurprisingly, Swinburne's work often offended Victorian readers and was frequently banned.

Tennyson, the Victorian Poet Laureate, was more in tune with Wordsworth's view of nature and certainly less controversial than Swinburne. The sea was a geographical and physical entity, described in lush detail, inspiring a sense of beauty, wonder and fear. But it was also entangled with, and intrinsic to, his imagination. Ultimately he saw it as a means of representing his internal thought processes. When his friend Arthur Hallam was drowned in 1833, aged 23, Tennyson looked out from Clevedon over the muddy waters of the Bristol Channel. The incessant

breaking of the brown waves reflects the dull rhythm of his grief:

Break break break
On thy cold grey stones O Sea!
And I would that my tongue could utter
The thoughts that arise in me

Later, D.H. Lawrence extended this Romantic concept of a synergy between body, sensibility and element. In a late poem, *Mana of the Sea*, Lawrence describes plunging in rough waves (possibly Atlantic breakers rolling into Zennor in Cornwall, where Lawrence lived in 1916) with Byronian exuberance:

And is my body ocean, ocean
Whose power runs to the shores along my arms
And breaks in the foamy hands, whose power rolls out
To the white-treading waves of two salt feet?

I am the sea, I am the sea!

Rupert Brooke's writing also formed a bridge between Romantic sensibilities and a modern outlook. Between 1909 and 1914, Brooke lived in the village of Grantchester, near Cambridge. His lifestyle seemed to echo the idealistic aspirations and unorthodox ways of the Romantic poets who had lived a century before him, as well as anticipating the laid-back peacefulness of the hippies who would emerge fifty years after his death. He lived a Bohemian lifestyle – wandering around Grantchester barefoot, wearing few clothes and living on honey, eggs and milk supplied by benevolent neighbours.

Like Byron, Brooke was extremely good-looking. Glamorous and charismatic, he attracted a coterie of intellectual and creative visitors from Cambridge and hosted many gatherings at his lodgings. His succession of guests included Augustus John, Ludwig Wittgenstein, Virginia Woolf and E.M. Forster. The Grantchester group was dubbed the 'Neo-Pagans' by Virginia Woolf, because of their close relationship with nature. They spent their time walking, camping, picnicking, discussing art and philosophy, debating, crafting their vision for a Utopian society and bathing in the river – all vestiges of their Romantic heritage. Bathing was an important social ritual for the Neo-Pagans. Both men and women swam naked. This was relatively commonplace for men, as shown in the contemporary paintings of Henry Tuke, but it was revolutionary for women.

Jacques Raverat (above) and Noele Olivier (below), both members of the Neo-Pagans.

Although he was writing early in the twentieth century, Brooke's relationship with nature and the landscape was essentially Romantic. But his sense of the sublime union with nature through immersion in water is darkened by a sense of fear and foreboding. While this resonates with Shelley's vision, it feels more sinister and is undeniably modern, begging a Freudian interpretation:

At 10pm alone, very frightened, I steal out into the ominous open and bathe by night. I am in deadly terror of the darkness in the wood. But when one, beginning to bathe, throws off ones garments then all is surprisingly well. You no longer feel disliked, an outsider, you become part of it all, and bathe. The only terror left is of plunging head foremost into blackness: a moderate terror.

In 1912, during a visit to Berlin in stiflingly hot weather, Brooke famously gave poetic expression to his longing for Grantchester. In this poem, Brooke eulogises the British landscape. *Sweating, sick and hot* in Berlin, he longs for the cool river where Byron swam and *the shadowed waters fresh lean up to embrace the naked flesh*:

> *I only know that you may lie*
> *Day long and watch the Cambridge sky,*
> *And, flower lulled in the sleepy grass,*
> *Hear the cool lapse of hours pass,*
> *Until the centuries blend and blur*
> *In Grantchester, in Grantchester*
> *Still in the dawnlit waters cool*
> *His ghostly Lordship swims his pool,*
> *And tries the strokes, essays the tricks,*
> *Long learnt on Hellespont, or Styx.*

Byron's Pool, Grantchester © Martin Parr/Magnum.

Byron's Pool

Brooke's poem inspires me to make a visit to Byron's Pool, near Grantchester, where the young poet famously swam naked with Virginia Woolf on a hot summer evening just before the world was plunged into war. I want to enter the river, breathe in the thrilling sweet and rotten unforgettable, unforgotten river-smell and pay my respects to those handsome poets, Byron and Brooke, both of whom died young, far away from home. So in Romantic spirit, on a Sunday afternoon in July, I set out.

It is hot, 24 degrees, but overcast. The sky is laden with heavy, yellowish clouds pierced by the occasional flicker of lightening. Every now and then there is a downpour so fierce that I can barely see through the windscreen, even with wipers going full tilt. I push on through the traffic on the M25 and up the dreary M11. When I finally arrive at Grantchester, the rain has stopped and a steamy heat presses down. The place is so pretty and well-tended it feels like a pastiche of Englishness. Every hedge is trimmed, every bed weeded, every delphinium staked. I peer into the dark interior of the Rupert Brooke pub, study the church clock, admire the hollyhocks. I wander through the Orchard Tea-Gardens, where queues of visitors patiently wait their turn for scones and cream. Seeing the sign for Byron's Pool I take the path through the woods towards the river. I had hoped for a solitary experience, but find myself following a party of visitors from the US, many of whom are optimistically wearing sunhats and pristine trainers. They all clutch guide books.

Their slow progress is frustrating so I make a detour through the wood and walk briskly along the river-bank, away from the voices. The trees in full summer leaf make the path seem dark. There is very little undergrowth. The river is brown, swollen with the recent downpours, fringed with mud and nettles. On the other bank I can see thick beds of rushes, and beyond that the flat yellowish fields stretching towards the bulging clouds on the horizon. I think about Brooke and his friends, and about Byron. Perhaps they walked this same path to get to the pool?

I have often pictured Byron's Pool. I imagine the water to be deep, cool and inviting, surrounded by open meadows. Clear, fresh water flowing over fine white gravel, where one can float, contemplating the fields beyond.

The river widens out and I hear the sound of rushing water… this must mean that the weir, where the pool is situated, is close. I emerge onto a patch of scrubby grass and mud. The weir is certainly here: water curves and spills from a higher pool down into the river. But the softness of the bank has been squared off with angular concrete walls. Two pipes stick from the pale facades, each spouting a torpid trickle. The pool is edged with nettles, a scum of old plastic bags, sweet wrappers and mud. Mid-stream, a broken branch sticks forlornly out of the water.

The concrete slabs are topped with municipal railings. In front of these, an Environment Agency sign reads:

Byron's Pool. No unauthorised access. No swimming. No fishing. Danger – strong currents.

I am dismayed. I sit for a while on the patch of scrubby grass, contemplating the place where Byron and Brooke dreamed and drifted. I feel I should swim, having come all this way. Furtively, I undress and put on my costume, looking over my shoulder for the tourist group who eventually arrive and spend just a couple of minutes inspecting the pool, before heading off for lunch. They seem unimpressed. I need to move quickly before the next tourists arrive. Poking tentative toes into the mud, worried about the strong currents, anxious about breaking the law, I make a quick plunge towards the broken branch, then retreat.

This could be the most glorious spot – a place where people could bathe in the spirit of Brooke and Byron and contemplate the English landscape stretching away from the banks of the river across the flat fields, towards the sky. Instead, my swim is rushed, fearful and unpleasant: the antithesis of Romance.

the story of swimming

The democratisation of bathing

As a child, I could hope for no better treat than a visit to Brighton. Ghost trains, rock, candy floss, dodgems, slot machines, helter skelters, donkey rides, ice cream and hot, salty fish and chips wrapped in newspaper – bliss. Gradually, I developed a soft spot for the resorts that seem stuck in a time warp like Broadstairs, Ventnor and even Skegness, with its delightful model village. Here you will find the optician's, Seymour Clearly, and the underwear shop run by Lucy Lastic being smartened up by painter and decorator W.E. Slapiton.

But now it takes a lot to make me venture into the larger, busier resorts like Blackpool or Margate. As I walk past the blaring arcades and tacky gift shops or push through the crowds gorging on chips and fudge, I shudder and wish I was on a quiet beach in the middle of nowhere. I thought this snootiness was a symptom of me being middle aged, middle class and increasingly intolerant of noise and crowds. It is of course. What I didn't realise is that I am also re-enacting tensions that were first played out on Britain's beaches one hundred and fifty years ago. And bathing was at the heart of what was essentially a class-based conflict.

During the nineteenth century, resorts around the coast of Britain, from Bridlington to Bexhill, experienced a massive escalation in the numbers of summer visitors, all heading to the sea in pursuit of health and enjoyment. Fashionable Brighton led the way in resort development. Blessed with the Prince Regent's patronage, Brighton had flourished as the vogue for sea-bathing transformed it from an *ill-built place* to *Old Ocean's brightest bauble*. At first, summer migration to the south coast watering-place was relatively restricted. Accessibility by stage coach meant that only wealthy Londoners could enjoy the benefits of bathing. And it was a gruelling journey: in 1762, it took at least twelve hours to travel from London to Brighton. Improved road surfaces and better coach design meant that the journey gradually became shorter and more comfortable. By 1791, it was possible to reach Brighton in nine hours, and by 1811 the journey lasted only six hours. The draw of the resort was such that plenty of people made the effort, despite the arduous journey. The summer of 1837 saw a total of 50,000 visitors travelling to Brighton by stagecoach.

But just thirteen years later, 73,000 holiday makers would arrive at Brighton in one single week. And Brighton was not alone in experiencing this escalation in visitor

Bathing was at the heart of a class-based conflict.

The Railway Station by William Powell Frith (1863).

numbers. Other south coast resorts like Margate and Ramsgate, within striking distance of London by stage-coach or steamboat, formed the first wave of seasonal expansion and growth. Seaside towns remote from London, like Scarborough and Tenby, continued to cater for noble and genteel health seekers but also began to attract wealthy merchants and farmers from the surrounding areas. As the nineteenth century unfolded, provincial resorts like Blackpool, Llandudno and Weston-super-Mare mushroomed, their sands thronged with crowds from centres of population in Lancashire, North Wales and the South West. And in the later years of the nineteenth century, more remote spots like Cromer, Swanage and Whitley Bay started to welcome increasing numbers of holiday-makers seeking a more secluded seaside break.

What brought about this massive summer migration to the coastal towns of early Victorian Britain? One major factor was the advent of rail travel. The network of rail

connections spread rapidly across the entire UK during the 1830s and 1840s, linking major cities with remote seaside towns and allowing hitherto landlocked centres of population to gain fast, cheap and direct access to the beach. Intense competition between rival rail companies meant that journey times and cost were constantly being cut.

Those who could afford it were able to make prolonged visits. By the middle of the nineteenth century it was fashionable for middle class mothers to bring their children (with nursemaids in tow) to the seaside for a few weeks during the summer. Fathers continued working during the week and would visit the holiday lodgings at weekends.

Charles Dickens, writing in the magazine *Household Words*, in 1851, described the scene at his seaside abode, Broadstairs. Here, sea-bathing was a part of the daily ritual even for the very young:

So many children are brought down to our watering place that when they are not out of doors as they usually are in fine weather, it is wonderful where they are put. In the afternoons you see no end of salt and sandy little boots drying on upper windowsills. At bathing time in the morning, the little bay re-echoes with every shrill variety of shriek and splash after which, if the weather be at all fresh, the sands team with small blue mottled legs. The sands are the children's greatest resort. They cluster there, like ants: so busy burying their particular friends, and making castles with infinite labour, which the next tide overturns.

But the middle classes couldn't keep the seaside to themselves for long. Cheap, fast railway travel soon made weekend visits and even day trips a possibility for mill and factory workers and members of the lower classes. By the early 1850s, numerous cut price excursion packages were on offer, enthusiastically promoted by the railway companies. On a summer weekend, The Lancashire and Yorkshire Railway could deliver up to 12,000 trippers from the industrial heartlands of the North West to Blackpool. And the growth continued. In 1861, Blackpool's stations received 135,000 visitors. In 1879, one million holiday-makers disembarked and headed for the sands. And 1902 saw three million people arrive in Blackpool during the summer season.

The railways were not the sole cause of the seaside boom. The phenomenon was rooted in the developing wealth and organisation of industrial Britain, particularly in the North. As the prosperity generated by cotton, textile, steel and other industries accumulated, working conditions and pay improved. Although there was still wide-spread poverty, it became possible for factory and mill-workers, often with the help of Friendly Societies or 'Going Off Clubs' to put sufficient money aside for a trip to the seaside. The Factory Act of 1850 meant that working hours were reduced, and in 1871 The Bank Holiday Act enshrined holidays with pay on Boxing Day, Easter Monday, Whit Monday and the last Monday in August. Suddenly, people who had never previously ventured outside their home towns had enough time and just enough money to enable them to go to the coast.

In Lancashire and Yorkshire, the new bank holidays supplemented traditional local holiday periods known as Wakes Weeks, during which many mills and factories closed down entirely so that the mill machinery could be overhauled. Wakes Weeks may have had pre-industrial origins related to the founding of local churches and chapels but were quickly appropriated into the industrial schedule. They were traditionally celebrated with local festivities and fairs. Rail travel enabled factory and mill-workers to transfer their Wakes celebrations to the seaside, with fair showmen and vendors hot on their heels. The timing of the Wakes Week varied from district to district. This was good news for the nearest seaside resorts, as they could expect fairly constant numbers of holiday-makers from different inland industrial localities throughout the summer.

It made economic sense for factory and mill-owners to tolerate strongly rooted pre-industrial traditions such as the Wakes Weeks. Suppressing them brought the risk of disruption, absenteeism and ill-will. Employers were quick to see the advantages of promoting, supporting and even subsidising seaside visits for their work force. An annual trip to the seaside, carefully planned and long anticipated, had the effect of rewarding loyalty, promoting good will and improving productivity. The presence of work colleagues and families on an outing also ensured that employees' behaviour could to a certain extent be monitored and regulated. This benefit was not lost on workers' organisations like the Bolton Cottonspinners, and the Non-Conformist church and the Temperance Societies, which throughout the second part of the nineteenth century organised thousands of seaside trips, particularly in northern England.

THE INGRATITUDE OF SOME SERVANTS
You give them a change by taking them to the seaside—all they have to do is to look after the children—and yet they don't seem to appreciate it.

The ingratitude of some servants. From *Mr Punch At The Seaside*, 1910.

Train Arrangements.

THE TRAINS will START from Burton Railway Station (St. Paul's Side Platform), and, on returning, from Platforms Nos. 1 & 2 at the NEW EXCURSION STATION, Londesborough Road, SCARBORO'.

☞ Remember to bring ALL your Railway Tickets, and have them ready at Burton and Scarboro' Stations.

All Persons will be required to show their Railway Tickets at the **Doors at the Main Entrance**, and at the **Barriers** at the top of the steps, at **Burton Station**, and **none but Excursionists travelling by these Trains will be allowed upon the Platforms.** The Tickets will also be examined at the **Platform Barriers at Scarboro'** before leaving for Burton, and must be given up at the **Barriers at Burton Station at Night.** Persons using the Tutbury Special, and the Barton and Walton Train, will, of course, show their Tickets in the morning, and give them up at night when alighting at their **own** Station.

The **Foremen** and **Men** employed in the various Departments, **with their Wives,** and others for whom they have obtained Tickets, must travel by their OWN Train—both going and returning—as under:—

No. of Train.	DEPARTMENT, &c.	OUTWARD JOURNEY.		Departure Platform at Scarboro'.	RETURN JOURNEY.	
		Depart Burton.	Arrive Scarboro'.		Depart Scarboro'.	Arrive Burton.
1	Mr. Ollis—Blacksmiths, Coppersmiths, Excavators, Painters, Platelayers, Plumbers, Tailors, Cloggers, Wireworkers, Wheelwrights, Electric Light, and Fire Brigade	A.M. 3-40	A.M. 7-30	1	P.M. 8-30	A.M. 12-40
2	Mr. Ollis—Bricklayers, Fitters, and Joiners ...	3-50	7-35	2	8-40	12-55
3	Mr. Bull—Middle Yard	4-0	7-45	1	8-50	1-5
4	Mr. Clubb—Repairing Cooperage	4-10	7-55	2	9-0	1-10
5	Middle Brewery ... Mr. Clubb—Steam Cooperage ... ... Mr. Elson	4-20	8-15	1	9-10	1-15
6	Grain Department ...	4-30	8-20	2	9-20	1-20
7	Mr. Williamson—Railway Department ... Hop Stores ... ... Gas Works and Electric Works ...	4-40	8-35	1	9-30	1-35
8	New Brewery ... Bottling Stores, Shobnall ... ... Mr. Ollis—Office	5-0	8-55	2	9-40	1-40
9	Old Brewery ... Mr. Ollis—Shobnall ... ... Mr. Oliver	5-10	9-15	1	10-5	2-5
10	Mr. Spalton—Stables ... ... Local N.S. Railway Special from Tutbury, &c.	5-20	9-35	2	10-15	2-20
11	The Customers ... This Train will take up and set down Customers at WILLINGTON and at DERBY.	5-30	9-40	1	10-25	2-30
12	The Estate, Farm, and Gardens at Rangemore and Byrkley ... This Train ONLY will take up and set down at BARTON and WALTON, and at BRANSTON.	5-40	9-45	2	10-35	2-50
13	Clerks ... This Train will take up and set down Passengers at WILLINGTON and at DERBY.	5-50	9-55	1	10-45	3-0
14	Mr. Walters and Friends	6-0	10-0	2	10-55	3-5

Placards will be found affixed to each Train, both at Burton and Scarboro', plainly indicating the **number** of the Train. There will also be Boards—with the number of each Train—placed at the **bottom of the Steps** leading to the Platform (to the **Right** hand) at Burton. Prominent Notices will also be found on the **New Excursion Station Platforms at Scarboro'.**

SPECIAL NOTE.—Third Class Passengers **must travel 10 in each Compartment—5 on each side**—the same as ordinary passengers—and this must be **strictly carried out in all the Trains both ways.**

VERY URGENT.—It is **imperative** that all persons should **travel both ways by their own Train,** and most urgently does this apply to the **earlier Trains on the Return Journey.** The North Eastern Railway Company are **most particular** about you travelling by **your own Train,** and **seeing your Ticket,** so be fully prepared at Scarboro' at night.

Train Arrangements continued over.

Bass excursion railway timetable, 1914.

In addition, across the country, independent philanthropists put on trips to the seaside for groups of urban poor, with a view to exposing them to the health-giving qualities of sea water and the self-improvement that could be gained from immersion. In 1858, one Dr Miller persuaded the South Devon Railway to offer the poor of Exeter a six penny fare to Dawlish so that they could enjoy the improving experience of sea-bathing. The condition was that they had to travel on the first train down and the first train back, giving them an hour and ten minutes to enjoy the sea water. This they did with gusto. The *six penny dippers* then jumped onto their return train, leaving sedate Dawlish with feathers somewhat ruffled.

Major work excursions to the seaside were still being supported by the big employers like Lever Brothers, coal pit owners, industrialists and manufacturers, right up to the start of World War I. The entire works would close down and the outings were planned in meticulous detail and timed down to the minute. In 1914, Bass (Ratcliff and Gretton branch) published a handbook to help their employees make the most of their outing to Scarborough, due to take place on Friday 24th July. Trains departed Burton station every ten minutes, and the immensely complicated timetable fold-out specifies exactly which train was to be taken by each trade in the company. Blacksmiths, coppersmiths, excavators, painters, plumbers and platelayers needed to catch the 3.40am and would arrive in Scarborough at 7.30am. The Steam Cooperage department could catch the 4.20am while the Hop Stores and Gas Works needed to wait for the 4.40am. The timing of the return trip was equally precise, the last holiday-makers leaving Scarborough on the 10.55pm and arriving back at Burton at 3.05am.

The pamphlet details the amenities, conveniences, refreshments and entertainments awaiting the excursionists at Scarborough, directing employees towards Rawling's bathing machines on the North and South Beaches, where bathing costumes and towels could be hired for the special rate of 4d. The section on bathing ends with the following enigmatic *Advice to Bathers*:

Do not bathe immediately after a hearty meal, and after bathing taking a brisk walk. The good effects of a bathe are in proportion to the vigour of the re-action experienced after leaving the water. Sea Bathing is, like many things, excellent for those whom it suits but very detrimental to the health of those with whom it does not agree.

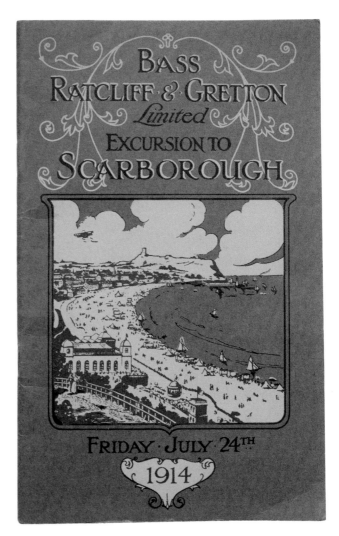

above: Bass excursion programme, 1914.
below: A card sent to a workmate on holiday.

above: The beach at Ilfracombe with Professor Harry Parker in the water.
left: Professor Harry Parker.

The gentlemen's tidal pool, Ilfracombe.

The Tunnels, Ilfracombe.

The seaside business boomed. Local speculators bought block bookings from the railway companies and sold them on. Even inland businesses jumped on the seaside band-wagon. Grocers and tea-dealers in Oldham used excursion-fever to boost their sales: customers could get a free ticket to the Lancashire coast with every purchase of 4lbs of tea. By the turn of the nineteenth century, even land-locked photographic studios were capitalising on seaside trade by manufacturing cards that could be sent from those at home to those on holiday.

Of course, seaside merchants and tradesmen also bene-fited directly from the holiday trade. Proprietors worked flat out to construct and maintain bathing machines. In season, considerable manpower was necessary to manage the horses and oversee the tricky manoeuvre of getting the bulky, heavy machines in and out of the water with the occupants undamaged. The building trade boomed as row upon row of houses, hotels and lodging places were erected to accommodate the visitors. Massive engineering projects were undertaken, as local authorities gave the go-ahead for the construction of sewage works, sea walls and promenades, where people could stroll and enjoy the sea air.

Engineering skills that had developed within the industrial world were adapted specifically to enhance local facilities in seaside towns. For example, in 1823 a doctor from Torquay – Thomas Stabb – hatched a plan to open up hitherto inaccessible coves to the increasing numbers of bathers who were arriving in the small town of Ilfracombe on the North Devon coast. Stabb got together with some local entrepreneurs to form the *Ilfracombe Sea Bathing Company*. A team of Welsh miners was employed to carve tunnels through the rocky outcrop and construct three tidal pools that offered sheltered bathing for three hours on ei-ther side of low water. Men and women could walk down through the tunnels and bathe on separate beaches. A bugler was stationed on the outcrop to sound an alert if any gentlemen strayed too close to the ladies' area.

The vision and high-risk entrepreneurial spirit that drove the project in 1823 were rewarded when Ilfracombe's Tunnel Beaches became a visitor attraction of international repute, drawing crowds to explore the network of rock pools (made famous by naturalist Henry Gosse, who dis-covered new species of coral and other sea creatures there) and to bathe. Professor Harry Parker's swimming displays also pulled in the punters… he performed all kinds of feats in the water: lighting a cigar, drinking cham-pagne, escaping from handcuffs, swimming blindfold and imitating crab, porpoise and submarine.

Even before the railway arrived, Ilfracombe developed rapidly from isolated fishing harbour to tourist hot spot, with hotels, guest houses, parks and amenities springing up. The main beach – Rapparee – which is directly accessible from the town, established its own bathing business and became famous in its own right in 1878, when proprietor Alf Price encountered Kaiser Willhelm

Mobile studio and postcard shop, Bailey's photographers, Bournemouth.

"BY THE SAD SEA WAVES"

Landlady (*who has just presented her weekly bill*). "I 'ope, ma'am, as you find the bracing hair agree with you, ma'am, and your good gentleman, ma'am!"

Lady. "Oh, yes, our appetites are wonderfully improved! For instance, at home we only eat two loaves a day, and I find, from your account, that we can manage eight!"

[*Landlady feels uncomfortable.*

P.S.   145   K

Landladies practised strict economies. From *Mr Punch By The Seaside*, 1910.

doing pistol practice on the beach, his target being the numbers on Alf's bathing machines. After a brief exchange, Alf Price made his mark on history and the Kaiser returned to his hotel with a bloody nose.

Predominantly female and middle-aged or elderly, lodging keepers also prospered from the influx of visitors to the seaside, eking out the seasonal income with strict economies that verged on penny pinching. Some embezzled food and drink, charged for extras like table linen and bed sheets and crammed as many guests as possible into their houses.

Another new technology evolved in parallel with the seaside holiday and developed rapidly to meet demand. In 1839, the year that work on the London to Brighton railway line began, Fox Talbot discovered how to fix images made on paper by light rays. In February 1846, he produced images of the Royal Pavilion, the earliest known photographs of Brighton. Early photography was an expensive business, involving costly chemicals, fragile glass plates and bulky equipment. Initially, it was only available to the well-to-do in the form of *carte de visite* portraits, formal landscapes and stereoscopic views. But as reproduction processes improved, dry plate and hand cameras gave photographers increased mobility. Gradually, the photograph became more accessible to the middle classes, as portrait studios sprang up in every town and travelling photographers took to the road, visiting beauty spots and beaches and even going into the water to photograph bathers. They were initially treated with suspicion.

By the turn of the century, when the working class seaside holiday was reaching its peak, photographs could be cheaply mass-produced in the form of picture postcards, which were available to everybody. Low postage rates encouraged the postcard boom: in 1894, it cost a half-penny to send a card (as opposed to 1d for a letter). Most people could afford to pose in a seaside studio or on the beach and send the resulting postcards back home, or keep them as a memento of their visit to the seaside.

" Now, mind, if any of those nasty people with cameras come near, you're to send them away ! "

Photographers were treated with suspicion. From *Mr Punch By The Seaside*, 1910.

A FIND. "What is it?" The "Dainty" Series.

Photographs at the seaside.

Pier construction was another technology that had evolved rapidly in response to the new seaside leisure market. Ironwork became cheaper to produce, while advances in engineering skills and the railways meant that the components of piers could be pre-fabricated in inland factories and then transported to the seaside to be erected. Originally designed for the purpose of landing and embarking boat passengers and goods, piers were soon found to be excellent venues for promenading, a process that allowed seaside visitors to converse, display summer outfits and flirt whilst enjoying the salubrious sea air and admiring the view. Entrepreneurs and shareholders were quick to catch on to the business potential for this. The 1860s saw a boom in pier construction. At least 21 were completed, many gracing the resorts of North Wales and Lancashire.

Most piers were set up as businesses and funded by shareholders. Local tradesmen, merchants and lodging-keepers often pledged support, as they knew the piers would bring them business. Some projects even attracted investment from inland businesses: tradesmen in Preston and Manchester helped to fund the construction of Blackpool's piers. In an effort to meet the demands of the new leisure market, piers became less functional and more flamboyant and exotic in design, with oriental style pavilions, domes and delicate filigree work, the best example being Brighton's Palace Pier.

As demand grew, new piers were planned to make provision for commercial entertainment. This trend was first apparent at Blackpool, Weston and Margate, resorts that were among the first to receive large numbers of excursionists. By the 1880s and 1890s, new piers were being designed and older ones re-vamped to accommodate a range of all-weather facilities: dance floors, concert halls, refreshment rooms, shopping arcades, swingboats, fun fairs, arenas for gymnastic and swimming displays and theatres. Despite all these supplementary attractions, simply promenading along the pier continued to be a popular way to spend time at the seaside.

As the range of other entertainments on offer widened, bathing quickly ceased to be the sole purpose of a seaside visit. In the first half of the nineteenth century, resorts had responded to the need for supplementary entertainment by encouraging activities that would be improving as well as enjoyable. After bathing, visitors were urged to explore the natural environment (the rock pools at Ilfracombe being a good example) to identify and collect plants, ferns, fossils and butterflies and study local buildings and monuments of historical interest. In 1803, visitors to Swansea were even advised to walk along the canal in order to admire the copperworks, forge and steam engines. Bathers were also encouraged to take warming exercise in the form of sports such as tennis, croquet, archery and golf.

With the arrival of middle class children at the seaside, more family-based entertainments started to appear on the sand: donkey rides, Punch and Judy, pierrots and minstrel shows all becoming a common feature of beach life. But a tension arose between the needs of middle class families and those of excursionists and the poorer classes. Not surprisingly, the latter wanted to cram as much enjoyment as possible into their often short visits to the seaside. They preferred drinking and having fun to worthy, morally uplifting activities. Some resorts responded to this market by providing ever more elaborate entertainments and spectacles. On a day trip to Blackpool in 1874, you could goggle at firework displays, acrobats, naked classical tableaux and tight-rope walkers, try your luck in shooting galleries, and marvel at wax-works, menageries and human cannon-balls. And thanks to the town's relaxed licensing laws, you could do all this in a well-lubricated state.

Winter gardens and pleasure palaces sprang up around the coast of Britain to provide all-weather entertainment for the hordes, and, in Blackpool and New Brighton, magnificent Eiffelesque towers rose into the sky. A quiet

Promenading along the pier.

drive or stroll along the sea-front was likely to be anything but and this came as a shock to those who foolishly visited the seaside in the old-fashioned way, with a view to improving their health.

But while resorts like Brighton and Blackpool flourished, many smaller, less commercially resilient seaside towns struggled to deal with the advent of the masses, attempting in vain to legislate against noise, drunkenness and rowdiness, regulate entertainments and restrict the informal fairs, sideshows, stalls, hawkers, peddlers and prostitutes that followed in the wake of the lower class visitors. In 1856, the growing sense of outrage at the impact of cheap railway fares at Whitsun was evident in a Weston-super-Mare newspaper:

The dregs of St Philips, Bedminster and other disreputable neighbourhoods destroyed every quiet retreat.

If these conditions continue the future of Weston as a fashionable resort is at stake. What invalid would dare to emerge from lodgings on such a day?

Thirty years later, things in Weston had not improved. In 1886, the Local Board complained that *of late the noise and annoyances on the foreshore have become intolerable through the Rabble that frequent there with their Swing-Boats, Shooting stands and Galleries, Games of Aunt Sally, Shows of every description, Occupants of Tents etc.*

These comments show how, in the middle of the nineteenth century, the British seaside was an arena where upper, middle and lower classes – rich and poor, pious and ungodly, sedate and rowdy – found themselves sharing the same space and competing for the same facilities. Dickens describes some of the comical consequences of such a social mix in Broadstairs:

A cartoon from *Mr Punch By The Seaside* highlighting the rowdiness of a seaside promenade.

171

A QUIET DRIVE BY THE SEA
A Brighton bath-chairman's idea of a suitable route for an invalid lady

Ramsgate Sands by William Powell Frith (1852-54).

Some tip-top 'Nobbs' come down occasionally – even Dukes and Duchesses. We have known such carriages to blaze among the donkey-chaises, as made beholders wink. Attendant on these equipages come resplendent creatures in plush and powder, who are sure to be stricken disgusted with the indifferent accommodation of our water-ing-place, and who, of an evening (particularly when it rains), may be seen very much out of drawing, in rooms far too small for their fine figures, looking discontentedly out of little back windows into bye-streets.

But despite the availability of so many entertainments and distractions, on arrival at the seaside most people, whatever their background, headed onto the beach and straight into a territorial struggle over bathing traditions.

Pressure on small strips of sand grew with the arrival of the crowds. The problem was worse at high tide, which re-stricted the available area even more. Bathers of different sexes and from different class backgrounds ended up piling together into the waves, and into controversy:

There is not even the slightest pretension to common decency. The men gambol about in a complete state of

nature, and the ladies frolic in very questionable bathing garments within a few yards of them, while the sands are crowded with spectators of the scenes, of all ages and both sexes.
(*The Observer*, 28 August, 1859, article on Ramsgate.)

The outcry about indecency on the beaches reached its peak in the middle of the century, fuelled by the prudery that characterised the era. Two factors were to blame. Firstly, bathing trends were changing. People were not just taking a brief, discreet, medicinal dip but were starting to swim and to stay in the water for longer. Men, who traditionally bathed naked, could easily swim away from the segregated machines to areas where they could mingle with scantily clad women. Women were also spending longer in the water, often not so much swimming as lolling, as an *Observer* journalist, visiting Margate in 1856 commented:

Females do not venture beyond the surf and lay them-selves on their backs, waiting for the coming waves, with their bathing dresses in a most degagee style. The waves come and carry their dresses up to their neck, so that, as

THE BATHING QUESTION
Master Tommy is emphatically of the opinion that the sexes
ought not to bathe together.

above: Cartoon from *Mr Punch At The Seaside*
addressing the question of mixed bathing, 1910.
below & right: The erotic charge of sea bathing.

*I'm waiting for the tide
to go out.*

far as decency is concerned, they might as well be without any dresses at all. And all this takes place in the presence of thousands of spectators… the gentlemen are there with their opera glasses.

But the main catalyst to outrage was the problem of the lower class bathers, like the six penny dippers at Dawlish, who could not afford to hire bathing machines or bathing drawers. They would bathe naked. The postcard opposite, with its rather sinister inscription, shows a number of naked boys frolicking in the waves at Hove. Possibly this scene depicts local children or an outing of orphans or poor boys, perhaps organised by a Sunday School or some

Snap Shots at the Seaside — *Intruders*

THE SEA HATH ITS CHARMS AT HOVE.

Boys swimming naked at Hove.

local philanthropist. It shows how poor bathers behaved very differently from the middle classes, who were frequently satirised in the pages of Punch.

Different resorts tried to resolve the bathing question in different ways. Some places tried to price out working class bathers by increasing the cost of bathing machines, just as some authorities had levied an entrance fee for the piers in order to make them more exclusive. Some tried to legislate against nude bathing. Some authorities started to ban mixed bathing. In the 1860s, bathing by-laws proliferated. But these had a potentially problematic economic impact for lucrative seaside businesses: families would simply stop coming to beaches where mixed bathing was banned. And upper class, wealthy and aristocratic male bathers, who had always dipped naked, were not inclined to change the habits of a lifetime. Bathing machine

proprietors at Scarborough opposed the proposed by-laws with the view that: *first class visitors object to wearing drawers while bathing.*

In Scarborough, a compromise between morality and market forces was finally reached with the establishment of bathing timetables in certain zones: in the main bathing area, men must wear drawers except before 7am and after 9pm. Elsewhere, people could bathe as they pleased *to prevent the exclusion of the labouring classes and others who might be unable to provide themselves with drawers.* (*Scarborough Gazette*, 9th August, 1866.)

In some resorts, there was concern that banning nude bathing would mean excluding local townspeople, who themselves could not afford machines or costumes, from the benefits of immersion in the sea. David Sawyers

Bathing machines were expensive.
North Sands, Scarborough.

NORTH SANDS, SCARBOROUGH.

explains how the Brighton Sea Swimming Club originated when a group of tradesmen decided to enable the townspeople to experience the sea, gain mastery over it and thereby to move along the path to self-improvement:

'My grandmother's grandfather had been a founder member in 1860. He was one of the handful of North Street tradesmen who re-appropriated the beach in the name of Brighton's ordinary people. They were in the water literally for what they could learn through exploring the link between action and understanding. That movement of self-improvement was taking as given that one could develop one's conceptual powers almost indefinitely. My forbears were desperately trying to make something of themselves and one of the ways they thought they could do so was by extending their bodily powers and capabilities. In learning to swim, they would be teaching themselves how to think productively and therefore how to take charge of their lives and literally succeed. The club was founded in order to bring this capacity for self-realisation and self-determination to the youth of the town.

'Great great grandfather was not a fast swimmer but performed the most marvellous feats in the water. To demonstrate that what they were about was mastery of
the water, they undertook tea parties, to cook a steak, change clothes in the sea.

'Because you weren't allowed to undress on the beach you were compelled to use a bathing machine. Bathing machines were expensive so that meant that ordinary people could not have access to the sea except at dawn and at dusk. It's not surprising to find on record someone saying: "Swimming has become comparatively rare here amongst the townsmen."

'So: swimming classes, literally breaking new ground for ordinary people who were going to undress on the beach. Swimming classes were held from 6-8. They started by 1858. In the winter of 1860 a little handful decided they'd gained so much they were going to form a swimming club. And they did.'

By the end of the century some resorts were taking a more relaxed approach to mixed bathing. The main reason for this was that families wanted to enjoy the water together, with Papa joining the fun and not being despatched to some secluded cove. In addition, the UK's horrifying drowning statistics highlighted the fact that many people, particularly women and children, could not swim. Every year between 1860 and 1900, over 2,000 people accidentally drowned in Britain. 1878 was the worst year: a shocking 3,659 accidental and 369 suicidal drownings were recorded by the Royal Humane Society. This was the year that Thames paddle steamer *The Princess Alice,* returning to Woolwich after a moonlit cruise to Gravesend, sank in the heavily polluted river after a collision. Of the 650 drowned, the majority were women and children. Drowning accounts for between 200 and 500 deaths per annum these days, according to the *Royal Society for the Prevention of Accidents*. While still a grim statistic, it is a quarter of the toll that the late Victorians might have expected.

Given these figures, it is hardly surprising that drowning was a recurrent theme of much Victorian literature, where it was often symbolic of punishment, sacrifice or the relief of suffering. In *Daniel Deronda*, Gwendolen contemplates her brutish husband Grandcourt struggling in the water, having fallen from their yacht. Unable to bring herself to throw him a rope, she watches him drown (something she has long wished for), then throws herself into the sea in a fit of suicidal remorse. The evil Quilp goes under and meets a suitably horrible end in *The Old Curiosity Shop*. Estranged siblings Maggie and Tom Tulliver are finally reconciled in a watery embrace at the climax of *The Mill on the Floss*. Charles Kingsley, in *The Water-Babies*, even represented drowning as a magical, transformative experience, reminiscent of Celtic shape-shifting. The abused chimney sweep, Tom, runs away from his master, tries to wash away his dirt and ends up *with a pretty little lace-collar of gills around his neck and as clean as a fresh-run salmon:*

Tom was so hot and thirsty and so longed to be clean for once that he tumbled himself as quick as he could into the clear cool stream. And he had not been in it long before he fell fast asleep, into the quietest, sunniest, cosiest sleep that ever he had in his life. The reason of his falling into such a delightful sleep is very simple; and yet hardly anyone has found it out. It was merely that the fairies took him.

With drowning so lodged in the Victorian psyche, it became increasingly clear that swimming and life-saving needed to be taught much more widely. If men, women and children could bathe together, more could learn to avoid the danger of death by drowning:

Who better to teach a timid wife or daughter to swim

Mary Wheatland, Bognor's celebrated bathing woman.

than the man whose home they adorn?
(*Daily Graphic*, 1895.)

Dippers (who had originally accompanied bathers into the water for their medicinal dip, pushed them under then pulled them out) evolved into lifeguards. The postcard above shows Mary Wheatland in 1908. Known as *Bognor's mermaid*, she had started work in 1850 as a dipper, but by the age of 72 had saved 30 lives. Her life-saving medals are pinned to her chest.

With the re-establishment of mixed bathing, all-in-one bathing costumes became *de rigeur* for both sexes. Women's costumes became increasingly elaborate and

Mixed bathing at Margate.

This costume is not worn at Ostend. They look a draggled lot at that place.

WE DO SEE 'SIDE' AT THE SEASIDE

left: Bathers continued to assert their taste and superiority abroad. *right:* Stylish bathing costumes attract attention.

decorative, although often sufficiently revealing to provide an erotic charge for onlookers.

The end of the century saw the rowdy behaviour of the early excursionists improve as the poorer classes became more accustomed to taking holidays and managing the space and rituals of the seaside. Resorts like Blackpool and Brighton provided such a range of entertainments and activities that they acted as a magnet for pleasure seekers, and lifted pressure both from their own beaches and from the quieter, more sedate resorts. Upper and middle class holiday-makers who were reluctant to welcome the poor to their beaches sought out more secluded seaside spots around the coast of Britain, where excursionists wouldn't

Bathing tents on Folkestone beach.

Ventnor, Isle of Wight, showing bathing machines.

bother them. Or they de-camped to the Continent, where they could continue to assert their taste and superiority.

Meanwhile, the end of the century saw a new spirit of tolerance and egalitarianism. The lower classes were reconfigured as valued and valuable contributors to resort economy, people who deserved rest and refreshment as much as anyone else:

We love our haunts by the sea; the poorest amongst us regards his favourite seaside resort pretty much as the rich man does his country seat – as a place of relaxation from the hurly burly of life, and yet a home withal. How the eyes brighten at the sight of a familiar spot! And how vividly the old associations crowd back to the mind – memories of glowing, careless days that gave new life to the jaded worker and caused the brain-weary to forget their ineffable tedium vitae.
(*Round the Coast*, 1895.)

As men and women became accustomed to bathing to-gether and the mingling of the sexes on the sand was an increasingly common sight, the need for the bulky, labour intensive and expensive bathing machines declined. Peo-ple still needed somewhere to change, but tents and huts served the purpose well and were more flexible, and cheaper to hire.

Now in his early 80s, Jim Blake remembers seeing bathing machines in the water at Ventnor on the Isle of Wight when he was little. His great great grandfather started a bathing machine and boating business (*Blake's Longshore-men*) in 1830. The machines were made of wood and had

Jim Blake, Ventnor, Isle of Wight © Martin Parr/Magnum.

Beach huts at Ventnor, Isle of Wight © Martin Parr/Magnum.

brass nails and hinges and canvas roofs. The enormous metal wheels were three inches wide and five feet in diameter. Rather than being drawn into the water by horses, they were winched up and down the sand by capstan.

Jim stills run Blake's Longshoremen from his wooden hut on Ventnor beach and is proprietor of a small museum of bathing memorabilia on the front, displaying some threadbare examples of beachwear from the turn of the century and yoked buckets that were used by his grandfather to carry seawater up to lodging houses.

While his boat-hire business has been scuppered by health and safety regulations, Jim is still pretty busy in the summer hiring out deckchairs, sun-loungers, windbreaks

and beach umbrellas. He also rents out beach huts, which are the original bathing machines minus their wheels. The machines were sawn in half and made into huts by his father, just after the First World War. You can still see the axles where once the great wheels were fixed.

The Ladies' Pool, Ilfracombe

The radio is issuing severe weather warnings for the South West: thundery showers and torrential downpours. But as I wind along the tight road that leads to Ilfracombe the air is humid, the sun is strong and only the slightest breeze ruffles the high hedgerows and cow parsley.

I arrive at Tunnel Beaches and walk down through the sudden dark of the rock passage towards the light and noise of the sea. It seems the weather forecast was right after all. The wind has got up and, although I entered the tunnel in sunlight, I can see a shower of rain at the other end, where a cluster of visitors, hurriedly donning anoraks and plastic macs, shelter and peer up into the sky.

I dash through the rain into the second tunnel leading down to the ladies' beach, and the only one of the original three seawater pools still intact. The shower passes and I emerge onto a grey beach of grit and shale – no sand. Two elderly women wearing rain hats who are making their way back up through the tunnel seem to have given this beach the thumbs down for this reason: *'What a shame there isn't any sand. It's not very inviting'*. But I think it is stunning: the grey grit at the top of the narrow strand gradually ceding to tiny, rounded slates near the water's edge. All easy on the feet. Smooth black rocks slope into the water and, beyond that, jagged limestone jutting out from the sea, pointing north. I turn around. The cliffs looming over the beach are black, bursting out of their tight, mossy coat. I can just glimpse the roof tiles, elaborate chimneys and fancy cream and red brickwork of a Victorian house perched on the cliff edge, looking out to Lundy and across the channel to the Welsh coast beyond. Behind the house, clouds pile up.

The sudden wind has whipped up waves. The tide is coming in but has not yet reached the sea pool, which is clearly outlined by cemented walkways that run between the large smooth rocks. The water in the pool is greeny-black, the surface rippling. I quickly change and then step down from one of the little walkways (which has a deep, clear rock pool on the other side) onto the soft shale and move slowly into the water. It feels cool and beautiful.

I swim gently across to the other side of the pool, where it gets deeper. As I swim, my underside, arms and legs are stroked by the soft red fronds of the seaweed. Everything feels smooth and quiet. Low down in the pool I am

protected from the wind. I can hear the tide approaching – the pool will be covered in half an hour – and every now and then I can see a splash and spray of foam as water hits rock.

The sun comes out and instantly the water turns from black to milky turquoise. I float on my back and contemplate the beach, where a few families with toddlers and babies are sitting. A mother drags her buggy backwards up the steep beach, its wheels churning in soft shale. Every now and then, visitors emerge from the tunnel and stand blinking in the light and gazing around. A few people walk around the pool and take photos of the sea and the cliffs. No-one else is swimming, but at the other end of the pool, a mother and son, clad in life-jackets, are trying out a kayak with much shrieking and hilarity. One hundred years ago, they would not have been allowed to have fun in the water together: mixed bathing was only permitted here in 1910.

After my swim I feel cold in the wind, so buy a cup of tea from the shop then take it down to the beach and sit warming my hands. The lifeguard tells me that no-one will swim today (apart from me) because people think that bad weather makes the water temperature drop, whereas in fact it stays fairly constant through sun, wind and rain. He will go in later with a wetsuit to do his triathlon training. He says that, on a hot day, many people bathe in the pool – which is safe for children – and also go in from the beach at high tide.

I sit watching as the water swirls noisily up towards the high tide mark and think about the amazing feat of tunnelling through 160 metres of rock to give access to beaches that could previously be reached only by boat. I last came to Ilfracombe twenty years ago. The tunnels were neglected, the town felt run down, and I feared that the pools would disintegrate and this extraordinary part of Ilfracombe's heritage would be lost. But, thankfully, Jamie McLintock and his partner have taken on the project of restoring the tunnels and building up the business again. Despite the lack of sand, families are attracted by the pool where it is safe to paddle and use inflatables, the smart new play area and café, the rock pools and the quirky history of the place. Jamie says that a warm August day can see 2,000 visitors make their way through the tunnels down to the grey beach and turquoise water, more than the total number of visitors for the whole of November.

This, plus the fact that a number of elderly regular swimmers have recently died, and rigorous health and safety legislation, has led Jamie to close the Tunnels in the winter.

This remarkable bathing place is one of the hundred-odd tidal pools built by businessmen and philanthropists around the coast of the British Isles during the nineteenth and early twentieth centuries. From La Vallette in St Peter Port, Guernsey, to The Trinkie, at Wick Bay in Caithness, the pools allowed bathers to enjoy sea water in safety, regardless of tide and weather conditions. While many have fallen into disrepair, like the Portsoy Pool on the north east coast of Scotland, around thirty tidal pools are still in use, and some continue to welcome swimmers throughout the year.

Rules and pools: the regulation of swimming

The Victorians were great organisers and administrators, whose rule-making vigour extended beyond government and legislation to permeate every aspect of social and domestic life. Household management, fashion, gardening, even table decoration – all became highly regulated activities, governed by strict codes of correctness. Sporting activities were also transformed by this pervasive organisational zeal. During the latter part of the nineteenth century what had been loosely structured sporting practices, largely determined by variable local traditions, slowly became formalised and standardised across Britain.

Organisation on such a scale was necessary because sport was becoming increasingly popular. The second half of the nineteenth century saw the growth of trade across the Empire and the consolidation of the great British industries, boosting prosperity and financial security and leading to improved standards of living for many. The middle classes found themselves with more disposable income and more leisure time in which to dispose of it. The working classes also started to enjoy better conditions, restricted working hours and guaranteed holidays. Seeking ways to pass this new leisure time, middle class people turned enthusiastically to cultural activities, to scientific pursuits such as collecting fossils, butterflies, and bird-watching and to sports and games. Archery, angling, tennis, croquet, rowing and golf escalated in popularity, each attracting aficionados who formed clubs and associations and worked industriously to promote competition and improve technique.

Swimming was no exception to this process of formalisation. Opportunities to bathe and to learn how to swim were increasing. Every summer, the railways would bring hundreds of thousands of holiday-makers from inland cities to the coast where many seized the opportunity to dip in the sea. Inland, thousands of bathers took to Britain's lakes and rivers: during the hot summer of 1873 a total of 356,813 people were known to have bathed in the Serpentine. In addition, the last quarter of the nineteenth century saw municipal pools being built in towns and cities across the United Kingdom, providing even the most land-locked populations with opportunities to get into the water.

Public interest in swimming was further boosted on the 25th August, 1875, when Captain Matthew Webb's second attempt to cross the Channel ended successfully

Prize winning swimmer, Yorkshire Amateur Swimming Association.

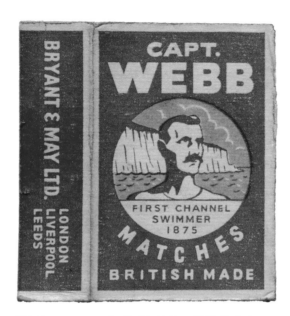

Matchbox commemorating Captain Matthew Webb, the first person to swim across the English Channel in 1875.

after 22 hours in the water. Webb became a popular swimming hero, crowds turning out to meet him wherever he went, and he inspired people either to get into the water for the first time or, if they could already swim, to work on improving their speed, endurance and technique. Sadly, Webb was to drown just eight years after his Channel achievement while attempting to swim across the Whirlpool Rapids, below Niagara Falls.

The sheer number of people taking to sea, lake, river and pool meant that the practice of swimming, previously something of a free-for-all, had to be organised and systematised. Primarily, it was important to manage large numbers of swimmers of both sexes in close proximity, preserving both their safety and decency. However, other factors also drove the regulatory process, not least the growing interest in competitive swimming and the quest to improve technique and performance under controlled conditions. Every aspect of swimming became regulated: who could swim, where and when; who could compete; who could join which clubs; what swimmers should wear and which strokes they should use; how life saving and swimming should be taught, and so on. Swimming clubs and associations were established (with constitutions, rules and regulations of Byzantine complexity). Books, magazines and manuals were published and elaborate training courses formalised and set up across the UK.

Class and cleanliness

In the first part of the 19th century, as Britain's industrial cities grew, increasing numbers of people were compelled to live in close proximity, often in unsanitary conditions. In 1842, Edwin Chadwick's report on the living conditions of the labouring classes had made clear the link between over-crowding, lack of sanitation and disease. Epidemics of flu, typhus, diphtheria and scarlet fever were common. Cholera was caused by drinking contaminated water (although this link was not demonstrated until John Snow analysed the source of the outbreak in Soho in 1852). Eventually, the *Great Stink*, during the hot summer of 1858, precipitated a debate in the newly built Houses of Parliament on the management of sewage. Engineers and town planners were tasked with improving sanitation. Elaborate engineering programmes, like the one led by Joseph Bazalgette in London, resulted in the construction of the great municipal drainage and sewerage systems across the UK, radically improving living conditions and raising standards of public health.

Despite these advances, few houses had private toilet or washing facilities. The Baths and Wash Houses Act was passed in 1846 in order to rectify poor standards of hygiene by providing the public with access to facilities for bathing and washing clothes, at a reasonable cost. The aim was to promote personal cleanliness, thereby improving the health of the nation. An anonymous tract published in 1834 (*Constant Use of Cold or Swimming Baths of Great Importance in the Prevention of Disease and the Preservation of Health*) probably informed the Act. This made explicit the connection between swimming, hygiene and health and as a result many local authorities incorporated small plunge pools in their municipal washing facilities. In 1878, the Act was amended to endorse the building of large municipal swimming pools, thereby formalising the connection between swimming and cleanliness. The financial viability of swimming pools was assured, guaranteeing local authorities a year-round income from their investment, as they could be closed in the winter months – when the water would be unheated – and used as gymnasia or dance halls.

A wave of public building followed the 1878 amendment. Pools sprang up all over the UK. In 1845 there was only one municipal pool in England (in Liverpool). By 1880, 83 were in existence. By 1900, 206 pools had been built and by 1912 there were 600. By the start of the First World

Brill's Baths, King's Road, Brighton, built in 1869.

The Free Swimming Baths, Derby, built and donated in 1873 by brewer Michael Bass.

Posters advertising the Goulston Street Baths, London.

War, every town with a population over 100,000 had access to a municipal swimming pool, although there was a higher concentration in London and the industrialised areas of Britain – Lancashire and Yorkshire in particular – than elsewhere.

The building of swimming pools attracted the support of philanthropic businessmen as well as local authorities. The men and boys of Derby, that same hot summer of 1873, welcomed the advent of the Free Swimming Baths, lavishly designed open air pools built and donated to the community by brewer Michael Bass.

As increasing numbers of people started to use swimming pools to exercise and keep themselves clean, certain technical and logistical issues arose. Pools thronged with

grubby bathers quickly became dirty and had to be emptied, scrubbed out and refilled on a regular basis – efficient systems for chemical management and filtration not being developed until 1918. The Baths and Wash Houses Act reinforced social divisions by authorising municipal establishments to provide several separate classes of baths. Second and third class pools were usually smaller (say 75 x 35 feet as opposed to 100 x 40 feet for first class swimmers). Where it was not possible to build a set of separate pools on one site, different classes swam at different times, a form of time-zoning that was also in place on many beaches, where poorer people had to bathe very early or very late. In the pools, first class swimmers and higher class patrons were allowed to swim on the clean water days.

Swimming and female emancipation

Against the backdrop of debate about the benefits and propriety of exercise for the weaker sex, mid-Victorian middle class women started to engage enthusiastically in some of the newly fashionable sporting activities such as archery, bicycling, golf and tennis. In 1879, as the Suffragette movement was gaining momentum, a female doctor gave a talk to the Women's Union in which she listed the benefits of swimming for women. Swimming exercised the lungs, freed the body from the constraints of stays and corsets, released internal congestions, allowed unhampered movement of limbs and muscles and stabilised the nervous system. This sounds startlingly up to date compared with the case made for female swimming 40 years later in *The Swimming Magazine*, which centred on more traditional womanly qualities:

Swimming is an exercise peculiarly adapted to girls by virtue of its gentle action and absence of strain. There is nothing that reaches the masses which so materially preserves youth and beauty, or so effectively develops grace and ease of movement.

The Baths and Wash Houses Act of 1846 had protected the right of women to bathe and wash in privacy. This meant the separation of men and women's facilities. The Act also legislated for the strict definition and separation of men and women's areas in public bathing places, a law that was re-stated in the Town Police Clauses Act in 1847 but inconsistently implemented on British beaches. Of course, it was much easier to enforce the rules within the confines of the swimming pool than on the beach.

Many authorities complied with the law by building separate pools for men and women. Again, social divisions – this time between the sexes – were reflected in the relative sizes of the pools. Women were thought to need less room for swimming, so their pools were considerably smaller, certainly than the men's pools, and even than the lower class pools. For example, in the Clapham and Brixton Baths, built in 1873, the men's pool measured 150 by 60 feet and the women's pool 65 by 30 feet.

Where provision of separate pools was not possible, the time-zoning approach was adopted, this time to keep the sexes apart. This kind of segregation continued well into the twentieth century. In the September 1915 edition of *The Swimming Magazine*, a correspondent known as Lady Dorothy wrote a column complaining about the size of women's pools: often half the size of men's, they charged the same admission fee. When the same pool had to be shared, Lady Dorothy condemned the fact that men were offered more favourable times to swim.

During the middle part of the nineteenth century a number of swimming clubs and associations were set up, many of which excluded women other than as spectators of the races and competitions. Even this raised a problem as it meant that the male competitors could not swim naked, as they had been accustomed to do. Regulation came to the rescue and by 1890 the *Amateur Swimming Association* (ASA) had laid down strict rules about the wearing of swimming costumes by male competitors:

Any Competitor who is discovered to have swam without drawers or with the leg portion turned up is thereby disqualified, and the promoters of the Meeting may report him to the Association.

When women were eventually allowed to join the ASA and to take part in swimming races, they too had to observe a strict dress code. They were required to wear stockings and skirted costumes that had at least a four inch sleeve and were cut straight around the neck to preserve decency. Between 1890 and 1918, ASA regulations about swimming attire for women proliferated. Lady Dorothy, clearly a vociferous supporter of women's rights, sent a letter about the issue from America to *The Swimming Magazine* in April 1917:

She contributed some trenchant opinions on the costumes lady swimmers are perforce compelled to wear, by virtue of the rulings of the Amateur Swimming Association. She stoutly maintained that English lady swimmers were severely handicapped by having to wear four inch sleeves. She was also dead against stockings on the grounds that they were untidy, ungainly, never matched the bathing dress in colour, hung off the ends of the feet when wet, tended to make the wearer slip, pulled the costume out of shape, were generally soon full of holes and made the swimmer look ridiculously over-dressed. She added: 'I'd like to take some of those men, hang long stockings on them and then make them swim races in rough weather.'

According to Lady Dorothy, American women were starting to favour the more streamlined knee length costumes worn by men and were of the opinion that stockings

Ladies' bathing fashion went through many changes.

became water bags that retarded the swimmers. She reported that her American friends wanted to know whether they should wear hats and shoes when swimming.

Although this was clearly meant as a joke, images of early Victorian bathing attire show that female swimmers in Britain had indeed worn hats, coats, shoes and even corsets into the water. Fashion had imposed its own strict codes on swimwear for women and bathing costumes reflected the rapidly changing styles and trends of the second part of the 19th century. Decency took priority over functionality. Costumes were made from thick, dark material, usually serge or linen, to avoid becoming transparent when wet. Many were so elaborate and cumbersome that they must have made it extremely difficult for the wearer to float and move freely through the water.

In the 1860s, women swam wearing the bloomer bathing suit: ankle length trousers topped with a tunic like jacket, some adorned with epaulettes and the whole outfit topped off with a hat. Bathing shoes, like ballet slippers tied with ribbons, protected the feet from stones. During the 1870s, under-trousers became shorter and by the 1880s women were wearing combination-like garments, topped with a jacket or coat and accessorised with a wide belt, a bit like a corset. This gave a pleasingly slim shape but must have

Fin de siècle bathers, wearing costumes with 'leg o'mutton' sleeves.

The cover of *The Swimming Magazine*, July 1917, showing streamlined bathing attire for women.

rules laid down by the *Amateur Swimming Association*, swimwear started to reflect the process of rationalisation that was becoming evident in women's fashion more generally, spurred on by the Suffragette movement. Engaging more in physical activity, and increasingly aware of the damaging impact of tight corsetry, women were gradually being released from the imperative to wear restrictive and cumbersome clothing. Corsets and bustles were laid aside and a more natural and streamlined female shape started to emerge.

The Swimming Magazine, which advocated for mixed bathing and championed swimming for women, drove the point home by depicting on its cover a young woman preparing to dive into the water. She has bare legs and is wearing a close fitting sleeveless costume, similar to that worn by her male companion. Obviously it would be easier to swim wearing such a costume, not weighed down by folds of material and hampered by tight sleeves and bodices. Swimwear was finally becoming fit for purpose.

Despite the numerous rules and regulations about swimwear, and their limited access to pools, recreational swimming was extremely popular amongst late Victorian women. Agnes Campbell's survey of municipal baths, published in 1918, shows that thousands of women were making use of bathing facilities. This sporting revolution was mostly confined to middle class women. Unlike working class women, they could afford the time to learn and practise swimming strokes, pay the entrance fee to their local pool and purchase the costumes.

However, some working class women did break into the world of competitive and display swimming, doing long distance swims, racing for prize money and performing in aquatic entertainments. This was off limits, other than in informal galas, for the middle class female recreational swimmers, who were only allowed to start competing in ASA championships in 1901. The first women competitors and performers were often part of swimming families, the daughters of teachers who were known as *professors*. In 1875, Miss Agnes Beckwith, aged 14, swam from London Bridge to Greenwich for a wager of £100. She covered the distance of five miles in 1 hour, 7 minutes and 45 seconds, despite reputedly wearing a dress with a full skirt, pantaloons and stockings. She went on to campaign for women to have more practical bathing costumes, adding a swimmer's voice to the call for female emancipation, a cause later taken up by Annette Kellerman.

been extremely restrictive to wear in the water. Straw hats, with the brim tipped over the face, protected bathers from the sun. These were later replaced by the more practical *Normandy*, a kind of mob-cap or turban that could keep the hair dry and be trimmed with different colour ribbons.

By the 1890s, bare legs were out and stockings were in vogue, displayed by the shorter hemlines. *Leg o' mutton sleeves* (a billowing upper sleeve tapering down to close fitting lower sleeve) also became fashionable for day and evening wear. Despite their lack of practicality as regards swimming, these too were incorporated into stylish bathing suits for *fin de siècle* bathers.

In the first decade of the new century, despite the strict

Clubs and associations

Clubs and associations were an important part of Victorian and Edwardian life and as much a part of the legacy of the era as railways and sewerage systems. Clubs promoting bathing had started to appear in the early part of the 19th century and represented the first attempts to organise the sport. The first clubs to be formed were for masters and students of Eton College and Cambridge. The elite *Philolutic Society* enrolled 200 members between 1832 and 1849 and was dedicated to promoting bathing and swimming. A small sub-section of this group formed the *Psychrolutic Society*, made up of men who were passionate about bathing in cold, wild, open water (a prototype for today's *Outdoor Swimming Society*). Records show that the select company of 26 Psychrolutes bathed in Scottish lochs, dipped in English rivers and swam across the Hellespont.

In contrast to this esoteric group, a more traditional, formal body dedicated to swimming was founded in 1830: *The National Swimming Association*. Although its aim was to organise swimming on a national scale, the association only really had an impact in London, providing instruction and mounting competitions and races in the Thames. It evolved into the *British Swimming Society* (BSS), founded in 1841, which aimed to *promote health, cleanliness and preservation of life by the practice of bathing and teaching and encouraging the art of swimming* through lessons, races and even essay competitions. However, the BSS was also short-lived, only surviving for 4 years.

In the 1850s and 1860s, large numbers of independent swimming clubs and societies sprang up across the UK. These first appeared in London and along the coast, but, as municipal pools were built inland, clubs were founded in the most land-locked towns and cities, from Huddersfield to Yeovil. The first London based clubs included *The Ilex Swimming Club* (1861), *The Serpentine Swimming Club* (1864) and *The Otter Swimming Club* (1869), the latter two of which still exist today. David Sawyers talks about the *Brighton Swimming Club*, an organisation of which his great great grandfather, a North Street tradesman, was a founder member:

'There were bathing facilities on the West Pier and the club used them and carried out its races, performances and annual fete under the full gaze of the public – marine acrobatics and all the rest of it. By that time swimming was taking off. By the late 1890s there were something like 25 separate swimming clubs in the Brighton region alone. The railway works had its own swimming club. I think the post office had one as well. In fact most large organisations did.'

These amateur clubs were dedicated to promoting public interest in the art of swimming through putting on galas, races and displays. Local swimming events attracted considerable interest in the press:

The Lambeth Baths was the scene, on Monday evening, of an animated fete, into which the London Swimming Club had contrived to include a number of aquatic amusements of a strikingly novel and amusing character. There was, first, a 'hurdle-race' for a cup, contested by youths under sixteen who had never previously won a prize. The hurdles consist of poles floated on the water. Next there was an egg-diving contest. Next there were trial heats for a silver Leander medal, trial heats for a goblet, and an extraordinary 'pole-walking' competition by members of the club. The great feature of the programme was the race for the captaincy of the London Swimming Club. The whole distance swum was 400 yards, in ten lengths of the bath.
(The Penny Illustrated Paper, 29 September 1866.)

A national body dedicated to swimming finally emerged in 1886 in the form of *The Amateur Swimming Association* (ASA). Its evolution was fraught with debate and conflict over definitions of amateur versus professional status, mirroring what was going on in other sports, particularly football and cricket. The distinction was largely class based, as professional swimmers (who earned their living by competing for large sums of money) tended to come from lower social groups. Conflict over rules and regulations, particularly over swimming races and prize money, led to bitter controversy and the formation of numerous splinter groups, each accusing the others of being professional, not amateur.

The formulation of a definitive set of rules led to the resolution of the conflict: amateur and professional swimmers came to exist peaceably side by side. The ASA slowly extended its jurisdiction, establishing coherent representation, governance and control across the different regions of Britain. In 1887, Queen Victoria's patronage of the Association put the royal seal of approval on swimming and stimulated more public enthusiasm. Britain started to play a part in international competitions, entering swimming teams into the 1900 Olympic Games in Paris and of course into the London Games of 1908. In that year, an international conference on swimming led to the foundation of the *International Amateur Swimming Federation*. Its first general secretary was British, and most of its policies and rules were taken from the ASA handbook. Thus, the British talent for regulation influenced swimming organisations in Europe, throughout the colonies and even the New World.

Different strokes

Competitive swimming became extremely popular in the nineteenth century. Early races seem to have been pretty wild, unregulated affairs, attracting competitors from all backgrounds, some of whom were not afraid to cause a spectacle and provide a flagrant affront to decency:

The Morning Herald of Monday last contained the following announcement: SPORTING NOVELTIES. A SWIMMING RACE twice across the Thames by AQUATIC JOCKIES will take place at Cremorne house, King's Road, THIS DAY. Upon entering the grounds, we observed a number of faces familiar to us, amongst which were the Duke of Dorset, the most noble the Marquis of Waterford, Lord Waldegrave, and Count D'Orsay. "Here come the jocks!" saluted our ears. We turned round and beheld a file of stark naked adults, marching round the grounds, in order to show themselves, prior to plunging into the bosom of old father Thames. These were the aquatic jockies. The Duke of Dorset was the first to fall into the line. His Grace's skin had a shrivelled, yet very glossy appearance.
(*The Town Magazine*, 1840.)

As swimming clubs and associations proliferated, such flamboyant spectacles became increasingly rare. While professionals battled it out for prize money, middle class recreational swimmers took part in amateur championships and competed to win medals, cups and trophies. Although some races, such as the amateur championship, continued to be held in the Thames or in the sea, local galas and competitions were commonly staged in swimming pools, where there were no worries about the weather and conditions were consistent. A good swimming speed was seen as the highest achievement, and almost a moral duty:

Speed and endurance are of the utmost value when the

use of swimming has to be put into practice and the varied nature of racing competitions encourage these important details. Speed is imperative if a drowning person is to be reached in time to do most good, and endurance is needed in the effort and oft-times the struggle that follows.
(Frank Sachs *The Complete Swimmer*, 1912.)

Competitive swimming was boosted by advances in the understanding of dynamics and physics. The Victorians turned their attention to technique, minutely analysing the various different strokes in order to improve their efficiency and enhance the teaching of swimming. Breast stroke, side stroke, over-arm stroke, and back stroke were described in painstaking detail. Some strokes were sanctioned – they were correct, official, 'recognised styles' – while others were disparaged.

The Trudgen (a very fast stroke introduced to Britain by John Trudgen, who had learned it from swimmers in South America) became popular, as it enabled the swimmer to move through the water at a great speed, at least for a short period of time:

The mode of swimming is applicable in cases where a great degree of rapidity is required for a short distance. The body is lifted at each stroke and at each swing of the arms seems to be hurled forward.
The Swimming Record, 1873

While they were certainly fast, Trudgen-users were not elegant. *The Badminton Library Book of Sports and*

A relay race in a municipal swimming pool (from *The Badminton Library Book of Sports and Pastimes: Swimming*, 1893 edition).

Postcard sent in 1907, showing different strokes including the Trudgen.

Pastimes: Swimming, first published in 1885, was damning about the 'slovenliness' of the stroke. Nevertheless, the Trudgen caught on and was taught until it was superseded by the crawl. Mr John Phillips, who in 1999, at the age of 88, was still swimming in the sea at Ryde on the Isle of Wight, was a self-taught swimmer. As a boy he developed a kind of hybrid stroke that suited him, but that would not have been officially sanctioned:

'I learned at 12, 13 and you just swam by going in the water and walking out far enough and taking your feet off the bottom and learning how you could manage to avoid to sink. We just taught ourselves. In those days the crawl had not been invented and we used to call it the Trudgen. The Trudgen was an overarm double sided action with a scissor kick with your feet. And that was how the people who were taught, that's what they used. When I was in my teens I went to Southampton to work and I did do a bit of bath swimming, pool swimming there and I joined the swimming club but it was too late for me to try to learn any decent stroke because I got too inured with what I learned myself, a breast stroke I mainly settled with. Then the side stroke. That was very popular. You lay on one side and you did scissor kick. I later got in the way of taking my left arm out of the water and it was a kind of side overarm, but it was very unofficial, very unofficial.'

Mr Philips' swimming methods would certainly have aroused the scorn of Frank Sachs, who wrote in *The Complete Swimmer: It is seldom that two men are found who swim exactly alike and the chief reason for this is that so many of the strokes they use are bad. They lack intelligent thought. They have just been allowed to come.*

In contrast to the Trudgen, the crawl was a fast, elegant stroke that could be maintained over considerable distance. *It revolutionises everything,* wrote Frank Sachs. *It is an import from Australia and is faster by several seconds than any other stroke. Its greatest exponent has been the American C.M. Daniels, who created records of 1 minute 32⅖ seconds for 150 yards in Manchester in 1898.* The stroke was minutely analysed and quickly taken up by swimming clubs and competitive swimmers around the world.

Alongside this scientific approach to swimming techniques, the quest to improve the swimmer's buoyancy and performance engaged the engineering inventiveness of the late Victorians and Edwardians. *The Badminton book*

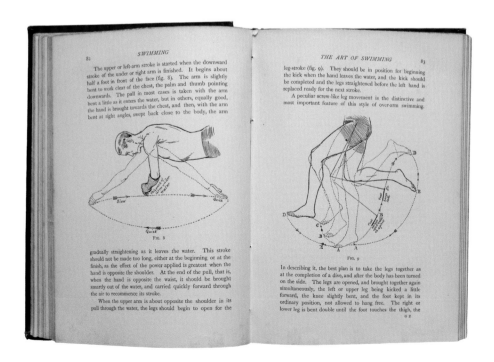

A scientific approach to swimming strokes (from *The Badminton book*).

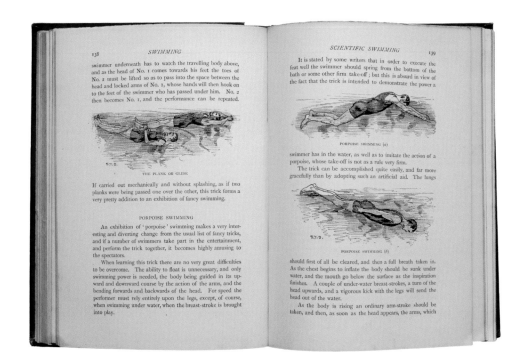

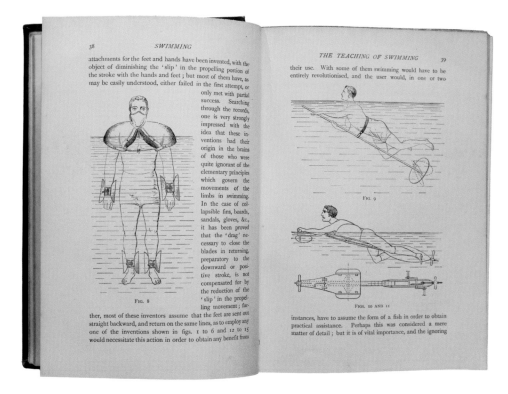

Scientific swimming techniques, and aids to buoyancy and propulsion (from *The Badminton book*).

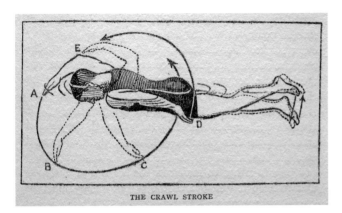

THE CRAWL STROKE

From *The Complete Swimmer* by Frank Sachs (1912).

features some of the Patent Office's more extraordinary buoyancy aids, hoists and devices to aid propulsion such as attachable leg fins and a kind of underwater bicycle.

The peak of formalisation was reached with *scientific swimming* (which would be known today as *synchronised swimming*). Practised almost exclusively by men, it involved tricks such as smoking, eating and drinking under water and undertaking various manoeuvres such as swinging like a pendulum or revolving on the surface of the water, either individually or as part of a team. These tricks were entertaining to watch and transformed local amateur swimming galas into an extremely popular spectator sport. Scientific swimmers were trained to execute the required moves correctly:

In this branch of the art, more than any other, practice of a careful and painstaking character is compulsory. A number of tricks can only be accomplished after very steady trials and any swimmer who attempts them in public before attaining perfection risks the chance of making his exhibition ludicrous and absurd.

Although his great great grandfather practised scientific swimming in the early days of the Brighton club, David Sawyers feels that competitive swimming was to prove a distraction to swimmers. They no longer enjoyed the benefits brought by learning to manage an unpredictable sea. The stable conditions of the pool meant they could focus their efforts solely on improving their technique and increasing their speed:

'Brighton's North Road Baths arrived in the late 1880s. That was the beginning of the end. Pool swimming – because of the controlled conditions, because you could count on the water conditions being exactly replicable from one moment to the next – became where one could measure one's performance. Racing took over and the attitude of mind that prized co-ordination, prized the scientific management of human resources. We were getting the beginnings of the industrial society: time and motion studies, ergonomics. And that killed sea swimming as it had been. Everything was focussed on the pool and this business of refining performance, of being faster and swimming more strongly, more precisely, more ergonomically. Being concerned about the stroke. In fact Brighton's swimming club had become practically entirely pool based with just a handful of people swimming in the sea.'

The teaching of swimming

The teaching of scientific swimming – and swimming in general – was regarded as a serious business, to be tackled in a rigorous manner. The different strokes were carefully studied and analysed and the correct techniques instilled through comprehensive swimming drills that took place both in the water and out of it. Archibald Sinclair and William Henry devoted a whole chapter of *The Badminton book* to a detailed description of the most effective teaching methods that would enable the pupil *to acquire a thorough knowledge of the correct movements necessary to attain speed.*

The land drill was a first starting point for the novice and had the great advantage that it could be practised in winter before the bathing season began. The teacher was advised to be clear, firm and concise in giving directions:

At the command: 'Prepare for breaststroke' raise the hands in front of the chest with the thumbs and forefingers nearly touching, palms downwards, fingers closed. The elbows should be close to the side, the hands pointing upward.

Once having mastered the arm and leg strokes separately, the pupil moved on to using them both together, while lying on his front on a bench or table. Only then did the novice move into the water and begin the water drill, which was also graded to build up buoyancy and confidence.

Land drill from *The Badminton book*.

But swimming had not always been taught using such precise methods. The July 1917 issue of *The Swimming Magazine* carried a feature on Mr B.P.W. Smyth, who had recently died at the age of 97. Mr Smyth was taught to swim at Eton, presumably in the late 1820s in a much more casual style:

Swimming was taught in a rough and ready way. A bigger boy would say: 'Can you swim?' On being told 'No' he would reply: 'Then it's jolly well time you learned' and you were chucked into the Thames and left to scramble out as best you could, choking and half drowned. We never changed our clothes afterwards and would sit for hours in our half dried garments. It was certainly in those days the survival of the fittest.

Mr Smyth was one of the privileged boys taught at the great private schools before mass education arrived in the latter part of the nineteenth century. According to the

authors of *The Badminton book*, most renowned public schools were teaching swimming using convenient bathing places in nearby rivers or lakes. The boys at Charterhouse learned to swim in the Wey, those from Shrewsbury in the Severn, while Rugby boys learned in the Avon and so on. Coastal schools also made use of nearby natural resources, some in more extreme ways than others. Around 1900, a limestone pavement near Swanage in Dorset was blasted to create a swimming facility for Durnford Preparatory School. The pool was known as *Dancing Ledge*.

Harrow was the first school to create an area specifically for swimming (known as the *Duck Puddle*) by digging out a pool and diverting Thames water into it. A pupil at Harrow, Lord Byron swam wearing long trousers to conceal his disability and keeping himself apart from the other boys. The Duck Puddle was maintained and improved over many years (parts of it were even tiled) and was the focus of many nostalgic outpourings, as evidenced by a poem written in 1881 by Mr J. Roberston, an ex-pupil and master at Harrow:

*How sweet when the summer rejoices
The heart with the glow and the breeze
To plunge in the pool while the voices
Are ringing from under the trees.
Ah! Long in the sober hereafter
Shall linger in ears far away
The sound of that innocent laughter
The splash of the spray.*

Dancing Ledge tidal pool, Dorset © Harriet Short

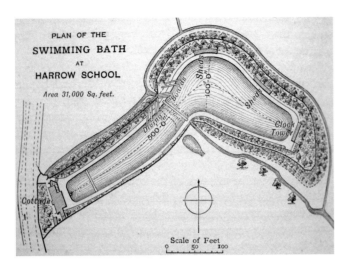

PLAN OF THE
SWIMMING BATH
AT
HARROW SCHOOL

Area 31,000 Sq. feet.

The Duck Puddle, from *The Badminton book*.

Such a carefree approach to childhood bathing was not to last. As the nineteenth century progressed, the so-called *Clarendon* schools (those reviewed by the Clarendon Commission in 1861) established swimming drills and tests, mounted competitions and inter-school swimming matches and started to build their own indoor pools, although many continued with river swimming as well.

As state education became established, many teaching methods and practices were transferred from the public to the state schools. By 1910, the government was committed to the teaching of swimming to children and young people across Britain. Swimming became part of the curriculum for boys and, somewhat later, for girls. Unlike the public schools, most state schools had to make use of local municipal pools for their lessons. Their limited access to bathing places meant that most state schools used land drills to teach the basics:

There are many who will scoff at the idea of teaching swimming by means of a land drill, but it is a practice that has produced tens of thousands of swimmers across the country. A land drill can be carried out at times when instruction in the water is impossible, will lighten the task and hasten the acquisition of the strokes very sensibly indeed.
(Frank Sachs, *The Complete Swimmer*, 1912.)

Swimming lessons were supplemented by the teaching of life saving techniques, as the late Victorians sought to reduce the high number of deaths by drowning which were occurring in Britain each year. Rudimentary methods for rescuing a drowning person had been developed by *The Royal Humane Society* (founded in 1776) which provided boatmen to keep an eye on swimmers in the Serpentine and other popular bathing spots on hot summer days. *The Life Saving Society* was established in 1891, its aim being to teach every young person in Britain to swim and save life. The Society made explicit the link between learning to swim and being able to save the lives of others. This changed the culture of swimming. Instead of merely being seen as an enjoyable, entertaining and healthy activity, swimming became a moral duty.

Life saving was promoted with great zeal through publications such as *The Badminton book* and *The Swimming Magazine*. The Society set down codes of practice, educational principles, teaching drills and a repository of stories of daring rescues that inspired converts to the cause. The annual report of 1895 showed that life saving was being taught in all public and state schools and was being learned and practised by hundreds of thousands of young people. By 1914, it was seen as an essential skill for the nation's youth.

Life saving was promoted by awards and competitions sponsored by commercial firms (for example the Lever Brothers 'Sunlight Challenge Shield') and techniques were disseminated through practical displays, demonstrations, lectures, lantern slides and of course the new technology of photography. Life saving became an unquestioned part of one's education. John Philips could still remember what he had learned from his life saving lessons 75 years previously:

'And the back stroke came along and of course the Life Saving Society was formed and to save somebody who was drowning the back stroke became quite important. You just approached somebody on the breast and then you turned them over and as you turned them over you held them the best as you could then using the feet only you swam the back stroke more or less underneath them and that's how you pulled them ashore.'

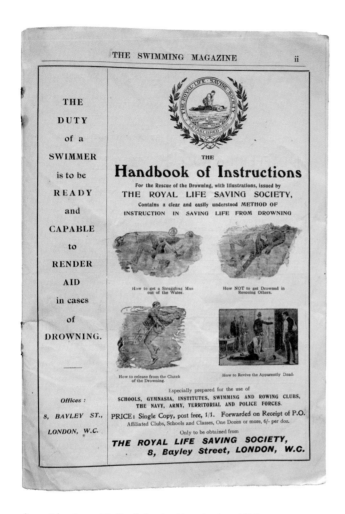

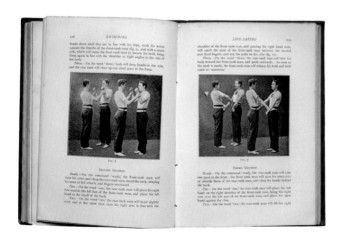

above: Advertisement in *The Swimming Magazine*, June 1917.
below: Life saving drill, from *The Badminton book*.

The documentation of swimming

Another sign of the regulation of swimming was its documentation in various specialist books and periodicals dedicated to the sport (including *The Swimming Magazine*, *Swimming Notes* and *The Swimming Times*). The fact that these publications were established, co-existed and survived for some years is evidence of the huge popularity of the sport. Of course, they are also evidence of advances in printing, production and distribution as well as the growth of literacy.

The documentation of swimming was not limited to describing techniques, strokes and manoeuvres. The late Victorians were passionate about indexing and *gazetteering* places of historical, geographical or natural interest. *Round the Coast* is an album of photographs of the chief seaside places of interest in Great Britain and Ireland. It was published in 1895 and presents large format black and white images of 284 different towns and villages around the British coast, each accompanied by text that systematically describes points of interest and details local bathing facilities.

Many hang-overs from the era of regulation are still apparent today. Henleaze Swimming Club in Bristol, which was founded in 1919, still issues its members with lists of rules, the wording of which has changed very little from the original. Health and safety concerns now mean that many more rules have been developed in order to protect the swimmers from danger and the club from litigation. Warning signs are displayed around the lake side. One notice board, in particular, lists forbidden activities in alphabetical order.

For David Sawyers, the competitive ethos that emerged during the age of regulation still prevails in modern club swimming. The relentless focus on improving performance in standard conditions is, for him, one dimensional:

'It's not us cripples who are seen but the able-bodied, the fast strong swimmers. The press does that too and is perpetuating entirely the wrong picture. Coping with the sea is not about being a strong swimmer but a reflexive swimmer. Thinking with one's body and having the confidence and courage to let that happen. This is where the sea is so unlike the pool. Wind conditions are constantly varying and this means the height of the waves is never the same from one day to another. The height of the waves also depends on the shore bottom,

which is constantly being shifted. And then there's the force of the tide. Tide and time, phases of the moon, you can plot where everything is and what is happening, through the way the sea is behaving. Developing that sort of responsiveness, that sort of feel, becoming no longer frightened but at home amid the forces of the movement of the waters. I've talked to people about it. 'You're not in the water to battle, but to be. Relax. Find yourself in the water'. Incomprehension. The pool people have no interest to find themselves in the water.'

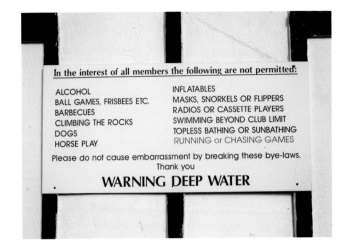

By-laws at Henleaze Lake © Susie Parr.

Tenby, from *Round the Coast*, 1895.

Swimming with Ye Amphibious Ancients, Broughty Ferry, Dundee

Ye Amphibious Ancients Bathing Association (known locally as the Phibbies) is a swimming club that was founded for its workers in 1889 by the North British Railway Company in Broughty Ferry, on the banks of the Tay. The association's mottos convey an ethos of challenge, hard work and self improvement: *'Labor humidus et subriguous'* (damp and watery work); *'Aqua sine mercede'* (water without mercy) and *'Come with us and we will do you good'*. These, together with the club website, make ominous reading for someone like me, uninterested in speed or endurance swimming and unable to do the front crawl:

Across the years, the purpose of the Association has been to foster and encourage the sport of open water swimming and though the emphasis today is much more competitive, because the sport has broadened its horizons, there is still the basic enjoyment of the challenge and the personal satisfaction in achievements and ambitions realised.

The founding Phibbies set swimmers the challenge of swimming in the cold waters of the Tay, even developing new units of distance based on local topography. *A Single Tay* was the distance between Broughty Ferry and Tayport on the opposite bank of the river (about two miles across). Miss Topsy Johnson was the first woman to swim a Tay in 1906, seven years before my mother was born. Since then, many Phibbies have achieved Singles and also *Double Tays* (over the river and back), a distance first swum by Bill Blair in 1905. More recently, Robert Saunderson crossed the Tay back and forth seven times without a break (*a Treble Tay plus one*). Members of the club also ventured further afield, successfully swimming the Channel and crossing numerous lakes including Lochs Ness and Lomond in Scotland and Windermere and Ullswater in the Lake District. Phibbies have even swum up the Suez Canal and across Lake Zurich.

Despite hard times and dwindling numbers in recent decades, the club now seems to be going through a renaissance and is attracting press interest and new members. It has a modern clubhouse on the harbour wall with hot showers, toilets and heating (luxuries the founding members would have deemed totally unnecessary). Indoor swimming lessons and training sessions are offered at a local pool in the winter and the club runs a lively programme of open water distance swimming events in the summer. It also oversees charitable events like the popular *New Year Dook* which sees hundreds of merry makers entering the freezing river in fancy dress on January 1st. The club takes safety very seriously and stipulates that each cross-Tay swimmer must be accompanied by a rowing boat with a pilot and a lifeguard on board, so each event demands considerable human resources. Outdoor training sessions – that take place in Broughty Ferry harbour in the summer months – are overseen by experienced coaches. Open water swimming ends at the beginning of November when the air temperature can reach as low as 42 degrees (6 celsius) and the water 44 (7 celsius). Wetsuits are banned.

I have come to Broughty Ferry to see where my mother learned to swim and to join a training session. I am a bit early, so I sit by the clubhouse looking across the harbour to the castle. It is a grey, breezy evening and the river is gleaming in the low light, ebbing fast, rushing out towards the open sea. The water flows so quickly past the entrance to the harbour that I resolve not to venture out beyond the protective stone walls that keep the water within dark and still and deep. As I gaze down, a young seal raises its head to look at me, then silently dives, its back rounding before it disappears. As I try to follow its movement underwater, I notice two large jellyfish floating dankly near where an iron ladder descends from the harbour wall. I find it hard to believe that anyone would want to climb 12 feet down into such uninviting sea, but at 7pm people start to appear and go into the club house to change. Soon, about twenty swimmers are standing on the harbour wall, exchanging jokes and banter. The coach appears, wearing a tracksuit, wielding stop watch and clipboard and emanating a no-nonsense air.

One by one, the Phibbies go down the ladder and start plying back and forth across the mouth of the harbour, most doing the crawl, while the coach shouts encouragement and instructions and counts each person's number of passages to and fro. It strikes me that they are using their harbour like a pool, using the distance between harbour walls to measure and improve their time.

My mother's swimming teacher used the same unorthodox methods that Mr Smyth experienced at Eton: she was thrown into the cold Tay water from Broughty Ferry harbour wall and literally had to sink or swim. This experience did not seem to put her off. I remember her saying that swimming was the only sport she could do well in, because she was so short sighted. She used to swim myopically across the harbour with the Phibbies, heading towards the castle, the shape of which she could dimly make out. I want to swim in her memory, but feel anxious about the cold and the pressure to go quickly. The iron rungs of the ladder dig into my feet as I go down. The water feels shockingly cold and I can see my arms turning bright pink as I set off using my slow and stately breast stroke, trying not to think about the jellyfish. I manage one passage across and the return journey. This is just one sixteenth of a mile in total, the coach informs me as I emerge, gasping and shivering. I swiftly repair to the club house to change into warm clothes as the Phibbies continue their training and the coach counts them across and back.

Swimming with Ye Amphibious Ancients, Broughty Ferry
© Martin Parr/Magnum.

Swimming through the twentieth century

It is a well-worn cliché to say that the twentieth century was a period of dramatic change for Britain. Nevertheless it seems extraordinary to think that someone born at the beginning of the century, when Victoria was still on the throne, could, in old age, be familiar with the concepts of space exploration, supersonic flight, nuclear power and the Internet.

Two world wars helped to spark off and speed the most comprehensive transformations within British industry, technology, transport, and communications. British women gained suffrage and moved towards equality and power. Young people broke long established rules and came into their own as consumers and arbiters of art, taste and fashion. Against this backdrop of change, the simple practice of bathing and swimming – at least in Britain's rivers, ponds and lakes – remained constant. On a warm summer's day in 1910, 1950 or 1990, young people would appear at local swimming holes, just as they had done in Everard Digby's Cambridgeshire, Sir John Floyer's Staffordshire and Wordsworth's Cumbria.

In this sense, swimming can truly be described as a timeless activity:

Summer after summer the walks took the same route. Nothing changed – not even the demonstration that Aunt Betsy put on daily by a deep pond where the boys sunbathed and swam in the nude. Betsy always got worked up about the nude bathers long before we reached the pond. 'Did you see that, Grace? What are we coming to? There's no shame.' On and on she went, her moist face becoming scarlet. By the time we reached the pond, her stick was raised like the sword of an avenging angel. By then the swimmers had slid down the muddy bank into the water.
(*The Road to Nab End*, William Woodruff, 1933.)

Yet throughout the twentieth century the practice of swimming was influenced by many different factors: the world wars of course and later, more localised conflicts; industrial and economic growth and decline; the constraints of poverty and class; legislation; the diversification of transport; growing awareness and understanding of the environment; changing concepts of health, education, beauty and fashion. Swimming even took on a political aspect, becoming briefly linked with Fascist ideology, a factor in various political scandals and a symbol of feminism and sexual liberation.

A river swim.

Workmates and neighbours at the seaside together.

Prior to 1914, life in British seaside resorts continued much as it had in previous decades. In the summer of 1913, Blackpool welcomed four million visitors, mainly drawn from the industrial heartlands and mill towns of the North West. Some holiday-makers were day trippers, excursionists whose outings were organised and funded by employers, philanthropists or by the church. Others made use of savings schemes like the 'Going Off Clubs' in order to fund their week in seaside lodgings. Landladies made the most of the seasonal demand. Most operated a traditional apartment system, letting out rooms to entire families who had to share limited and cramped facilities, crammed in with other boarders. The boarders would supply their own food, which the landlady would cook and serve. Any extras such as salt and pepper, crockery and even bed linen had to be paid for. Boarders were evicted from their rooms early in the morning and not allowed to return until evening, no matter what the weather. Indeed, it was his miserable childhood experience of Barry boarding houses that led Billy Butlin to develop the idea of the holiday camp: a place that would cater for the needs of all holiday-makers, old and young, all day long, no matter what the weather.

These short pre-war holidays were often communal affairs. Entire communities would cram into trains and descend on Blackpool, Scarborough and other northern resorts during Wakes Weeks when the mills and factories closed down for maintenance. It was not unusual to bump into workmates and neighbours strolling down the promenade, to sit together on the sand and to bathe together as a group. The presence of home communities at the seaside helped to regulate the holiday-makers' behaviour, at least to a degree.

But such communal get-togethers at the big resorts were not the only form of holiday experience in the earliest years of the new century. More sophisticated and affluent holiday-makers sought to distance themselves from the hordes by catching a train or steamboat to more remote destinations. The exclusive *Queen* newspaper pointed its readers in the direction of quaint seaside towns such as Cromer, Clovelly and North Berwick. Here, the discerning visitor could appreciate the seascape, admire a ruined castle, visit a museum and bathe from a relatively secluded beach. The aristocratic and really wealthy continued to holiday abroad as they had done for decades, combining the long-established tradition of the cultural Grand Tour

with sea-bathing at various up-market continental resorts such as Ostend.

Another type of British holiday tradition was established around the beginning of the twentieth century. The first holiday camps often had a religious or political ethos and were set up to provide an improving experience for men and boys, who were accommodated in Spartan conditions in rows of canvas tents. Joseph and Elizabeth Cunningham started organising camps for underprivileged boys from Liverpool. From this philanthropic seed grew a lucrative business which they ran on the Isle of Man from 1904 until 1945. For an all-inclusive tariff, the male campers were provided with basic accommodation and were served meals in a purpose-built dining pavilion. Entertainment was laid on in the form of a golf course, swimming-pool, theatre and concert hall. Although drinking, gambling and swearing were banned, the camps were enormously successful, attracting 60,000 campers to the Isle of Man in 1936. This was the same year that Billy Butlin opened his first camp in Skegness, having previously visited Cunningham's to check out the competition and to learn what he could about setting up organised, all-in holidays.

In 1906, grocer John Fletcher Dodd established a holiday camp for working class men and trades union members at Great Yarmouth. At the Caistor Socialist Holiday Camp a collective ethos prevailed. Campers helped out with the chores, exercised, swam in the sea and attended lectures and talks given by intellectuals sympathetic to the Labour movement including George Bernard Shaw, Bertrand Russell and Keir Hardy. The camps were so successful that, by 1912, Dodd could afford to expand, replacing the original bell tents with huts, each boasting the luxury of its own tap. By the time Dodd died in 1952, the camp was attracting 1,000 holiday-makers per week, although its socialist ethos had faded somewhat.

These early camps were very much in tune with and probably influenced by the contemporaneous Neo-Pagan movement, which originated from the ideas of Edward Carpenter. Formerly an academic and a priest, Carpenter lived the lifestyle advocated in his book *Towards Democracy* (published in 1883) by setting up a utopian community at Millthorpe, on the edge of the Derbyshire moors. He lived what he called the 'simple life'. Carpenter wrote political books and tracts, grew vegetables, made his own sandals and clothes and swam naked in the rivers and ponds. He promoted socialism and solidarity with the working classes and denounced the evils of urban living and industrialisation. His community attracted a stream of curious visitors and disciples as well as interest from leading socialists and thinkers of the day. Rupert Brooke and his Grantchester coterie replicated this kind of lifestyle, in which bathing played a significant part, in the years leading up to the war.

World War I and the Great Depression

After the glorious summer of 1913 the outbreak of the First World War brought utopian dreams and care-free seaside holidays to an abrupt end. Hundreds of thousands of young men were sent to the trenches. Shipping was suspended and excursion steamboats requisitioned for the war effort, plunging holiday venues dependent on boat traffic, such as Douglas on the Isle of Man, into financial ruin. Coal became scarce and increasingly costly; railway companies were forced to restrict the fares they could offer to the essential routes. The shortage of fuel meant that trips to the coast by private car (which were popular for the well-to-do before the war) became too expensive to contemplate. In addition, hotels, holiday lodgings and boarding houses were requisitioned by the military. In Scotland, the traditional hydropathic hotels offering water treatments were taken over as convalescent homes for injured soldiers.

Seaside towns, particularly those on the southern and eastern coasts, were seen as vulnerable to enemy attack, with drastic results for their appeal as relaxing places to stay. Holiday towns on other coasts made safety and security a selling point in a bid to attract at least some customers (now predominantly older people and women with children). Scarborough Town Council even ran advertisements in the Scottish press advising potential holiday-makers that fears of enemy attack were groundless. Unfortunately, Scarborough and Whitby were shelled by the German navy in December, 1914. The raid destroyed the upper storeys of Scarborough's Grand Hotel and, with it, the reputation of the resort as a haven of peace and tranquillity, although local businesses strongly denied the dangers.

Advocates of swimming responded proactively to the pressures and restrictions imposed by the war. *The Swimming Magazine* continued to be published throughout the war period. This was somewhat against the odds as pools across the country were closed down (being too expensive to heat and maintain) and swimming clubs were suspending their activities because their members were in the trenches. In April 1917, the editor, William Henry wrote: *The only journal of its kind should be kept going until normal times come around.* Henry asked readers to send their subscriptions of 5 shillings without delay so that he could purchase the correct quantity of paper (which was becoming scarce and expensive) and print the next issue without waste. Poignantly, every issue of the magazine published between 1914 and 1918 contained tidings of death or injury:

In the daylight air raid on London on June 13, 1917, severe injuries were sustained by PC Blackmore one of the best known of the present members of the City of London Police Swimming Club.

We have heard of the death of Alfred Fazakerly, one of the most promising Birkenhead swimmers.

Lieutenant B.G. Sampson of the Royal Fusiliers, killed in action, was a fine swimmer and skater.

Clearly an optimist, William Henry interspersed this gloomy litany with news of swimming activities at home and up-beat messages from the front: *We have received a cheery letter from Lt Frank Beaurepaire who is now with the Australian forces in France. He is feeling fit and sends his regards to all old swimming friends. It will be delightful to renew old friendships when the war is over.*

A postcard from Scarborough, showing the pool, opened in 1915, and refuting the threat of Zeppelin raids. It reads: 'Scarborough's New Bathing Pool, Bungalows, Café are right on the shore. It's all moonshine about Zeppelin Raids. Scarborough has never seen one.'

An outing by charabanc.

Henry also sought to galvanise the swimming community into responding positively to the restrictions imposed by the war. He devoted the editorial of the issue of July 1917 to making a plea that *ardent swimmers should seek bathing pleasures closer to home*, using their local rivers and swimming holes. He called upon the local authorities in riverside towns to identify suitable spots and erect bathing chalets and tents, to allow mixed bathing and to establish riverside bathing clubs in order to promote exercise and competition.

Towards the end of the war, Henry also made a strong case that local authorities should re-open pools and actively promote swimming, using well-established teaching methods in order to improve the health, welfare and morale of troops, to protect against illness and epidemics and to advance the health of the nation generally: *We have a system ready to hand. All that is needed is to organise.* In the April 1917 issue, he had expounded his theory that the act of closing the pools would lead to the 'moral hydrophobia' of the nation, encouraging a disinclination to bathe and contaminating the whole being, moral and physical, reducing the populace to a *lower scale of animal existence.*

Sadly, Henry's warning about the menace of illness was proved correct. The influenza pandemic of 1918-1920 claimed over 50 million lives worldwide, killing more people than had perished in the war.

The industrial landscape of Britain changed after the First World War. The traditional industries largely based in the North (coal mining, ship-building, steel and cotton) enjoyed a brief period of prosperity before slipping towards decline. However, in the South East and Midlands, the new automobile, light manufacturing and electrical industries flourished, bringing full employment and welcome prosperity, at least to some communities. Car ownership was on the rise. In 1921, the Ministry of Transport Whit Week traffic census recorded 21,676 vehicles travelling between Blackpool and Preston, 925 of which were horse drawn vehicles and 9,704 private motor cars. Motor coaches and charabancs were also popular, particularly for days out for firms and factories.

By 1933, one million private cars were on Britain's roads. Car ownership meant that holiday-makers could travel independently of their neighbours and work colleagues, go further afield and explore remote and isolated parts of the

The growth of motorised transport was reflected in studio photos and private snapshots.

country and coast. More rural counties such as Dorset, Devon and Cornwall were opened up to the holiday trade. By the late 1930s, traffic jams, congestion and parking problems had become a common feature of south coast seaside resorts like Bournemouth, and many column inches were devoted to these issues in the local papers.

For many mill, mine and factory workers, the years leading up to the General Strike of 1926 and the Great Depression (1928-1932) were times of great hardship and deprivation. Many went cold and hungry – taking a holiday or even going on a day-trip to the seaside were unthinkable. The relentless poverty of those years is described by Walter Greenwood in his novel *Love on the Dole*, published in 1933. Unemployed engineer Harry Greenwood longs to escape from Hanky Park in Salford with his sweetheart Helen. He dreams of living in Blackpool, for him a place of freedom, peace and pure air, a far cry from the smoke, grime and poverty of his home town.

William Woodruff's memoirs of his boyhood in Blackburn during the 1920s also paint a bleak picture of hunger and misery. However, in 1924, when he was eight, the cotton

mill where both his parents worked experienced a brief period of recovery. With money in their pockets, the family was, for once, able to make the most of the Wakes Week holiday. They packed one case with food for the week and took the excursion train to Blackpool, where the children were instructed to rush through the barrier without a ticket. The entire family shared one bedroom in a crowded boarding house:

Aside from the smells and queuing for the toilet, everything was bliss. We abandoned our parents on arrival and only joined them for meals. Sitting on benches in sand-streaked bathing suits we ate twice a day with all the other families in a large room downstairs. Nobody dreamed of grumbling. We'd come from the same town, some from the same street. We belonged together. As long as the weather was fine, we spent our time on the beach or paddling in the sea. What the adults did was their business. A week later, with long faces, we caught the train home. After Blackpool, the Blackburn air hung like lead.
(*The Road to Nab End,* William Woodruff, 1933.)

In the late 1930s, the extraordinary Mass Observation project focussed on Bolton (given the pseudonym Worktown) documenting the details of the day-to-day life of the town's working class people. Trips to Blackpool, the nearest resort, were described and photographed by Humphrey Spender. One respondent talked about putting his wife and daughter on the train to Blackpool then signing on the dole and cycling the 37 miles from Bolton to join them there. Spender's photographs show the beach crowded with people, women wrapped up in coats and wearing hats and men in caps, suits and ties. A footnote reads:

There are notes in the archive showing how little people bathed. For example at 11 o'clock one bright and warm August morning there were 63 people in the water and 8,000 on the beach. One sunny afternoon at the beginning of September on a half mile stretch there were two in the water and 6,200 on the beach.

This suggests that sea-bathing was in decline at Blackpool, other than for drunks, as observed one Saturday night in July, 1939:

On the sand and sea-edge four boys so obviously have been drinking that the liquor smell is perceptible ten yards from them. Fully clothed they are running deep into the rough incoming tide, wrestling with one another, tempting one another to go deeper.

For holiday-makers in Blackpool it seems that the attractions of sea-bathing were being displaced by land-based pleasures: drinking, gambling and sex. William Woodruff recalls how, when he was very young, his mother took him to Blackpool for a week and made him sit outside their boarding house during the day while a series of men went in to visit her for a while, emerging to tousle his hair and give him sixpence.

Poverty was not confined to the industrial cities. On hot summer afternoons, Dorothy Watts, who was born in 1900, used to take her daughter Joyce from their house in Sharpness to the Gloucester Sharpness canal and to the Severn estuary, where they would bathe and swim in the muddy water. Joyce recalls seeing some neighbours heading for the river, not to bathe but to wash:

'Mrs Thomas had 12 children and they were very poor. They lived in a very poor terraced building. Her husband was a docker and work was short. Sometimes they had work down in Avonmouth and sometimes they had no work. To save money they went down to the Severn on a hot night with their bar of soap and that was their bath night. I've seen that with my own eyes when I was there with my mother. They'd be having their bath in the river, and she'd be washing them.'

I wish you were here
IT'S GREAT

Cheerio!

— This is forgotten! —

For workers from the industrial North, the seaside seemed like paradise.

We certainly don't want to
come back yet.

don't stand and
shiver like this, but
go straight in

Seaside studio photographs.

Sea-bathing, sunbathing

Images of poverty are very much at odds with representations of British seaside that were becoming more prevalent, particularly in southern resorts. In the early 1920s, ideas from the Continent were starting to filter into Britain regarding the health giving properties of sunlight. These had emerged as early as 1903, when Auguste Rollier opened a sunbathing clinic in the Alps for the treatment of tuberculosis. Rickets had become endemic during the war and consequent medical research suggested that sunlight could both prevent and alleviate the condition. Hans Suren's *Man and Sunlight* (originally published in Germany) arrived in Britain in 1927, instantly becoming a bestseller.

Sunlight was understood to be a remedy for anaemia, debility, bronchitis and catarrh. It was to be sought out, not avoided. In Britain as in Germany, it became fashionable for men and women to engage in outdoor activities such as hiking, camping and of course swimming – anything that exposed them to as much sunlight as possible. Naturism became popular as this allowed the maximum exposure. For some, physical fitness was not a matter of fashion but a demonstration of supremacy, as in the case of the campers who attended Oswald Mosely's summer gatherings on the south coast in the mid 1930s – Worthing apparently being a favoured location. Blackshirt campers would hike and swim every day and carry out camp chores as well as attending lectures and debates. Newsreel footage shows followers saluting Mosely as he goes in for his daily dip.

Of course, sunbathing had its merely hedonistic aficionados, more concerned with glamour than demonstrations of political vigour. After the war, wealthy and aristocratic Britons, able once again to holiday on the Continent, were drawn to the Riviera, previously only fashionable during the winter season. There, new hotels were being designed with sloping terraces to provide guests with a platform on which they could expose themselves to the sun's rays. Once shunned as a symbol of manual labour, a sun-tanned skin became an indicator of wealth and privilege.

These ideas slowly filtered across the Channel, precipitating a transformation in British fashion and seaside architecture. Every resort produced comprehensive guides and brochures to entice visitors, listing the average hours of sunshine that could be expected. Resorts competed with

Sunbathing started to take over from sea-bathing as a popular holiday pursuit.

Whitley Bay, London and North Eastern Railway poster.

each other to advertise the best sunbathing opportunities and play up their facilities and health-giving assets. Even northern resorts such as Whitley Bay that were habitually exposed to Atlantic gales or cutting east winds played the sunshine card, although some were more honest about the likely weather conditions: *'Skegness is so bracing'* was the strap line for one of the most memorable posters produced in 1933 by the London and North Eastern Railway.

The promotional efforts of the seaside resorts were boosted by the railway companies, fighting back against the rise of the motor car. The independent regional rail companies vied with each other to produce the best designed brochures and most eye-catching promotion for the destinations they served. The Great Western Railway Company capitalised on the fact that Cornwall and Italy have similar outlines, and produced a poster showing young women bathing on the Cornish Riviera in February. Trading on its catch phrase: *'South for sunshine!'* Southern Railway produced fabulous posters depicting sunny scenes at its various destinations including Eastbourne, Ramsgate, Broadstairs and the Isle of Wight.

Every year between 1923 and 1940, Southern Railway also published an illustrated brochure called *Hints for Holidays*, each with a beautifully designed cover. The booklet listed all the southern resorts on the network, described facilities and advertised boarding houses and hotels. Of the booklets that were published between 1930 and 1940, most featured beach activities, including swimming and diving. The last *Hints for Holidays* was produced in 1947, just prior to the nationalisation of the railways.

The images on the covers of *Hints for Holidays* demonstrate the dramatic changes in British women's bathing costumes that took place in the 1920s and 1930s. The slow advance towards functionality during the first decade of the new century had been impeded by the modesty imperative. Mixed bathing was still forbidden in many places. In addition, women had protected their skin from the sun's rays with hats, parasols and long sleeves and legs. As a tan became linked with concepts of health, beauty, youth and wealth, women's costumes shrank so that eventually the greatest expanse of skin could be exposed to the sun. Arms, legs, shoulders and necks were gradually revealed. Sleeves, high necks, trouser legs and overskirts slowly disappeared.

Hints for Holidays 1932.

left: Jantzen logo © Gail Symes.
Women were increasingly engaging in vigorous swimming and diving and their costumes reflected this change.

This transformation in fashion was also driven by changing perceptions of women, who, having played such an important role in the war, had finally achieved suffrage for women over 28, in 1918. They were increasingly engaging with vigorous swimming and with diving and needed appropriate dress to do this.

Indeed, in 1926, the first woman swam the Channel, beating the male record by two hours. Six more women followed suit in 1928. The increasingly minimal bathing costumes may have raised eyebrows amongst the older ladies on the beach but they were extremely functional, allowing for complete ease of movement in the water. They dried quickly and were perfectly adapted both to swimming and sunbathing. The pioneering rib stitch swimsuit company Jantzen, founded in Portland, Oregon in the US in 1910, was quick to make the link between their products and the more energetic lifestyles that women were taking up. In 1921 Jantzen came up with a catch phrase that conveyed the transformation: *'The suit that changed bathing to swimming.'*

Competitive swimmers wearing functional costumes.

Dorothy Watts at Weston-super-Mare, around 1925.

Seaside comic series.

IT ALWAYS MAKES ME SHIVER WHEN I GET AS FAR AS THIS!

The more stream-lined costumes left little to the imagination.

Whilst the new-fangled swimming suits could look glamorous and enticing when worn by a slim, athletic young woman, the comic potential when adorning more ample shapes was irresistible to cartoonists. The image of the larger lady clad in a bathing suit became iconic of the slightly risqué fun of a seaside holiday. It is a curious anachronism that humorous postcards poking fun at stout swimmers and sunbathers, many by Donald McGill, can still be purchased today at most British seaside resorts. They provide 21st century tourists and day trippers with a direct link back to the attitudes of one hundred years ago.

Aside from these caricatures, women bathers, whether tanned and athletic or soft, vulnerable and exposed, were alluring and had an erotic appeal that could be used to sell everything from rail tickets to cars. The link between sexual power and swimming, while largely subliminal, was openly articulated by D.H. Lawrence in the novel *Women in Love*, published in 1920. Sisters Ursula and Gudrun are walking by a local lake when they spot a naked man running towards the water, plunging in and swimming vigorously up and down. The swimmer is Gerald Crich, a local mine-owner, who will become Gudrun's lover:

Gudrun stood by the stone wall watching: 'God how I envy him', she said in low desirous tones. … She stood motionless gazing over the water at the face which washed up and down on the flood, as he swam steadily. From his separate element he saw them and exulted to himself because of his own advantage, his possession of a world to himself. He loved his own vigorous, thrusting motions, and the violent impulse of the very cold water against his limbs, buoying him up. 'God what it is to be a man! The freedom, the liberty, the mobility!' cried Gudrun, strangely flushed and brilliant.

This use of swimming to represent sexual freedom recalls the scene in *Room with a View* by E.M. Forster, published a decade earlier, in which the heroine Lucy comes across her young brother, a friend and a middle-aged vicar swimming naked in a local pond. For Lucy, the woodland encounter highlights the directness, aliveness and spontaneity of the man she loves – George Emerson – and shows up the stuffy behaviour of her convention-bound and controlling fiancé, whom she subsequently rejects.

As trade picked up in the aftermath of war and competition between resorts became more intense, local authorities struggled to out-do rivals in the provision of modern facilities for the holiday-maker.

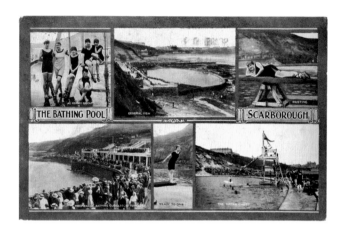

There was fierce competition between resorts. The message on the back of this card reads: 'This place beats Blackpool to a frazzle.'

The Midland Hotel, Morecambe, built 1933.

Tarlair pool, Macduff, Banffshire.

In the early 1930s, the stolid, traditional design of British seaside buildings ceded to a modern style known as Art Deco. Even humble seaside towns erected magnificent hotels, pavilions, dance halls, cinemas, car parks and shelters. Sleek outlines and simple shapes in dazzling white concrete made Morecambe and Bexhill seem, for a time, as exclusive as Biarritz or Cannes.

This was also the era of the lido, which became as critical to the seaside industry of the 1930s as piers had been to the mid-Victorians. Magnificent temples to sun and water worship sprang up everywhere, inland and on the coast (where they were filled with salt water), even in the most rugged regions of the far north. The wonderful Tarlair pool was built on the site of a popular traditional bathing hole just east of Macduff on the north east coast of Scotland in 1931. Its elegant design and ample facilities attracted thousands of bathers from Banffshire and beyond to the remote and rocky shoreline on summer evenings and weekends from the 1930s until the mid 1970s.

A little further west, in Portsoy, a more modest sea water pool had been constructed in the 1920s. This also became a real focus for the local community as Gilbert White recalls:

'It was a sun trap, a big day out. It is sheltered from the south west wind. If you got a wind from the north it could be pretty chilly, but overall it was a suntrap. You had diving boards, a spring board and a big high diving board. I've seen hundreds of people down there in the mid 50s through to the mid 70s. That was the place to be back then. When our family came along I've seen the wife go down there and there'd be hardly a space left by the pool at 11 o'clock in the morning. Whether it was pouring rain, a gale, the tea room was open. You'd spend the rest of the day down by the pool and there were races, gala races against Macduff, competitions against the teams. It was run by volunteers. In the winter we had dances to gather up money for the pool. It was a bottle of juice and a sandwich and a dance. Happy memories.'

Although they seemed exclusive, the lidos played their part in the democratisation of swimming. Many local authorities were continuing to charge people to use the beach and forcing them to make use of expensive facilities in the form of bathing machines, huts or tents. Some authorities even banned *mackintosh bathing* – in which the bather changed in his boarding house or hotel room

New Brighton Lido, London, Midland and Scottish Railway poster.

and came down to the beach with a coat over his costume, thereby avoiding the expense of changing on the beach. The seaside lidos spelled the beginning of the end for the old sea-bathing industry, offering swimmers and sunbathers changing facilities and access to water and sun for one modest, all-in charge.

Lidos provided the perfect setting for the fitness mania that prevailed in the late 1930s in Britain and on the continent. This was boosted in 1937 by the Physical Training and Recreation Act, which undertook to provide facilities that would improve the health of the nation through exercise and recreation. Grants were offered to local authorities for the construction of gymnasia, playing fields, swimming baths and camping sites. Some pools were so huge they could double up as stadia. Indeed, the lido at New Brighton was emptied for a mass display by schoolchildren to mark the coronation of George VI in 1937.

Lido poster for Farleigh and District Swimming Club.

The lido at Skegness Model Village © Skegness Model Village.

When the Holidays with Pay Act was passed in 1938, 11 million workers were able to enjoy the luxury of a week off at their employer's expense. Seaside resorts thrived. Some seaside authorities accommodated the increasingly sophisticated taste of holiday-makers, investing in modern facilities, stylish buildings and up-to-the-minute features. Others, like Eastbourne, adhered to traditional seaside architecture, or simply added Art-Deco clocks and ornamentation to existing buildings, in a clash of styles. Everyone tried to cash in, particularly local landowners who made a killing selling off plots to speculators, developers and do-it-yourself builders. Informal seaside settlements made up of huts, chalets, bungalows, camp and caravan sites began to straggle along miles of Britain's coastline. Often erected without planning permission, many did not have any sewage system. Cesspits filled up, then flooded into the surrounding land, leaching into rivers and streams and eventually into the sea.

In inland towns, the lidos hinted at the elegant proportions of the ocean-going liner and brought a breath of sea air to the most land-locked locations.

The alluring imagery of the lido was so powerful that it was even used by the river clubs to attract members although, in reality, they offered very different bathing facilities. The poster which *Farleigh and District Swimming Club* used into the 1960s hinted at the sleek lines of an Art Deco pool, complete with diving board and sun-terraces, whereas the reality was simply a river, a field and a hut.

Even those who could not afford the lidos could share something of the seaside dream. In 1934, 1,500 barge loads of sand were dumped beside Tower Bridge in London. The object was to give East End children a taste of the beach life that they were unlikely to experience for real. On the opening day, Tower Beach attracted thousands of children, who were given free buns and lemonade. The beach operated from 1934 to 1971 (when it was closed due to pollution fears), except during the war. Even though the tide meant that it was only available for two hours each day, people would queue to get in. Children dug in the sand, played, paddled and even swam in the grey Thames water as it rose and fell with the tide.

Londoners relax on Tower Beach, 1952.

World War II

The Second World War broke out on 3rd September, 1939. For the second time within twenty five years, southern and eastern coastal resorts were virtually closed down. Hotels and guest houses were requisitioned as soldiers' billets. An enemy invasion seemed only too feasible, as Hitler's forces progressed across northern Europe and established themselves in the Channel Isles. There was a scramble to shore up defences along miles of vulnerable coastland. Beaches were mined, huts and chalets dismantled, bunkers dug, pill boxes erected and barbed wire unfurled along the sands.

Hoping that it would be business as usual, some southern resorts produced guidebooks for the summer of 1940. That year's issue of *Hints for Holidays* opens with the optimistic statement that *to keep fit one must have holidays and Southern England is natural holiday land*. Many of the towns covered by the Southern Railway network were particularly vulnerable, so the handbook promoted Cornwall as one of the safest places for a holiday, claiming *many people will find here the rest and recuperation so much needed as a counter to the stress of war*. To drive the point home, a photograph of six young women shrieking with laughter as they surf-ride Cornish waves seems to capture the carefree pleasures that were in danger of disappearing. The 1940 issue of *Hints for Holidays* was re-published in 1946, the front cover stamped with a warning that some services advertised would not be available and that prices would have changed.

Hints for Holidays used the sea as a wartime symbol, representing freedom, frolics and fun for care-worn Britain. Enid Blyton's first Famous Five book, *Five on a Treasure Island* (published in 1942), also reinforced the idea that the south west coast, with its smugglers' coves and rocky islands, was a place where children could solve mysteries, enjoy adventures, and outwit dastardly villains. Here they could row boats, go camping and swim in the clear blue water, all without any adult supervision. Blyton's story, like Arthur Ransome's *Swallows and Amazons* (published in 1930), transformed free swimming in lakes and seas into the stuff of fantasy for hundreds of thousands of war-beleaguered British children.

The reality at most seaside locations was very different. The rolls of barbed wire and the mines meant that sea swimming became off limits, although Jean Perraton talks

Hints For Holidays 1940, re-issued in 1946 with a disclaimer on the front cover.

poignantly of a farewell swim with her father: '*My earliest memory is, as a two year old, crawling under the new tank traps with my dad and clinging to his back as he swam out to sea. That was his last swim before the war took him away from us for five long years.*'

Holiday accommodation was allocated to house British and allied troops as well as the thousands of evacuees fleeing the bombardment in industrial cities. Military training exercises took the place of donkey rides and sand castles on some beaches, most notably at Blackpool which, adaptable as ever, welcomed visiting GIs from a nearby base.

Billy Butlin had opened his first holiday camp in Skegness in 1936, his second in Clacton in 1938, and was planning his third for Filey in 1940. The camps, with their modern chalets, bars, heated pools and dance halls, were comprehensively advertised with the help of the railway companies that served the locations and had instantly proved a massive hit with holiday-makers. But throughout the summer of 1939 the holiday atmosphere was marred as the names of men who had to return home to sign up were intoned over the tannoy systems. Although the war could have been a disastrous blow for his business, Billy Butlin quickly adapted to the new situation. Within days of the outbreak of war, the Skegness camp became a billet for naval trainees. The once bright holiday chalets were painted battleship grey. Butlin made a deal with the government that he could build two new military camps and buy them back after the war. In a canny move, Butlin later opened a camp at Mosney in the Irish Republic, in order to take advantage of the lack of rationing. He was not the only businessman to look ahead. Fred Pontin also anticipated a major post-war holiday boom and started planning and erecting rival camps in Somerset and Devon.

People continued to swim wherever they could. Once again the maintenance and heating of swimming pools – including the new fangled lidos – were low priority. Many pools in towns and cities were commandeered by the fire service, others were closed and many would not open for years due to lack of maintenance and shortage of materials. The use of natural swimming holes flourished as a result, particularly during hot summers. At Farleigh and District Swimming Club in Farleigh Hungerford, group membership was negotiated for troops stationed at nearby bases. Several of these military club members were killed in action and in 1947 the Club erected a memorial diving board in their honour, now sadly dismantled. Local land girls also made the most of the swimming hole. It is said that Tim Woodman, a bomber pilot, would fly low over the club in order to buzz the girls as they bathed naked in the refreshing river water. This story is the 1940s version of the 1701 ballad in which an intruder spies upon three sisters as they bathe in a pond on a warm summer's night.

Evacuated from the coast with her sister and her mother to her grandparent's village in the Midlands, Jean Perraton also resorted to traditional inland swimming holes. The family swam in a pool in the River Nene at nearby Ditchford, where her father and grandfather had learned to swim: *'It wasn't the sea, but it was the next best thing.'*

Although the lake in London's Victoria Park had been closed in the early 1930s for public health reasons, the Serpentine Club continued to function throughout the

Jean Perraton in the River Nene during World War II.

war years, despite the threat of air raids and doodle-bugs. This was largely thanks to dedicated multi-tasking by Clary Read who took on many roles during the war years: secretary, treasurer, gardener, adjudicator and handicapper. He ensured the races and competitions continued, even when there were only a handful of entrants and no other club officials around. Commander Gerald Forsberg described sunbathing himself back to health at the Serpentine after an injury and thinking, with a mixture of dread and envy, about his fellow soldiers who were on the Dunkirk mission. In 1944, he was enjoying a swim when someone made off with his uniform shoes and he had to walk home through London in bare feet.

Henleaze Lake in Bristol also continued to operate during the war. Soldiers and GIs based nearby, or on leave, were given a special membership rate (6d). The committee encouraged members of other clubs to carry on their swimming activities at the lake. Convalescent soldiers were invited to watch competitions and events (even though these were pretty sparse compared with the peacetime programme) and the club committee sent regular consignments of cigarettes to members who were in prisoner of war camps. In the German bombardment of Filton on 25th September 1940, when stray bombs destroyed several nearby houses, one bomb fell into the water and is rumoured to lie there still, unexploded, in the mud at the northern end of the lake. Luckily, the magnificent ladies' changing room, with its wooden panelling and separate cubicles, emerged unscathed from conflict (having been used either as a first aid post or a troop billet in the 1914-1918 war) and still stands today.

When the war ended in May 1945, there was a resurgence of previous holiday activities as people celebrated victory and freedom, relaxing after six long, hard years of conflict. Helped by the fact that 1945 was a good summer, the fortunes of the big resorts began to revive. Extra trains were put on from nearby cities, each jammed with eager holiday-makers. On the last Sunday in July 1945, a staggering 102,889 passengers passed through Blackpool railway station en route to the beach.

Some traditions of communal holiday-making were resumed as towns closed down for Wakes Weeks or Glasgow Fair Week and workers descended on the coast, this time with the knowledge that they were being paid to holiday. By 1950, Blackpool was welcoming 7 million visitors per year. As before the war, families, streets and communities were transposed from industrial towns and cities to the beach. Some made encampments on the sand, marking the different gatherings of streets, factories or mills with flags.

But Britain was struggling economically with the aftermath of victory. While Germany and Japan were able to focus on re-building and developing their industrial capacity, Britain had to plough what remained of its resources into managing the defeated countries, negotiating relationships with Russia and the other allied forces and dealing with the fallout from the disintegration of the Empire. All this took an economic toll on a country struggling to get back on its feet. The USA cut off financial aid to Britain once the Japanese surrendered, plunging the country further into financial crisis. Times were hard. Rationing continued and would last until 1954. This meant that most holiday-makers had to have their fun on a shoe string. Camping and hiking, relatively cheap holiday activities, became increasingly popular. Railway companies fought back against the rise of the motor car by promoting walking, rambling, camping and caravanning (predominantly on fixed sites). People camped under canvas, in disused railway carriages and even in old double decker buses parked in rows in a field. Urged by the government *to lend a hand with the land'*, some people opted for working holidays, for example hop-picking in Kent.

There was great camaraderie at caravan and camp sites, to

which holiday-makers would return year after year. The communal urge – meeting up with old friends, helping each other out and having fun – seemed to be as strong for caravanners and campers as it was for the inhabitants of mill towns on Blackpool's sands. People were determined to have a good time, even if it was raining:

'If you had any problem, if anything went wrong which it did all the time it was part of the fun to help each other out. We did everything together. I'd go round all the caravans knocking on the doors saying 'Everybody out for cricket' or 'Right let's all play volleyball!' or 'Everybody in the sea!.' We'd go down to the beach to swim with a mac on over our costumes and a couple of army groundsheets to keep our clothes dry. We used to change on the beach with a towel.'
(Interview from *Some Liked it Hot*.)

The 1950s and 1960s

Such community spirit was a dominant feature of the post war holiday camps, with the indefatigable Redcoats chivvying holiday-makers to have fun. And there was always affordable fun to be had, no matter what the weather: *'When it's wet it's always fine at Butlin's'*. The 1950s and 1960s were boom time for Butlin's and three new camps were built to cope with the demand: Bognor Regis in 1960, Barry in 1966, and Minehead in 1968. Rivals to Butlin's (like Warner's and Pontin's) also did well.

One can see why the holiday camps were so attractive after all the demands and efforts of the war. First of all they were affordable (as the slogan put it: *'a week's holiday for a week's wage'*). But more importantly, everything was organised for you and all members of the family catered for, entertained and kept happy. A forerunner of the all-in package tours, the camps provided facilities and fun for children, and even catered for the very young. Baby listening patrols (the *Night Owls*) meant parents could enjoy a drink in the bar, safe in the knowledge that they would be called back to their chalet if their child was crying. Everyone could relax. According to promotional material from the 1950s, Mother would *feel like a bride again, recapturing with her husband the magic of their earlier years together amid the delights and attractions of a Butlin's holiday.*

Much of Butlin's promotional material, partly funded by railway companies, hinted at the rejuvenation of romance

Glamorous holiday-makers at Pontins Holiday Camp, Osmington Bay, Weymouth.

and sex in order to attract care-worn families to the camps. Technicolour advertisements, brochures and postcards showed attractive young people, with film-star looks, wearing stylish costumes and bathing in pools of clear blue water, both indoor and outdoor. Indoor heated pools were exuberantly decorated and some had viewing windows so one could sit and watch the swimmers below the water line.

Perhaps the most sophisticated camp rivalling Butlin's was built in Prestatyn by Thomas Cook Ltd in conjunction with the London Midland and Scottish Railway. A masterpiece of Modernist architecture, the thoughtfully designed site had every possible facility including a liner-style bar overlooking the swimming pool. It was soon dubbed the *Everyman's Luxury Hotel* and started attracting a more middle

class clientele, although campers paid the same as they would for a week at Butlin's.

Indoor and outdoor pools like the ones at Butlin's must have seemed all the more alluring to swimmers, some of whom were starting to be concerned by pollution levels in the sea, mostly caused by untreated sewage being pumped out, a long established practice around the coast. Writing in 1903, W.J. Dibdin had commented: *The universally considered panacea for the sewage difficulty at seaside towns was to run an outfall sewer into the sea as far as was convenient and to discharge the sewage at such time of the tide as was thought would effectively carry it away, but in some cases the flow of the tide has brought it back to the point of departure, sometimes right into the stretch of water used for bathing so that bathers have to postpone*

Glamour at Butlin's c.1960.

Be sure to have a sea water bath or swim each day you are on holiday.

Extensions to existing outfall pipes were, for many local authorities, the cheapest solution to the problem. And for many holiday makers and visitors to the seaside, pollution was a matter of course. Margaret Drabble remembers her holiday swims at Filey:

'When we used to swim in the 1950s we never gave it a thought. There was faeces. Tampax. I must have seen condoms but I wouldn't have known what they were, I was only 9. I didn't know what all this stuff was until my father told me. It used to come out of this big gate in the harbour wall at night. But there was a lot of sea and not much of that. We thought the sea was very big and all this stuff would disperse.'

The polio outbreaks that took place in the late 1940s and early 1950s alerted people to a possible link between contaminated water and the disease which killed and paralysed thousands of children all over Britain. Significant numbers of children affected by polio had bathed or played near an outfall pipe, but the government issued reassurances that salt water killed bacteria and was safe. Outbreaks of polio worsened during the summer months. Parents started to prevent their children from swimming in the summer, particularly in pools, as there was a fear that pool water spread polio. Ian Dury, the late pop singer, was thought to have contracted polio from a pool in Southend. The polio vaccine became widely available in the UK in 1954, but for some parents it was too late. An anti-pollution movement was started in 1957 by the parents of a child who had died from the disease. Despite media attention, concerns about sewage disposal were not taken seriously until the mid 1970s and not acted upon until the late 1980s.

Given this scenario, with sea and pool water potentially contaminated, it is not surprising that people started looking towards the Continent, particularly the South of France with its blue waters and sunny beaches populated with glamorous bathers. Flickering film footage of King Edward and his lover Mrs Wallace Simpson shows them swimming in the clear, apparently sewage-free waters of Biarritz, she in a stylish one piece costume and hat, the epitome of elegance. Humphrey Bogart, Rita Heyworth and Grace Kelly were amongst the other glitterati attracted to the Riviera, where it seemed so much easier to be glamorous than at

their dip until the unsightly flood has drifted on.

Fifty years after Dibdin wrote those words, deposits of faecal matter on the shore had built up into sludge banks that seriously contaminated beaches and bathing places. The problem got worse during summer seasons, when resort populations exploded, overloading elderly pipework as millions of tons of waste were pumped into the salt water. Despite the danger to bathers and to consumers of fish and seafood, bathing resorts were continuing to ignore the problem and even promoted their water as an asset to health and beauty: *Salt water improves the complexion.*

Butlin's Skegness. The allure of the continental seaside was confirmed in 1956 with the release of *And God Created Woman* starring Brigitte Bardot, a gorgeous 18-year-old sex-kitten, who started a new fashion on the beaches of St Tropez. Embraced by the French, the new bikini beachwear was so revealing that it was instantly banned when it first appeared on the beaches of Italy, Spain and Portugal. British bathers took to the bikini with gusto and appropriated it with traditional seaside humour.

Home and abroad

In the late 1950s, it became the vogue for middle class British holiday-makers to make the long drive down through France in order to visit the Riviera. Just emerging from a prolonged period of austerity, many travelled on a strict budget, camping or sleeping in the car. These adventurous Britons found French wine cheap and plentiful, the food delicious and the waters of the Med warm, blue and crystal clear: a complete contrast to things back home. British women arrived on the beach after the long, hot journey, to be confronted with the unnerving sight of Brigitte Bardot look-alikes:

'I'd imagined I was the height of fashion with my one-piece white swimsuit with embroidered guitars, then I saw all these beautiful girls in bikinis. When they weren't on the beach they were walking round town with their high heeled shoes, little poodles and big hats. My husband was nearly bumping into lamp posts, he couldn't take his eyes off these girls. But I was so pale and my swimsuit was so old fashioned.'
(Interview from *Some Liked It Hot*.)

Our family of five made the trip from Manchester to St Tropez in 1959 in an elderly Riley loaded up with an enormous canvas frame tent on the roof rack. I was 6, my brother was 14 and my sister 13. It was a complete contrast to our usual holidays in Dundee and the Lake District, where we were clad in sensible jumpers and rainwear. Our car laboured along for 800 long, hot miles, with tension mounting every time my father tried to overtake as the right hand drive meant he could not see the oncoming traffic. I remember my amazement at new tastes: *café au lait* with warm croissants and baguettes for breakfast and the delicious sourness of *citron pressé*. A cine film shows us pitching the tent, an hour long operation that involved

"YOU OUGHT TO SEE ME IN MY **TEENY WEENY BIKINI — I LOOK SMASHING !**"

British bathers took to the bikini with gusto. Seaside comic series.

all of us working as a team. My mother hated every bit of it, especially the campsite toilets. My father's cine camera would frequently stray away from the family activities to track the backside of some glamorous stranger passing by our tent. I spent every day on the beach dressed in a teeny weeny bikini and a big straw hat. Hours were passed lolling in the warm blue sea, so different from the bracing waters of Broughty Ferry. My brother got prickly heat and had to spend most of his holiday inside the tent, reading.

Britain's grey seas, wet summers, cardies and pac-a-macs seemed a long way away from this exotic paradise. But the British were not just looking to Europe for diversion from their bracing climate and humdrum routines. The appeal of Californian beach-life hit Britain's windy shores when The Beach Boys began producing their series of hits in the 1960s. And in 1953, Ian Fleming had published the first James Bond novel in a series which opened up an enticing world to austerity weary Brits. The Bond stories were mostly set in exotic locations and offered the reader a heady mix of sex, danger, and luxurious lifestyles. Fleming himself lived in Jamaica and he and his wife Ann attracted stars and politicians to their beachside penthouse. Hugh Gaitskell, the Labour Chancellor of the Exchequer was a regular visitor and, indeed, one of Ann's lovers. Her reports of Gaitskell swimming 'like a hippo' in the turquoise waters of the Caribbean offer a radically alternative view of an outwardly staid politician who, in his own words, lived 'such a circumscribed life' at home.

But even home-swimming could have its own sexual associations. Indeed, in 1961, one of the greatest British political scandals of the century began when a call-girl, Christine Keeler, swam naked in a pool during a party at Lord Astor's Buckinghamshire home. John Profumo, the then Secretary of State for War in Harold Macmillan's Conservative government, was an appreciative audience and his subsequent affair with Miss Keeler led to the ruin of his political career.

Although the domestic holiday trade was steady and far outnumbered foreign trade (30 million per year holidayed in the UK during the 1960s) Britain's seaside towns were becoming aware of the allure of other countries and cultures and attempted to jump on the glamour bandwagon.

But the reality was very different. In his song *I'm turning into Dad*, comedian Mick Artistik describes his Leeds childhood in the early 1960s. His Northern Irish father took an authoritarian approach to fun and recreation:

He'd take us to the beach. And then we'd have to swim in the sea. It was always bloody freezing. And none of us was any good at swimming. We'd have to step into that big dark grey thing. It had a certain malevolence. We got a shock to the genitals when we hit the water. Not like the pictures in the holiday booklets, glossy brochures showing holiday-makers with beach balls. The water's not like that in Scarborough.

One can see why, for people like the young Mick, warm indoor pools might have a certain appeal. In 1960, The Wolfenden Report on Sport in the Community recom-

Glamour at Whitley Bay, 1957.

mended to local councils that any new bathing pools should be built indoors, as part of all-in-one sport and leisure centres. So, from the mid 1960s, new municipal pools started to cut swimmers off from the elements and from their local and traditional outdoor swimming places, which slowly became forgotten and neglected.

It did not take long for entrepreneurs to come up with the idea of combining the all-in holidays, so beloved of the British, with the guaranteed sunshine on offer in Continental locations. Many of the earliest package tour operators started business using aircraft (and pilots) left over from the war. The first modern package tour is recorded as taking place in 1950. A Reuters journalist, Vladimir Raitz, chartered an old American Air Force Dakota, converted to carry passengers, to run a trip from the UK to a camp site in Corsica.

These early holidays involved flying in elderly, adapted DC3s and DC4s in unpressurised cabins, at low altitude, with frequent stops for refuelling. Passengers were often terrified by turbulence (which was worse at low altitudes) and problems landing at underdeveloped airports, where the runway was often just a strip cut in a field. But such experiences didn't put people off. Statistics from the British Travel Association show that holidays abroad numbered 1.5 million in 1951 but reached 5 million per year during the 1960s. By 1965, over 80% of workers had a fortnight's paid leave each year, which made a foreign package trip more viable. The annual holiday became one of the top three items on the list of major family expenditure, along with the mortgage and the car. Foreign holidays became a matter of course, for middle class families at least. By 1964, my *Smart Girl Annual* was offering teenage travellers sensible tips on preparing for that foreign trip:

Try to avoid wearing cardigans in the evenings. They stamp you as an English tourist straight away! If you do feel chilly throw your cardigan around your shoulders or get a stole to match your dress. Buy a sunhat when you're there, they are much prettier on the continent. It is always wise to pack Elastoplast, aspirin, TCP for bites and stings, cotton wool and plenty of paper tissues.

Although they might be willing to risk ditching their cardies, some British holiday makers held fast to other home traditions. It is reported that it was common for the earliest package tourists to have a whip-round for the pilot and give the air hostesses money for a drink.

In the late 1950s, Harold Mamburg combined forces with travel agents Peter Cadbury and Henry Lunn to negotiate air routes to Viareggio in Tuscany and to Majorca. The latter signalled the start of the British/Spanish tourist industry, a development encouraged by Franco as a way of bringing much needed foreign currency into impoverished Spain. Development along the Costa de Sol and Costa Blanca began with the help of government subsidies and grants and was unimpeded by planning and building regulations. Progress was rapid. In 1957, Benidorm was a fishing village with just 2,726 inhabitants and three small

IT'S WONDERFUL HERE BY THE SEA !

" WE'RE MAKING QUITE
A SPLASH HERE ! "

The allure of the British seaside holiday was starting to fade.

Towards the end of the 1950s, young people started to meet and spend time together at seaside resorts.

hotels. By 1959, 34 hotels had been built, accommodating 30,000 visitors. By 1960, 300 new buildings, erected to accommodate the tourists, fringed the shoreline.

Sex and the seaside

Spain was still a deeply conservative and religious country, and police patrols ensured decent behaviour on the beaches and in the streets. Bikinis and kissing in public were banned until 1967 and it wasn't until 1975, when Franco died, that the rules were relaxed somewhat. This was in marked contrast to behaviour in the UK. For the post-war generation, some of whom had been liberated by their years away on service, the seaside was the place for sexual adventures. Even the Wakes Weeks holiday trains

were hijacked, with young people commandeering entire coaches on what was known as the 'passion wagon'. Once at the seaside, it could be a challenge to escape the scrutiny of eagle-eyed landladies, so lovers had to find trysting-places wherever they could. Couples would meet under the North Pier in Blackpool to kiss, embrace and make love in relative darkness and seclusion, although their privacy was often disrupted by the regular beach patrols.

British seaside resorts had already become associated with sexual freedom during the nineteenth century, as holiday makers found themselves liberated, for a few days, from the rules and restrictions imposed by the workplace, community, church and chapel. The seaside offered a chance for young people to meet with each other in relative freedom.

This sense of sexual freedom, lubricated by alcohol, was encapsulated in Donald McGill's suggestive postcards, which he started to produce after the First World War. He classified his postcards in terms of their levels of vulgarity: *mild, medium or strong*. The strong cards were his best sellers by far throughout the ensuing decades. Bizarrely, in 1954 at the age of 80, McGill suddenly found himself in court, accused of contravening the Obscene Publications Act, 1857. He was found guilty and fined, many of the more suggestive postcards were destroyed and orders were cancelled. By the late 1950s, however, the moral pressure had eased off. The saucy postcard market recovered and still thrives today.

Towards the end of the 1950s, young people started to meet and spend time together in the resorts and seaside towns, away from the constraints of family, workplace and community. By the mid 1960s, numerous youth subcultures had begun to appear, including the mods and rockers, rival tribes that often invaded seaside towns such as Margate, Brighton, Bournemouth and Clacton on bank holiday weekends.

The 1960s saw the blossoming of youth culture, more progressive attitudes and, with the advent of the Pill, increased levels of sexual freedom. Young people became visible and increasingly regarded as consumers in their own right. Recognising this purchasing power, some Butlin's holiday camps started to offer holidays for groups of unaccompanied teenagers. Unsurprisingly, the organised activities that had been so popular with their parents' generation were displaced by uncontrolled drinking, fighting and sex. Butlin's tried to exert control by separating the teenagers' accommodation from family areas and segregating and patrolling male and female chalets, to little avail. By 1968, bookings of groups of teenagers were no longer accepted and Butlin's struggled to re-establish its family brand.

Young people in the mid 1960s were indeed less inclined to submit to instruction and the organised activities so much favoured by the camps. It is ironic that some of the holiday high jinks of the camp Redcoats are not dissimilar to the kind of initiation rites that might have occurred in exclusive public schools:

'Over the tannoy came the announcement that our day would start down at the swimming pool. There were

From the earliest decades of the century the seaside offered young people a chance to meet together in relative freedom.

these Redcoats and they were getting hold of people and hanging them over the railings and passing them down to a Redcoat at the bottom and then he'd throw them into a swimming pool. I was terrified because I didn't like water and I couldn't swim. We never went back to the swimming pool and I thought 'Well if that's Butlins I'm not going any more and I never have.'
(Interview from *Some Liked it Hot*.)

This account, like Mick Artistik's song lyrics, signals a change in attitudes towards swimming in Britain. Having been represented as healthy, pleasurable and sexy, it was starting to be seen as an unpleasant, almost punitive experience. Britain's holiday camps started to go into decline in the 1970s as campers signed up for foreign package tours, which offered high levels of security and organisation plus guaranteed sun and warm, clear, blue water. Butlin had tried to fight back by opening a holiday camp in the Bahamas, but this proved a financial disaster. The Pontinental initiative worked better, with camps in Sardinia, Ibiza, Majorca and Torremolinos. Here, along with plentiful sunshine and cheap alcohol, plain English cooking was guaranteed. As punters leached away towards Benidorm, the British based holiday camps started to look neglected and down at heel and the regimented communal activities became the butt of jokes on a Colditz theme.

The slow deterioration mirrored the gradual decline of British seaside resorts, which were also starting to lose out to foreign competition. The film *The Punch and Judy Man* (1962) depicted – in black and white – life in a small British seaside town, Piltdown. Parochial, rainy and grim, it was the perfect setting for Tony Hancock's hang-dog, gloomy performance in the title role. Two years later, *Summer Holiday* was released – a complete contrast. A group of young people, led by energetic, chubby faced Cliff Richard, take a London double decker bus on a trip to the Continent:

We're going where the sun shines brightly
We're going where the sea is blue
We've seen it at the movies
So let's see if it's true.

Holiday camps started to look neglected and down at heel.
Holiday camp chalet, Isle of Wight © Martin Parr/Magnum.

These two films mirror the changing ethos of the British holiday. Piltdown comes across as parochial, old-fashioned and unappealing, except to traditionalists. Piltdownians struggle to comprehend why people might want to holiday elsewhere:

'I don't know why folks bother flocking off to those foreign parts. Whatever they've got, Piltdown can provide: the bowling green, the promenade, the memorial garden....'

New Brighton symbolised the general decline. Having been extremely popular in the 19th and early part of the 20th century, attracting visitors from Lancashire's industrial towns, as well as from nearby Liverpool, it lost one of its main attractions in the late 1960s when tidal changes washed away the golden sands. The main complex, which included the Tower Ballroom, was destroyed by fire in 1969. The town became increasingly run down, although hot summer Sundays could still tempt day-trippers across the Mersey, even as late as the mid 1980s.

As numbers of domestic holiday-makers dwindled, some seaside towns started to regroup, attracting older people wishing to take cheap off-season holidays, as well as those who were looking to purchase reasonably priced retirement accommodation. So as the resort business shrank, populations grew, becoming poorer and increasingly homogenous. As attractions such as cinemas and dance halls closed down, town centres became increasingly dilapidated, bordered by ever expanding settlements of retirement housing. By 1976, only 53 of Britain's 85 piers remained, the rest having been destroyed by fire or storms. Those who still holidayed in the UK started to gravitate away from the busier resorts and were drawn to the relatively unspoilt coastlines of Devon and Cornwall and the range of activities, such as surfing, that were on offer. In 1971, a staggering 26% of UK tourists headed for the South West. People from Yorkshire, Lancashire, the Midlands and the South East started to abandon their traditional and historic watering places, opting instead to drive for many hours along congested motorways and the busy A roads leading down country.

The 1970s saw the optimism and consumerism of the 1960s give way to economic hardship, compounded by rising unemployment and industrial conflict. The Troubles began in Northern Ireland and regular mainland bombings deepened the general sense of gloom. Living standards

New Brighton could still tempt day-trippers across the Mersey. New Brighton Lido, 1985 © Martin Parr/Magnum.

declined in Britain between 1974 and 1978. The economic crisis reached a climax in the freezing January of 1979, when public service workers protested against the pay rise restrictions imposed by the Labour government. The misery of that 'winter of discontent', when piles of rubbish lay uncollected on the wind-swept streets, and bodies were stockpiled in morgues, was sharpened when TV images were transmitted showing the then Prime Minister, Jim Callaghan, attending a summit in Guadalupe. While Britain shivered, Callaghan was pictured enjoying the Caribbean sunshine, sunbathing, and swimming in clear blue water, something he casually mentioned at a press conference on his return. Callaghan's swim symbolised a lifestyle that seemed cruelly beyond the reach of most. On his return to the bleak, strike-torn capital, Callaghan's *'crisis, what crisis?'* attitude helped to end his premiership and, indeed, opened the door to Mrs Thatcher.

Despite the economic problems and the increased cost of living, 9 million people holidayed abroad in 1978 (30% choosing to go to Spain). In 1979, 10 million people headed away from Britain for their summer break and by 1987 that number had doubled. It became fashionable to have the 'main' holiday abroad and to use the remainder of the increasingly generous holiday allowance to go on UK-based mini-breaks, or improve one's home with gardening and DIY, leisure activities that were becoming industries in their own right. People were not just heading to Europe. In 1970, the first jumbo jet landed at Heathrow and in 1977, Freddie Laker launched his Skytrain, the first low-cost no-frills airline linking Gatwick with JFK, New York. For the more adventurous and sophisticated holiday maker, advances in air travel offered long-haul alternatives to a package holiday on the Costas.

By 1980 the British were spending more abroad than those holidaying in the UK. Foreign holiday expenditure continued to rise through the 1980s and 1990s as more exotic and expensive holiday options and locations became available. The British Tourist Authority statistics suggest that 1987 was the worst year ever for British seaside resorts, as numbers of people seeking a cheap holiday on the 'Costa del Dole' continued to increase. 26 million travelled abroad for their summer holidays in 1994.

Pollution, health and safety

Meanwhile, back at home, bathing in British coastal waters seemed less and less appealing. Britain had joined the EU in 1973 and, along with other member countries, became subject to environmental standards set out in directives from Brussels. The EU Bathing Water Directive published tables comparing bathing water quality in various member countries. Despite this shaming scrutiny and exposure, the pollution of British coastal waters by sewage and litter continued unabated through the 1970s, largely condoned by the public health organisations who wanted definitive proof that sewage was harmful to health before taking any action. Shockingly, in 1980, the United Kingdom was registered as having no inland bathing places and only 27 coastal bathing places that met the required standards. In the same year France was recorded as having 1,362 inland and 1,498 coastal sites where bathing water was of satisfactory quality or better.

Seaside authorities were more concerned with sustaining their dwindling economies and tackling problems such as erosion than with improving the quality of their water. Bathing came low on the list of priorities. Seaside towns such as Brighton turned their backs on the sea, building up their leisure, commercial and conference facilities in a bid to attract more visitors. The continuing polluted state of Britain's coastal waters was brought to international attention with an EU report in 1988 followed by another in 1993, which exposed unacceptable levels of coli form bacteria in sea water at Blackpool and at other major resorts. The report was countered by a local MEP who declared that *'people don't come to Blackpool to swim'*. He was right. Sea swimming at Blackpool and everywhere else was in decline.

Growing environmental awareness eventually made Britain start to acknowledge that it had a problem. Irish pressure groups objected vociferously to the dumping of radioactive waste from Sellafield into the Irish Sea, a practice which had been going on since the early 1950s. In 1983 the so-called 'Beach incident' took place when a local beach was closed due to high radioactive discharges containing ruthenium and rhodium. In the mid 1980s, pressure groups such as *Surfers Against Sewage*, the Scarborough-based *Sons of Neptune* and the *Marine Conservation Society* began to bring the issue of pollution to public attention. Local authorities, local water companies and

The pollution of British coastal waters with sewage and litter continued unabated. New Brighton beach, 1985 © Martin Parr/Magnum.

the government were still slow to act. In 1994, 71 of 500 beaches identified in England still failed to come up to Marine Conservation Society water standards, and 100 failed to reach the minimum EU standards for bathing water. Britain's coastal waters were effectively a health hazard, the exact opposite of their original status in the 18th century.

Ironically, many people in the 1970s were less alarmed by pollution in the sea than by the possible presence of underwater predators. Stephen Spielberg's terrifying movie *Jaws* (1975) awakened deep-seated folk memories of monsters from the deep. The fact that the film was set on the west coast of America made no difference. The shark's deadly attacks on innocent swimmers made even the

The pool at Gourock continues to attract swimmers © Martin Parr/Magnum.

hardiest think twice as they waded into the cold, murky British sea.

Pollution-wise, things were not much better inland. Industrial waste and sewage continued to foul city waterways as they had done for at least 100 years. Rural rivers were (and still are) poisoned by agricultural run-off saturated with herbicides, pesticides and fertilisers. The 1974 Control of Pollution Act started to police discharges of

pollutants more effectively and slowly the management of sewage improved. The big industrial polluters themselves were in decline. Since the late 1980s fish and other wildlife have gradually started to return to Britain's great rivers including the Thames and the Mersey. By 2000, 94% of English rivers were either *good* or *fair* in terms of chemical quality and over 90% *good* or *fair* in terms of biological quality.

However, inland bathing waters were subject to the same EU directives as coastal waters. In addition, health and safety legislation (in particular The Health and Safety at Work Act, 1974) had made staff and landowners responsible for the safety of visitors to their premises, including open water swimming places as well as pools and lidos. Most local authorities, reined in by the Tory government and reluctant to spend money on improving water quality or employing lifeguards, chose not to promote their open water facilities. Bathing was therefore discouraged and even banned, sometimes at places that had been traditional swimming holes for hundreds of years.

Many of Britain's elderly lidos, costly to maintain and with dwindling numbers of customers, were closed down in the 1980s and 1990s. Again, financial issues were not the only factor. A series of major accidents in the late 1980s [The Herald of Free Enterprise, 1987; the fire at Kings Cross, 1987; Hillsborough, 1989; Piper Alpha, 1988; and the Clapham train crash, 1988], raised the profile of health and safety initiatives and extended the jurisdiction of the Health and Safety Executive. Reviews, policies, procedures and regulations started to affect every aspect of work and leisure. The Health and Safety Commission's rules and standards affected the culture and appearance of the lidos. High diving boards were dismantled and notices proliferated, issuing warnings and prohibitions in order to protect the management from litigation. For many local authorities, the combination of financial pressure and legal worries made lidos unviable. The magnificent Tarlair pool near Macduff in Banffshire succumbed in

Notice at Portsoy Pool © Martin Parr/Magnum.

1996. Today it remains derelict, a sad reminder of the glory days.

As volunteers died and vandalism proliferated, nearby Portsoy pool also lapsed into dereliction and was finally closed by the council on health and safety grounds. Since then, the young people of the town have sought their thrills in other ways. Images of local youngsters tombstoning from cliffs and harbour walls have been posted on YouTube, to the dismay of many local residents.

Ironically, the decline of many lidos coincided with the inception of what was to be known as the *heritage industry*, a movement that saw the decrepit relics of Britain's industrial past transformed into living museums and commercial enterprises. In 1982, *Taking the Plunge*, a survey of the UK's bathing-related architectural heritage, drew attention to the pitiful state of many of the remaining lidos. In 1991, the *Thirties Society* published *Farewell My Lido*, a tribute to the pools that were fast disappearing across the UK. This came too late to save the New Brighton Lido, demolished in 1990 following storm damage. But, against the odds, some lidos managed to ride the wave of closures. The pool at Gourock, which opened in 1909 and is fed with water from the River Clyde, is one example of a lido that has successfully adapted to fluctuating demand, has won major investment and is still going strong.

Meanwhile, the massive road building programme initiated by the Thatcher government improved Britain's

Tarlair Lido, 2010 © Martin Parr/Magnum.

network of motorways and trunk roads, making it possible for people to travel by car to coastal towns for weekend mini-breaks or day trips. Travelling on holiday by rail and coach continued to decline. The convenience, freedom and independence offered by the car made it an essential part of family life. A number of towns in the South West, Suffolk and Norfolk started to attract more discerning visitors, drawing in the middle and upper classes with exciting restaurants, cultural venues and arts events. The growing popularity amongst the well-to-do of places such as Padstow, Seaview and Whitstable boosted the market for second homes that could be done up, then let out as self-catering cottages, as a result putting them well out of the financial reach of locals. The growing popularity of surfing and other sports, such as wind-surfing, drew a younger, richer set of holiday-makers, particularly to the wild and windswept beaches of the South West. Some towns, such as Newquay, rescued themselves from encroaching decrepitude by responding to the growing demand for equipment, tuition, catering and accommodation, becoming a hub for the new generation of British surfers who combine relative wealth with a relaxed and informal approach to life.

'Extreme' sports like bungee jumping, white water rafting, and sky diving were also becoming popular. Seaside towns started to add adventurous and challenging water activities, including deep sea diving, to their portfolio of attractions. Many of these leisure activities were highly dependent on elaborate kit. Technological advances, for example within wetsuit and board design, made surfing much more expensive and advanced its exclusivity. Sub-cultures of surfing have now appeared in the form of windsurfing and kitesurfing, each again dependent on expensive equipment.

Traditional seaside places such as Hastings and Brighton, if they could not guarantee ideal surfing conditions, survived by a process of diversification. English language schools, conference centres, stag and hen parties, folk festivals, and cut price offers for out-of-season coach parties drew in much-needed visitors. Blackpool continued to thrive as a traditional northern resort, its season extended into the winter months by the magnificent Illuminations. Some less vibrant places went downhill and became the dumping ground for council problems. Once elegant seaside guest houses ended up as Social Service-funded accommodation for disadvantaged families or asylum seekers, who could not be housed elsewhere.

Visiting any British beach at the turn of the century, one would be far more likely to see wet-suited surfers, wind and kite surfers and jet-skiers in the sea than swimmers. Visitors to Brighton, Clevedon or Broughty Ferry might watch with amusement and incredulity as members of the traditional swimming clubs entered the sea in all weathers and all seasons. Few would want to join them. Indeed, by the late 1990s Britain was seeing rapidly increasing rates of obesity, well on its way to its unenviable position at the top of the European league table. Particularly associated with poverty, and caused by poor diet and lack of physical activity, obesity was a sign that Britain was turning into a nation of couch potatoes.

Given all the competing attractions, simple swimming in British seas, rivers and lakes went into gentle decline throughout the second part of the century. Yet one man was taking a new approach to swimming in Britain, albeit in relative obscurity. In *Swimming Free*, written in 1972, Geoffrey Fraser Dutton poetically celebrated Britain's native waters:

Most people believe that scenes of great underwater beauty and power exist only in localities as romantic and inaccessible as the Red Sea, the Barrier Reef, or more suburbanly, the Mediterranean. And only available to those

skilled in the craft of Cousteau and Hass, who, gleaming with dials and cylinders and floodlights, sink to some remote, sophisticated depths. This is nonsense. This book is about swimming or about journeying in the water, about the world of the swimmer among sandbanks and shoals, through skerries and beneath great cliffs, up fast rivers and slow ones, of the swimmer islanded in the golden evening on some remote mountain loch.

Swimming Free
by Geoffrey Fraser Dutton, 1972.

Dutton's mission was to free British swimmers from *littered holiday reaches* and the *chlorinated rectangles* of public baths. With his snorkel and wet suit, *whose rubbery bliss provides you with a fucoid integument blending perfectly with the native seaflesh around you* Dutton entered the coldest and most inhospitable of native waters, following salmon and trout up rivers and playing in rocky coves with seals. Dutton's poetic celebration of Britain's watery underworld was prescient, foreshadowing the Wild Swimming movement that would come to Britain some 40 years later: *We are still at the adolescence of free swimming, still in the Alps before 1854 and a little overmuch enthusiasm, a sincere if clumsy mysticism may be excused in this Golden Age. No one has been here before; the waters are undisturbed and the clichés scarcely fingered.*

Henleaze Lake

During the lake season (May to September) I fall into the grip of a powerful addiction. I have to get to the lake every day, no matter what the weather. If I cannot go, because of work or visitors, I become crotchety, edgy, ill at ease. I manage to resist the call of the lake during working hours, but by 5.30pm the craving sets in and I have to abandon whatever I am doing. As it is about five miles uphill from where I live I usually drive but will resort to begging a lift or even to bicycle if necessary.

The lake is situated in Henleaze – a sedate area of north Bristol, near the Downs. Flourishing in the 1920s and 1930s, Henleaze reminds me of the England of the Janet and John books, with its arcade of shops, an old-fashioned cinema and rows of semi-detached villas with neat front gardens, privet hedges clipped and lawns mown. It feels so suburban, a most unlikely setting for a dramatic limestone swimming hole.

It is always a relief to leave the traffic behind and turn down quiet Lake Road. I drive through the entrance archway – an elevated, rickety structure bearing the legend 'Henleaze Swimming Club' in faded gold letters – down to the low black and white swing barrier by the superintendent's hut. There my card is inspected and I am waved on with a smile. And there is the lake, set beyond a grassy area, bordered with neat flower pots and planters spilling over with geraniums, begonias and busy lizzies. Long and narrow, as befits an old quarry, the lake stretches for over a quarter of a mile, and is edged with steep limestone cliffs.

The southern part of the lake is fringed with mature trees. My favourite is the willow that stands by the furthest ladder on the right, trailing its fronds towards the water. I walk up to the ladies' changing room. This is one of the best moments of a visit to the lake: mounted on an elevated framework, this black and white wooden structure is thought to have been a first aid post during the First World War. I enter, breathing in the grassy smell of coconut matting, my eyes taking a moment to adjust to the dim light of the panelled wood interior. Each changing cubicle is screened with a checked curtain and has a wooden bench, a small mirror, some metal hooks and a slatted wooden changing mat. Sometimes when you enter a cubicle there are traces of talcum powder on the floor. I change quickly, kick off my flip flops then grab my towel and walk down the ramp, past the spring boards and diving stages, across the grass to the furthest metal ladder that enters the water under the willow.

Descending the ladder and entering the water is the nearest I get, these days, to a religious experience. It always feels cool, and sometimes shockingly cold, but I never hesitate in my descent. I move steadily and smoothly and launch myself out. It is exquisite. The lake is spring fed and as you swim you can come across mysteriously warm channels, and bitingly cold ones. The water is green and opaque. This is probably a good thing because it means one is neither alarmed by the depth of the quarry nor by the fish. Some unnerving photographs of the anglers' catches are displayed in the tea hut. Massive carp, perch and even pike lurk here. The pike are partial to ducklings and renowned for picking them off one by one. Every year a once proud mother of six, seven or eight fusses over her gradually diminishing brood and usually ends up paddling along the lake edge, sad and alone. I generally try not to think about the fish, although occasionally am startled by the sight of a scaly back arching out of the water, the casual flick of a tail nearby or a sudden splash, marked by a set of expanding, concentric rings. I swim across the lake to the ladder on the other side, by the men's changing hut (which is not really a hut, more of a long, open-sided shack with a corrugated roof).

Holding onto the ladder, I take stock. On a warm evening several people will be swimming up and down in pairs or alone. The grass will be dotted with deck chairs and rugs where swimmers doze, read or picnic. Children and young people are drawn to the diving stage and the spring board, and the repetitive sound of bounce and splash accompanies most of my swims. If it is grey, overcast, or raining I may be the only swimmer and apologise to the lifeguard who has to leave the cosy hut and come and watch me from the lakeside, from under the shelter of a large umbrella. Yet the lake is at its most beautiful when it is raining and you can swim along with a close up view of the droplets as they fall into the water, each creating its own miniature indentation and splash on the surface.

When I first came across the lake in the mid 1980s, membership was falling. But now interest has revived and there is a long waiting list. Part of the appeal is the fact that – no matter what tumultuous world events or traumatic personal upheavals take place – the lake is always the same. I think about all the people who have swum here over the past century, finding in the stillness of the water and its surroundings some respite from the worries of war, recession and industrial strife. I swam here after the 9/11 attacks and the London bombing, throughout the war in Iraq and the summer of my father's final illness, calmed by the place and by my gentle rituals. I like the fact that very little changes from year to year. Any proposed developments, such as the controversial proposal to install a small sauna near the ladies' changing room, are subject to in-depth scrutiny by the committee and lengthy debate. Reaching a decision can take years.

I swim diagonally back across the lake and out to the club limit, marked in uneven letters in white gloss paint on the cliff side. Swimmers must not go beyond this point, other than during the annual long swims (when the feat of swimming up and down the entire length wins you a Mars Bar, a cup of tea and a certificate). Beyond this mark is the anglers' domain. As you look down the expanse of water you can see figures sitting quietly amongst the bushes, watching and waiting. Here on the limestone cliff at club limit there are little ledges where you can sit and lean back against the warm rock. The pigeons favour this place too as it offers a quiet perch, away from the splashes and cries of young swimmers. And, several times from this spot, I have been lucky enough to see the flash of a kingfisher on the hunt for tiddlers along the lake edge, his intense turquoise plumage startlingly out of place against the dull, muddy green of the water and marginal plants. I often sit for a while, up to my neck in water, absorbing the smells, sounds and sights of lake life. Sometimes, other people are there and we chat, usually something

Outside the ladies' changing room at Henleaze Lake © Martin Parr/Magnum.

along the lines of *'It's lovely once you're in, isn't it?'* and *'Not as cold as I thought.'*

I swim back down to my ladder, past a charming sculpture of a water sprite – a recent addition – that dances on a plinth mid-water near the lilies and kingcups. Up my ladder, wrap up in the towel and then walk slowly back across the grass to the changing room, passing by a commemorative bench and under a commemorative clock, both remembering swimmers who swim no more.

Resurgence: swimming in Britain's rivers, lakes and seas at the start of the 21st century

Farleigh Hungerford, July

I have come to interview Rob Fryer, Chair of the Farleigh and District Swimming Club, founding member of the *River and Lake Swimming Association* (RALSA) and author of *Rob Fryer's Wild Swimming Guide*. I am a bit concerned about finding the club as I know it is basically just a field with a shed, so as I approach Farleigh Hungerford and drive over two stone bridges, I slow right down and look carefully along the river banks trying to spot the place.

I see a large field of closely mown grass with a car parked at the far gate, beside which stands a figure in black swimming trunks. This must be it. Rob has been a member of the club since 1966 and is now its chair. For many years he has been campaigning in different ways for improved access to lake and river swimming in the UK.

It is a beautiful July day, bright and warm but with a lively breeze that spins the clouds across the sky and fills the air with the sound of rustling leaves. Rob unfurls two folding chairs from the back of his car and we sit in the shade to talk. He puts on his maroon Farleigh & District Swimming Club polo shirt, with a logo on the pocket showing a damselfly hovering over a water lily. He tells me about the club, about RALSA and about the labour of love that is his directory of swimming holes, which he started working on over a decade ago, inspired by Roger Deakin's *Waterlog*.

While we are talking, a battered Land Rover turns into the field and parks nearby. This is Philip Bryant, the farmer who owns the two fields occupied by the club, and who invited the swimmers over to his river bank in 1992 when the farmer on the other side started holding motocross events in his field. Philip has come to collect the rubbish, to get a water sample for lab analysis and to mend a broken gate post. He too is wearing a swimming club polo shirt.

Philip and Rob tell me that the club is very relaxed, run by about five or six committee members. Although it has some 2,000 members there are no lifeguards and very few rules, although the charming membership card (which I am given when I pay my £1) does give some advice on safe river swimming and also requests swimmers to observe *decency of language and behaviour*. Club opening times for fully paid up members are simply described on

The noticeboard, Farleigh and District Swimming Club © Martin Parr/Magnum.

Rob Fryer © Martin Parr/Magnum.

the card as *Anywhen*. I am so used to strict supervision, rules and time-keeping at Henleaze Lake Swimming Club that I am completely enchanted by this informality.

And it is a magical place. When we have finished talking, Rob says: *'Let's go for a swim.'* I quickly change and we go down the steps by the weir – which dates back to the 13th century – onto the gravel river bed and into the cool green water. Just by the weir there is a cluster of kingcups, where electric blue damselflies hover and swerve, skimming over the water, bringing the club logo to life. We swim along the length of the club field, past overhanging willow trees, the old diving board that was dismantled in 1999, and a couple of aluminium ladders that are fixed to the bank for swimmers to get in and out of the water. It is wonderful to

swim along in such a relaxed way in deep river water, sometimes chatting, sometimes silent, with no fear of fishermen, water bailiffs, local authority prohibitions, weeds or currents. We reach the end of the stretch of deep water and turn back. Rob spots a group of young men who have arrived in the field and climbs up a ladder to greet them and collect their membership fees. I swim back on my own through dappled light, breathing in the watery river smell, past the muddy banks, the tree roots, the trailing branches, the kingcups and the damselflies. Then I sit for a while on the stone ledge of the old weir, my feet trailing as the water flows slowly past.

* * * * *

Open water swimming in Britain during the first decade of the 21st century presents something of a mixed picture. The practice continues to face a number of significant obstacles and challenges. But new opportunities have opened up too. There is evidence of a growth of interest in competitive events and the Wild Swimming movement has attracted thousands of followers, many of them younger people.

Pollution, access, health and safety and legislation

Perhaps the most significant threat to the practice of swimming in Britain's seas, rivers and lakes, pollution seems to be a continuing and possibly a growing problem. In 2009, nearly half of the 769 British beaches tested for water quality did not meet Marine Conservation Society standards. Worrying data suggest that coastal bathing water quality has actually been deteriorating overall since 2006. Although the Environment Agency highlights improvements in water quality at some bathing places, it adds, somewhat ominously: *'We are not complacent'*.

Untreated effluent from flooded sewers is a particular concern, exacerbated by a series of wet and stormy summers. Heavy rainfall, combined with land erosion, means that pesticides and fertilisers are washed into rivers from farmland. Combined sewer overflows, built to manage flood water, mean that urban waste including oil and petrochemicals mix with raw sewage and are carried from flooded sewers out into rivers and onwards to the sea. The Marine Conservation Society (MCS), a charitable organisation and pressure group, recommends that more British beaches need to be tested and the regional water companies made responsible for improving design and capacity of sewage pipes so that they can cope better with heavy rainfall and flooding emergencies. Urban drainage systems and waste disposal need to be regulated (currently only about one quarter of the country's 22,000 combined sewage overflow systems are monitored). The MCS is also seeking to promote more sustainable farm management systems to prevent the erosion and run-off that allow agricultural pollutants to enter the system. It also wants more information made available to the public on the risks that they incur when bathing.

What seems certain is that water quality can fluctuate from year to year. For example, bathing water at Weston-super-Mare won recommendation by the MCS in 2008, but then in 2009 it only reached the minimum European standard. The sea was polluted by manure from farmland, animal faeces, human sewage and run-off water from urban areas, making bathing inadvisable. Weston was warned that new European standards for bathing water would be introduced in 2015, and beaches failing to reach a sufficient standard would have to impose a permanent ban on bathing. Similar levels of pollution were reported around the coast, particularly after heavy rain caused sewage systems to flood. However, things improved for Weston in 2010, as once again its water reached the higher standard.

The 2015 EU directive will establish new criteria and more stringent standards for water quality, based on current research. All bathing waters in the UK will be required to achieve at least *sufficient* quality by that date (the level above *poor*). This legal imperative is putting pressure on water companies across the UK to clean up their act, particularly in areas where current results are poor. The water industry spent more than £10 billion between 1995 and 2009 in order to meet EU directives, and more investment is planned. Between 2010 and 2015 Scottish Water will invest £2.5 billion while £12.5 billion will go towards improving sewerage services in England and Wales.

Unpleasant debris is one consequence of untreated sewage flooding into sea water: tampons, panty liners and condoms can give beach-goers an unwelcome surprise as they sunbathe, play football or build sand castles. In 2009, MCS volunteers collected and analysed litter from 397 British beaches, finding for example a total of 12,961 cotton bud sticks. But beach debris is not only sewage-related. The same survey listed 1,849 items of litter found

over one weekend, a worrying 77% increase on the results of the first annual survey in 1994. 63% of the collected litter in 2009 was plastic: bottles and bags being the biggest culprits. The primary source of the waste was identified as public littering, followed by commercial and recreational fishing. Plastic waste is not just unsightly. The fragments are understood to attract toxic chemicals which then enter the food chain when they are eaten by marine creatures.

Oil is another source of beach and sea water pollution. This does not only come about as a result of catastrophic tanker spillages such as the *Sea Empress* accident in 1996, but also from incidents at refineries around the coast. The flushing of fuel and oil tanks at sea – a practice that is impossible to monitor, particularly on busy shipping routes – also contributes to oil pollution.

Despite such significant problems with coastal pollution, a popular (and largely inaccurate) perception continues that the sea is cleaner than river and lake water, which is often considered too dirty to swim in. Fears about pollution form only one aspect of the challenges facing those who are struggling to establish rights to swim in English and Welsh rivers and lakes. Jean Perraton, a campaigning swimmer, feels some progress has been made at a national policy level. She detects an increased tolerance of the practice, largely thanks to the efforts of a number of pressure groups, such as the River and Lake Swimming Association, that have campaigned strenuously for better access, with some notable victories. As a result, The Environment Agency's head of recreation policy has stated that the press releases warning people not to swim in any river, lake or canal, which used to be issued each summer, will no longer appear as a matter of routine.

The Health and Safety Executive has amended its guidelines so that the requirements for lifeguards no longer apply to open waters where operators simply allow, rather than actively encourage, swimming. The Royal Society for the Prevention of Accidents, too, has modified its advice, which now concentrates on how to swim safely rather than not swimming at all in inland waters. Outdoor swimming now appears in some regional water recreation plans. However, Jean points out:

'These shifts do not seem to have percolated down to local authorities and other managers of recreational sites with lakes or riversides. "No swimming" notices still proliferate at many inland bathing areas. Even at Brereton

Heath – the site of landmark rulings – park managers remain adamantly opposed to letting people swim in the lake. And we still get regular warnings about not swimming in lakes and rivers from county fire services. The Cheshire service, for example, in the summer of 2010, issued a warning that lakes in Cheshire are "freezing cold" and alleging, without a shred of evidence, that most people who drown in open waters are good swimmers.'

Clearly, swimming in inland waters is still a contentious issue. Councils and landowners are eager to protect themselves from litigation, an outcome more easily achieved by banning swimming and highlighting its dangers rather than by actively encouraging it.

But commercial pressures also affect sea and inland swimming. In 1957, on a BBC *Panorama* programme, members of a local council strongly refuted concerns expressed by the parents of Caroline Wakefield, aged 6, who died of polio after bathing in contaminated seawater. Spokesmen continued to claim that sea water had cleansing effects. It would be irresponsible to spend public money on a treatment plant, given the negative impact that adverse publicity could have on the local tourist trade, the town's main industry. Fifty years later, local authorities are experiencing similar levels of pressure to promote the reputation of seaside towns as desirable and healthy destinations. Their mission is to boost tourist numbers, in the context of dwindling resources. One solution to fluctuating water quality standards is to discourage, or rather *fail to encourage* bathing, perhaps by not providing lifeguards or not taking a proactive approach to regulating fair water usage by different groups, such as speed boat owners, jet-skiers and windsurfers. Swimming can also be discouraged by adverse publicity that emphasises the danger of drowning.

Commercial concerns also impact on inland swimming. Many landowners and authorities enjoy the profits brought by lucrative fishing rights. Fishing is big business; when swimmers take to rivers and lakes then fishermen are disturbed and the sport potentially threatened.

The question of whether the public has a legal right to swim in lakes, rivers and ponds in England and Wales is unclear, unlike in France where swimmers have free access and in Scotland where the right to swim goes with the right to roam. In fact, it is legal to swim in navigable rivers and at traditional swimming holes. But swimmers often feel discouraged, fearing encounters with irate landowners and fishermen. Many wonder whether they risk prosecution by entering the water. The open water swimmer's status remains hazy, clouded by concerns about legality, safety and pollution.

Olympic frenzy

As a counterpoint to the on-going concerns about open water swimming, there has been a huge upsurge of popular interest in the sport in the first decade of the 21st century. Much of this is due to Rebecca Adlington, the young British swimmer who won two gold medals at the 2008 Olympic Games in Beijing, trouncing the competition in both the 400 metre and 800 metre races. Adlington's achievement made her the 21st century equivalent of Captain Webb, a hugely charismatic and popular figure. She is Britain's most successful Olympic swimmer in 100 years.

Open water swimming is a relative new comer on the international competition scene, despite the fact that it was very common in 19th and early 20th century Britain. It was only in 1986 that the event was added to the international competition calendar and it was not listed at Olympic level until 2008. Such events can cover a variety of distances, typically 5km, 10km and 25km and can take place in any large outdoor body of water: the sea, lakes, rivers, canals, reservoirs and even docks. At the 2008 Olympics, the sport's Olympic debut, three of the six available medals went to British swimmers: silver to David Davies and Keri-Anne Payne and a bronze to Cassie Patten.

British victories in Olympic swimming events, combined with the fact that London won the bid to host the 2012 Olympic Games (and comedian David Walliams's successful cross Channel swim in 2006) have inspired many children and young people to take swimming seriously, to join clubs, embark on rigorous training schedules and enter competitive programmes, mostly pool-based.

'Rebecca Adlington, she's cool. And Eleanor Simmons, the one in the Paralympics. When you watch the people on TV and they are so graceful and elegant you just really want to be like that. I go to the club twice a week and when I move up a group into Junior Gold I will have to go four times a week. We do lots of races against people in our squad and we get coached by some really good coaches. It's really good fun but really hard work. We do

Eliza Swinburn training at her swimming club © Kate Swinburn.

different strokes every week, drills on front crawl, breast stroke and butterfly and so on.' Eliza Swinburn, aged 11.

In 2009, as part of the Olympic initiative, the government introduced free swimming for children and pensioners. However, the recession hit such initiatives hard. In 2010, the Department for Culture, Media and Sport described free swimming as *a luxury we can no longer afford* and the scheme was quietly dropped.

Nevertheless, the popularity of open water swimming events has continued to grow, particularly under the auspices of the *Great Swim* series, sponsored by British Gas. These are mass participation open water swimming events, the first of which was held in Lake Windermere in 2008, attracting 2,250 entries. By 2010, a total of 20,000 people had signed up for four open water swimming events held around the country, two of which had to be cancelled because of an outbreak of blue-green algae. Five events are planned for 2011: in Suffolk, Windermere, Strathclyde, London and Salford. Swimmers of all ages and all abilities are encouraged to enter and swim in a safe and supervised event, often in a beautiful setting. Many undertake the challenge not just to raise their fitness levels and improve their technique but in order to raise money for charity, making the Great Swim events the aquatic equivalent of running a marathon. The Great Swim website gives training tips and advice on safety, and is creating a virtual community of swimmers.

The numbers attracted by the Great Swim are evidence of the growing popularity of swimming outdoors. But Britain also has a long and continuing tradition of smaller open water swimming events that have for years attracted people who want to challenge themselves, support their communities and raise money for local charities. Examples include the annual Padstow to Rock swim across the Camel Estuary, the cross-Tay swims in Broughty Ferry and the cross-harbour swim in Fowey.

While such events, both great and small, have a competitive aspect, racing is not compulsory. The popularity of competitive open water swimming is on the increase, as evidenced by the growing numbers of people taking part in triathlons. A triathlon is an endurance event that involves three sports: open water swimming, cycling and running, all undertaken in sequence and without a pause. The sport was granted Olympic status in 1989 and takes its most extreme form in the *Ironman* race, an event that involves swimming, cycling and running marathon distances consecutively, within a time limit. Despite the event's ominously macho title, women also take part. Ironman and triathlon events are now held across the UK and are growing in popularity. In Britain, an astonishing 650 triathlons and other open water events attract thousands of swimmers, all of whom embark on rigorous training programmes prior to taking the plunge:

'Swimming with 2,500 people when the hooter goes is like setting off for a swim in a washing machine. White water and bodies everywhere flailing, it's spectacular to watch and to be there within that mass of people. Everybody around you is knocking you and pushing you. If you ever see a pool with adult only sessions see how many triathletes there are – there's loads of them. They've sort of occupied the space. In the time since the triathlon started in Britain it has become so inclusive. Everybody does it. Every man and woman and kids and people with disabilities. People from every walk of life enjoy it. And if you can do it at your own level with people your own age. It's good. I've come to competing in swimming in my 50s, something I never did as a teenager, and it's great.' Kes Aleknavicius

Of course, success in such a sport is to a certain extent dependent on kit: athletes want the best swimming wetsuit, racing bike and running shoes. Kes comments: *'Wherever we go, we all look the same because the internet has spread this information far and wide. A British triathlete standing on a beach in Brazil will have the same wetsuit on as the guy next to him. It's become globalised. And the*

Padstow to Rock swim, Cornwall © Martin Parr/Magnum.

new technology is instantly everywhere. I always think there is more carbon fibre at the start of a triathlon than there is in a space shuttle.'

The growing interest in competitive open water swimming has stimulated in-depth scientific research into the effects of cold water on performance. The sporting context has, to a certain extent, started to dispel the negative associations of such research. These emanated from the fact that prisoners in Dachau were subjected to prolonged immersion in cold water as part of Nazi experimentation on survival rates.

Recent research into the physiology of cold water swimming examines potential problems for the swimmer such

as hypothermia (which is in fact much less likely to cause the death of a swimmer than cardiac arrest), muscle weakness and the cold shock response. Interestingly, the data suggests that regular exposure to cold water can enable swimmers to adapt and habituate their responses.

The first decade of the 21st century has also seen the development and growing popularity of water-based activities other than swimming. Surfing, windsurfing and kitesurfing continue to broaden their appeal. One notable newcomer is *coasteering*, which combines rock-climbing, jumping from cliffs and swimming in rough seas. This challenging outdoor activity is now available in some coastal holiday locations in west Wales and elsewhere.

Again, the levels of instruction and supervision needed, together with the compulsory safety equipment, make this activity far from cheap and perhaps only accessible to the better off.

Fitness fallout

Despite the fitness frenzy in some sectors of British society, there is worrying evidence that British children are significantly less fit than they were a decade ago, a problem that can be blamed on the sedentary lifestyle of what has become known as the *Playstation generation*. More children are spending time on line or in front of the TV rather than getting out and about, cycling and swimming. A study published in 2008 in the journal *Archives of Disease in Childhood* showed that fitness levels of the 300 British children studied over a period of ten years had declined by an average of 8%, as opposed to 4% in other European countries. The decline of school sports was cited as one possible cause, one result of a government initiative to generate revenue by selling off playing fields.

Fewer than one in three British children now play competitive sport at school, hence the growth of expensive private swimming, tennis and athletics clubs. Obesity, which is a problem for one in three British children over the age of 11, has somewhat overshadowed the related issue of fitness levels in public health policy. Generally speaking, the poorer a child's background, the more likely they are to be both fat and unfit.

Meanwhile, some children and young people have created their own version of extreme water-related sports in *tombstoning,* the practice of leaping from cliffs, high bridges, harbour sides or quarry edges into deep water. Despite, or perhaps because of, the fact that a number of young people have been critically injured or killed, the popularity of tombstoning seems to be on the increase, judging by its presence on YouTube. Tombstoning is an informal, totally unsupervised activity that needs no special equipment and which is guaranteed to send shockwaves through local communities. It is also free.

New Romantics: the Wild Swimming movement

'People don't always want to be sold experiences and holidays and to have leisure time packaged up in a shopping mall or 5 star luxury. It's quite nice to do something basic, just about you and your swimming costume and whatever bit of river you're getting into.' Kate Rew

The first decade of the 21st century has seen the arrival of a movement that has its roots in Romanticism, a phenomenon that has helped to revive the popularity of open water swimming in Britain. The term 'wild swimming' was coined by Roger Deakin, a film maker and writer with a keen interest in the environment and the natural world. His book *Waterlog*, published in 1999, describes Deakin's swimming odyssey across Britain, inspired by John Cheever's short story *The Swimmer* in which a man travels from pool to pool across Long Island. Deakin's journey has him travelling the length and breadth of Britain, swimming in seas, lakes, rivers, ponds, estuaries and the occasional lido. He visits all points of the compass from the icy waters round the Isles of Scilly to the treacherous whirlpool in the Gulf of Corryvreckan on the west coast of Scotland. He enters calm mill ponds, eel-ridden fenland ditches, muddy tributaries and secret limestone pools. His journey is random and quixotic, as he zig zags along in his battered old Citroen, occasionally repairing to his moated farmhouse in Suffolk. There, his delicate observation of the aquatic creatures and plants he encounters is suffused with his delight in the experience of immersion:

Swimming is a rite of passage, a crossing of boundaries: the line of the shore, the edge of the pool, the surface itself. You see and experience things when you're swimming in a way that is completely different from any other. You are in nature, part and parcel of it, in a much more complete and intense way than on dry land and your sense of the present is overwhelming. In wild water you are on equal terms with the animal world, in every sense on the same level. As a swimmer, I can go right up to a frog and it will show more curiosity than fear.

Deakin, who sadly died from a brain tumour in 2006 at the age of 63, was a great communicator. *Waterlog* documents his many conversations with swimmers across the UK, his delight in their eccentricities and his celebration of Britain's rich swimming heritage. His fury at the swimmer's restricted access to English rivers and lakes is

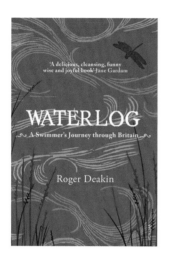

Waterlog by Roger Deakin, 1999.

aroused when he encounters landowners and water bailiffs, rendered apoplectic by the sight of him swimming up their lucrative fishing rivers or strolling along their private banks, clad only in his trunks and goggles. For him, swimming is a *sweetly subversive act.*

A true Post-Romantic, Deakin brings an eclectic sensibility to swimming, drawing on biology, geography, philosophy, geology, history and literature as he swims along at one with the natural world, reflecting upon the sights and sounds he encounters from his frog's eye vantage point. His writing style is idiosyncratic, combining poetry, science and humour, as in this passage describing a swim in the Helford River in Cornwall:

The tide was beginning to ebb, the water oozing from the mudbanks. The first hundred yards of this bayou were deep silky mud, the consistency of yoghurt, then a wallow of thin brown soup under a roof of outstretched oak boughs. The creek was much impeded by the serpentine hulks of fallen trees and floating festoons of tangled seaweed. I lay full length on my belly rowing myself along with my hands like a walrus. As there began to be a puddle's depth, I proceeded like one of the mud hoppers that live in the mangrove swamps of West African rivers. Feeling deeply primeval, like some fast track missing link in our evolution from the lugworm I eventually squirmed into the relative luxury of deeper water. As I left it behind, I thought how much I had enjoyed my communion with the slime and I realised that I had just re-enacted the evolution of swimming. The experience was so unexpectedly delightful and the mud so curiously warm and friendly feeling that I even began to wonder if I had stumbled upon, or wallowed into, a whole new form of therapy, something along the lines of the primal scream.

When it first appeared, *Waterlog* felt like an elegy for the fading traditions of open water swimming in Britain. Deakin delighted in seeking out swimming holes where

generations of the same family had bathed, swimmers who were now being displaced by local legislation. He railed against the powers that fence off ponds and rivers, or erect signs warning of death by drowning or the danger of Weil's Disease. He lamented the passing of old swimming places, like the lost pool of Madingley, described in 1781 as the coldest in England, which he finally tracked down, just a faint outline in the grass. He documented ancient traditions, as remembered by older swimmers:

The young Robert and his cousins learned to swim in three stages. First, in March they were driven forty miles in the open-back of the mill's lorry to their Great Aunt Ellen's house at Mundesley, on the north coast of Norfolk. Here they were taken to the shore clad in striped swimming costumes and totally immersed in the sea.
It was believed that wetting their heads protected them from chills. The old lady came in with them and the adage was: 'no bathe, no lunch' whatever the weather.
Swimming lessons were resumed at Mendham Mill where the children supported themselves by holding on to the tips of the willow twigs, gaining confidence from the sensation of actually swimming. They were then ready for Stage Three in the confluence of the main river with the mill's by-pass streams. Here they learned to use the traditional technique of the village children. It depended on a bundle of reeds about five feet long and eighteen inches thick, bent into a gentle V shape and tucked under the armpits to act as primitive water wings. The theory was that by the time the bundle had finally deteriorated the aspiring swimmer would no longer need its support. It worked too.

Roger Deakin was not the first to celebrate Britain's watery heritage through swimming: Geoffrey Fraser Dutton had already blazed that trail in 1972 with his book *Swimming Free*. But Dutton was before his time and it is significant that, although his book dealt with swimming in British waters, it was first published in the USA and seemed to lapse into obscurity. Roger Deakin, however, caught the spirit of his time perfectly in his yearning for wild places, his sense of the fragility of Britain's ecosystems and his dismay at the desecrations wrought by agriculture and industry. His whole-hearted appreciation of tradition and his free-spirited approach to the constraints of bureaucracy gave him a voice in a new narrative of Britain's natural world.

Deakin was the first in a line of modern wild swimming entrepreneurs, amongst them Kate Rew and Daniel Start.

Kate Rew at the 2010 Port Eliot Festival © Martin Parr/ Magnum.

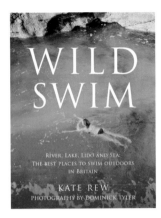

Wild Swim by Kate Rew and Dominick Taylor, 2008.

A passionate advocate of swimming, Kate Rew set up *The Outdoor Swimming Society* (OSS) in 2006, having successfully run a popular open water swimming scheme called *Breast Strokes* for two years (raising money for breast cancer care). The OSS's mission is to spread the joy of swimming outdoors, and Kate's charismatic style has attracted much media attention and thousands of members. Building on her extensive knowledge of outdoor swimming places, Kate published *Wild Swim* in 2008, a lavishly illustrated guide for Britain's adventurous swimmers.

Daniel Start's book *Wild Swimming: 150 hidden dips in the rivers, lakes and waterfalls of Britain* was published at exactly the same time as Kate's book, and he followed it up with *Wild Swimming Coast* a year later. This synchronicity is a sure sign that the topic was in touch with the zeitgeist in early 21st century Britain.

Daniel Start © Martin Parr/ Magnum.

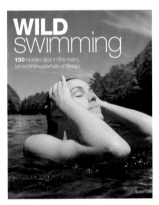

Wild Swimming by Daniel Start, 2008.

Both authors are philosophical about the serendipitous appearance of their works, which continue to sell well. They are intrigued by the evident allure and significance that wildness has for the modern mind-set:

'When my book came out there were five others that year with "wild" in the title. I think the non-commerciality of it appeals to people. I think we need to have experiences that aren't moderated by other people. It's very refreshing to go swimming, you come out feeling a bit more of yourself. It's a real, authentic thing. I think that's why it's taking off.'

'You can have a place that's wild in the city centre just as you can in the wilderness of Scotland. The wild is not a

million miles away, it's a state of mind, a way of seeing things. Even in quite a densely populated area you might come across a beautiful old gravel pit. You might have this dual carriageway thundering past, barbed wire fences around and yet there you are swimming in this beautiful spring fed lake in the ancient bed of an Ice Age river. For me that is wild.'

With their roots firmly in Romanticism, both Daniel and Kate nevertheless make expert use of modern internet technologies and social networking to promote wild swimming, thereby making it more accessible and extending its appeal to younger people. The Outdoor Swimming Society operates online and currently has over 11,000 members who receive e-newsletters and study the ever-changing interactive map of swimming holes.

As well as having an old fashioned explorer's fondness for maps, Daniel pores over satellite imagery and internet sites when researching new swimming places. He too has set up a Wild Swimming website, and regional Facebook groups are proliferating. Both writers are, in different ways, growing communities of wild swimmers, inspiring them, boosting their confidence and furnishing them with information through their books and websites.

Information is key to one aspect of the Wild Swimming movement: particularly concerning access to bodies of water in England and Wales. This issue, which so exercised Roger Deakin, is being tackled in different ways, from top level campaigning at the Welsh Assembly, forexample, to supporting local *guerilla swimming* activities. Daniel is clear about the issues and the potential outcomes:

'You're never going to be able to have right to roam for swimming across all of England. The transfer of values would go into tens of billions of pounds if you take rights away from fishermen to make it open access. A better way to do it is to work through involving providers like the water boards, the Forestry Commission and others and to get them to stipulate that there must be a certain amount of bathing places. In France, every single district has its list of bathing places and they are monitored. They have a very clear distinction between supervised and unsupervised. We could do exactly the same. We want the same rights as fishermen and sailors. We want return on the investments that the state has put in, we want to find ways to get the young people off the streets on a summer's day so they don't have to do crazy stuff, they can go and have a swim at the local lake, which is what they want to do.'

Substantial work on extending swimmers' rights had already been undertaken some time before the advent of the two attractive books that made wild swimming so fashionable. In 2005, Jean Perraton, a retired environmental planner based in Cambridge, published *Swimming against the Stream*, a meticulous examination of all the health, safety and access issues around swimming in Britain's rivers, lakes and ponds. In her book, Jean systemtically untangles the web of contention around the right to swim, taking an objective look at the statistics on drowning, disease and danger, EC water directives, litigation and legislation, environmental concerns, health benefits and risks and the private interests of landowners and councils.

Jean is now the president of the *River and Lake Swimming Association,* founded by Rob Fryer and Yakov Lev in 2003 with the mission of promoting swimming in Britain's inland waters, campaigning for increased access and countering excessive health and safety legislation.

Also a passionate river and lake swimmer, Rob Fryer found that *Waterlog* helped him reconfigure his identity and his sense of purpose as a swimmer at a time when both were starting to waver:

'We were almost thinking perhaps we were a bit odd, if everybody else thought so, at the point of conceding.

Rob Fryer's Wild Swimming Guide to Swimming in Rivers & Lakes in the UK, France & Overseas, (2011 edition).

So there was that point after Roger Deakin published his book we thought "We're bloody well not nutters! It's the rest. Who wants to swim in a concrete pool with chlorine? Not me." It's made us more conscious that we were right. We always knew we were right subconsciously. But we were almost beaten down. Now we're back with a vengeance. He gave us the confidence. That's when I started doing my book.'

Rob began documenting and following up the recommendations of visitors to the Farleigh and District Swimming Club on the River Frome. In 2009, after 10 years of research and exploration, he published *Rob Fryer's Wild Swimming Guide*. It contains detailed descriptions of over a thousand swimming holes in Britain and France, the entries organised along river courses rather than road routes. Rob's idiosyncratic commentary accompanies each entry and he adds some small, grainy black and white photographs, very different from the sumptuous colour imagery of the new wild swimming books. Rob continues to search for new swimming holes and is constantly updating his guide. His technique for finding places is to look at maps, follow water courses and tributaries – keeping an eye out for the tell-tale blue rope that indicates a river-swing – and chat to locals about where they swim, or used to swim, or where their parents or grandparents used to swim.

Although they may have different agendas and pursue aspects of wild swimming in different ways, these modern, entrepreneurial swimmers are in tune with each other, with Dutton and Deakin, and have a connection back to the Romantic poets. All are re-mapping Britain using water, rather than road or rail, just as the Romantic poets reconfigured the landscape by walking through it. All share a passion for immersing themselves in water and the intense communion with the natural world that ensues:

I began to discover the many different flavours of inland swimming – the relatively warm, placid waters of the Cam, swimming lazily behind a punt and once, by moonlight, with a boyfriend in Byron's Pool. Later I discovered the icy pools in the mountain streams of the Lake District and the delight of slithering over smooth black rocks to the pools below before drying out in the sun on soft damp mossy banks. I found too the shallow mountain tarns, which get surprisingly warm as their dark peaty bottoms absorb the heat of the sun, where, if they were too small to swim in, I could turn on my back and feel part of the world of water boatmen and dancing cotton grass. (Jean Perraton, *Swimming against the stream.*)

'It's the beauty of the location. Here you can see the damselflies flying over your nose when you're swimming along. I think that's fantastic and the comparison with indoor concrete and chlorine pools – well there's no comparison. It's extraordinary that people used to think that you could open a council pool and stop people swimming in the open.' Rob Fryer

'We plunged into this freezing lake and came round the corner and there was a big moon with storm clouds whistling past and the driftwood in the water was illuminated. And you just have this moment of transformation where everything that has gone before disappears and the whole world looks shiny and new again. It happens to swimmers all the time.' Kate Rew

'That urge to jump in water, it's not really an urge to swim. It's an urge to bathe, to immerse. It's about getting into the landscape and having a wild experience… it's the ultimate act of union with the landscape.' Daniel Start

Part of the appeal of wild swimming is the fact that it is not dependent on kit, other than togs, perhaps goggles and a towel. The wetsuit question is one that exercises many who want to immerse themselves in open water. For some, a wetsuit is a form of sensory deprivation to be avoided at all costs, something that detracts from the *'feral feel of water on your skin'* as Daniel Start puts it. Others put up with restricted sensation because a wetsuit improves their buoyancy and enables them to tolerate the cold for longer, so they can enter open water with confidence. And of course, some state of the art wetsuits can improve the swimmer's performance, an asset which is of great interest to triathletes and competitive open water swimmers.

Despite being fundamentally non-materialistic, wild swimming nevertheless has clear business potential. The Outdoor Swimming Society generates income to support its activities by selling merchandise, running events and providing training. In another initiative, passionate outdoor swimmer Simon Murie founded a wild swimming business in 2002 following his experience crossing the Hellespont, a swim he made to mark his 30th birthday. It had taken him a week to deal with the administration necessary for his crossing. The actual swim took him one hour. A business opportunity occurred to him: why not bring people together and enable them to tackle adventurous swims in interesting settings by handling all the organisational and safety issues for them? His company, *Swimtrek*, has flourished, offering adventure swimming holidays and trips abroad (Turkey, Egypt, Mexico, Croatia, Greece) and across the UK (the Thames, the Norfolk Broads, The Isles of Scilly and the Gulf of Corryvreckan). Although clearly running a successful business, Simon has not lost

The Clevedon sea swimmers enter the water for their daily dip © Martin Parr/Magnum.

sight of the values and principles that originally motivated him. Like William Henry, who edited *The Swimming Magazine* one hundred years ago, Simon passionately believes that everyone, particularly children and young people, should be taught how to cope with being immersed in cold water:

'We're trying to get schools and councils involved in some of our activities and there is still that feeling of 'we're taking a big risk here'. It's our argument that it's better to expose children to these kinds of environments so if they do get into trouble later they can get out of it. Whereas now, if they've been pushed into a canal by their mates, they can't react. So getting young people involved is important. We get schools on one day trips and give them exposure to the sea, to lakes. With safety support, instruction and technique.'

Of course, Wild Swimming – *'formerly known as swimming'* as one wag has put it – was going on well before these new trends arrived. Many traditional swimming activities still carry on in the same way that they always have, unaffected by trends, fads and fashions. Up and down the country, groups of people and individual swimmers enter the sea – some every day – or bathe in their local lakes, rivers and tarns and ponds. On hot summer days, groups of children and young people will appear, as if by magic, at traditional swimming holes that might have seemed forgotten but are clearly part of some local folk-memory. Organisations like the Brighton Sea

Swimmers at the Newnham Riverbank Club, Cambridge © Martin Parr/Magnum.

Swimming Club, the Bournemouth Spartans, the Clevedon sea swimmers, Henleaze Lake and Farleigh and District Swimming Club continue with rhythms and rituals that have been going on for decades.

Many bathing rituals are individual and informal. The swimmers who every morning at 9am enter the sea pools at La Vallette on Guernsey help each other in and out of the water, particularly when the tide is high. Once their swim is done they have tea and often exchange produce from their gardens. The swimmers at the Riverbank Club in Grantchester near Cambridge sunbathe on neatly trimmed lawns, behind hedges that shield them from the scrutiny of passing boats.

More formal, long established groups like the *British Long Distance Swimming Association* and the *Channel Swimmers Association* continue to grow in popularity. They, too, have not been slow to grasp the potential of the Wild Swimming phenomenon or to embrace new technologies: most of these venerable organisations now have websites and Facebook pages. Young it may be, but the Wild Swimming movement has enabled some traditional swimmers to see themselves differently:

'I got such lovely emails. "Thank you so much for doing what you're doing, before I was just the kind of crazy old guy and now I've got an identity. I'm a wild swimmer".'
Kate Rew

The success of the Wild Swimming movement is partly due to its eclectic and tolerant approach. There are no rules (other than the obvious safety recommendations), no exclusions, just the simple desire to spread the joy of swimming outdoors, to inspire people, link them up with others, and give them the confidence to swim, where and in whatever way they wish.

Any way you like: a typology of open water swimming in the 21st century

'You can swim any way you like. If you want to swim in freezing cold and crack the ice you can. If you want to float downstream looking at the clouds you can.'
Kate Rew

'The same individual may swim for different reasons on different days, I certainly do. The joys of swimming are sometimes silence and solitude, sometimes of communion with nature and sometimes the more friends that join you the merrier.' Roger Deakin

Having talked to many swimmers over the course of researching this book, I have come to realise that not everybody swims outdoors in the same way as I do, or for the same reasons. Cataloguing the enormous range of approaches to swimming and many different types of swimming experience has helped me to appreciate the diversity and vitality of a practice that I had feared was dying out. My typology of swimmers celebrates this variety. It is drawn from interviews and conversations with people from across Britain, swimmers who like nothing better than to enter into sea, river, lake or pond.

The traditional swimmer

Georgina Rose is one of the Clevedon sea swimmers, a small group of people who, every day at high tide, swim in the muddy waters of the Bristol Channel. The group members, whose ages range from mid-teens to mid 80s, have their club premises in one of the arches of the sea wall near the pier. Behind the barred gate there is a small recess, open on one side to the elements, where people can hang their togs and towels and store flippers and bathing hats (the group makes a concession for hats, gloves and shoes but disapproves of wetsuits). The recess contains a battered calor gas heater, a life saving ring, some plastic chairs and a blackboard where the times for the week's swims are chalked. The swimmers get changed and go into the water together. When they come out, they share hot chocolate and biscuits. As well as enjoying many get-togethers throughout the year, they put on fund-raising events and are often featured in the local paper.

As a girl, Georgina lived in Jersey. She loved competitive swimming and diving and trained regularly in the harbour at St Helier. But once she started working, her sea swim-

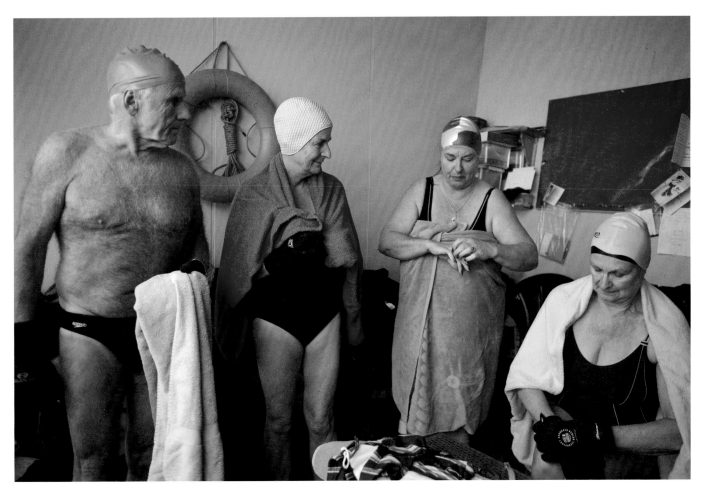

Clevedon sea swimmers warm up after their dip (Georgina Rose on the right) © Martin Parr/Magnum.

ming lapsed until 1999 when, living in Clevedon and struggling to recover from the death of her partner, Georgina bumped into an old friend who was a member of the group and who invited her to join them:

'I've never looked back. And that started me swimming from the beach and meeting all the really lovely swimmers. My immediate feeling was why haven't I done this before? The colour doesn't matter. It's the feeling of swimming and the open-ness of the water. I can't explain the feeling. You have to be a swimmer to understand.'

The Bristol Channel has the second highest tide in the world, so the group members are well aware of the power and danger of the sea. But their daily ritual means they are so familiar with the behaviour of the water, the different currents and tides, that – when conditions are right – mature and even elderly adults become as playful as children:

'One thing we love when the tide is right in the summer is we can pick up the current and we get swept back under the pier and it's absolutely exhilarating and we say come on let's do it again. We could get swept down to the bandstand if you get a really strong current but we know the tide too well. So we come back in, we can pull ourselves in. It's great fun. And of course we go round the end of the pier and that's a wonderful feeling to be right out there and it's so peaceful.'

Georgina and the other members of the sea swimming club were enjoying wild swimming long before it became fashionable and will continue to do so until they no longer

The political swimmer: Lewis Gordon Pugh at the North Pole, 2007 © Jason Roberts.

can. They are essentially wild swimmers because they are dealing with the tide and current and immersing themselves in an ever-changing and challenging environment. Sometimes, on summer evenings, they even swim in the dark.

The political swimmer

Although many wild swimmers enter the water in order to raise money for charity, Lewis Gordon Pugh is the best example of an overtly political swimmer, someone who uses swimming to make an explicit political point. So he has chosen his swims very carefully. Even though forbidden to do so by the Port Authorities until the very last minute, Lewis swam the entire length of the Thames in

2006 in order to raise awareness of climate change. He also swam at the magnetic North Pole and at the foot of Everest in order to highlight global warming. Lewis makes swimming a moral act:

'We live in a world that is absent of men and women who really stand for something that is important. We live in a celebrity culture and so I think we need people who stand for these important causes. I am often asked why I do it. At a simplistic level, I am passionate about swimming and I enjoy pushing boundaries. But there's a lot more to it than that. Through my swims I have had a unique perspective on climate change. I have witnessed retreating glaciers, decreasing sea ice, coral bleaching,

severe droughts, and the migration of animals to colder climates. It's as a result of these experiences that I am determined to do my bit to raise awareness about the fragility of our environment and to encourage everyone to take action.'

An SAS soldier and a Cambridge educated maritime lawyer, Lewis has always been a high achiever and pushed himself to the limit. When he combined his two passions: environmental politics and cold water swimming, he generated an image that caught the attention of press and politicians around the world.

Even though he does not regard himself as a hero, Lewis swims within an heroic tradition that extends back through Byron to Beowulf. His swims are daring, extreme, almost superhuman.

The celebrity swimmer

The Wild Swimming phenomenon has in recent years been given a boost by celebrity involvement. Comedian David Walliams's cross Channel swim for Sports Relief in 2006 attracted much public attention, transforming what had been perhaps perceived as an old fashioned, somewhat eccentric activity into a glamorous and worthwhile endeavour, embellished with political commitment and philanthropy. More recently, celebrity swimming took a confessional turn when actor Robson Green was filmed as he undertook various challenging wild swims, including crossing the Gulf of Corryvreckan whirlpool and swimming around Burgh Island.

Robson's goal was to swim from the mainland to Holy Island in memory of his father, who had taught him to swim in the cold north east seas. For him, the act of swimming would always be suffused with memories of his father so this was the perfect way to commemorate his life. In the programme, he veers between rugged action man and little boy as he struggles with the elements, the temperature, his fitness levels and his emotions.

The athletic swimmer

For Kes Aleknavicius, sports teacher and triathlete, open water swimming has become a passion. Kes is motivated by competing with others and trains three times a week to improve his speed and technique: *'I would train in my sleep if I could.'* The athlete's rigorous training schedule

The athletic swimmer: Kes Aleknavicius © Martin Parr/Magnum.

has roots reaching far back to Roman military drill and the tightly disciplined practice promoted centuries later by Victorian swimming teachers. Already a keen runner and cyclist, Kes became interested in triathlon events when they first arrived in Britain from America in the early 80s. At the time a virtual non-swimmer, Kes first tried competitive open water swimming in the gravel pits near Reading, then in Barry, Bedfordshire and the Cotswolds and, to his surprise, fell in love with this part of the event, even though he considers it the most challenging of the three activities.

Kes enters many triathlons both in Britain and abroad every year, even organising his holidays around

Ritual swim at
Lee Dam, West
Yorkshire, 1976
© Martin Parr/
Magnum.

competitions abroad. He has also completed 32 Ironman races worldwide. Although he trains at least three times a week, Kes is clear that his rigorous swimming gives him more than just exercise, particularly when he is training in open water. In fact, surprisingly for one with such a focus on improving technique and stamina, he is no stranger to the Romantic outlook:

'It's more than just the ploughing up and down. It's the connection with this element of nature. It's you moving under your own steam in this element which you feel connected to. Here we are in the middle of this lake, total peace and freedom. When you're training, you're not just training you're interacting with this fantastic thing. It's a bit like going for a walk in the countryside, but it's your countryside because there's nobody else there. A beautiful, still place.'

The swimmer as collector

Although the popular image of wild swimmers is of free spirits at one with the elements, some manage to combine a deeply Romantic approach to water with an unexpected level of nerdiness. These are the collectors, the aquatic version of twitchers, who are on a quest to notch up swims or swimming holes. These modern-day swimming-hole finders provide a link to the Victorian and Edwardian explorers and gazetteers who painstakingly documented the bathing places around the British coast. Meticulously, they pore over maps, plan their explorations and catalogue their finds. Surprisingly, key players in the new Wild Swimming movement (Rob Fryer, Daniel Start and Kate Rew for example) all, to a certain extent, take a collector's approach to finding and documenting wild places to swim. Each endeavour may have been sparked by a personal moment of spontaneity and inspiration, but has involved breath-taking levels of planning, organisation and commitment to be carried through to the end. The startling thing is that each individual's compendium of swimming places is so different in style, content and appearance.

And it is not just swimming places that are collected. Kes Aleknavicius is always adding to his list of triathlon and Ironman races. Lewis Gordon Pugh notches up extreme swims in hostile environments:

'I have now pioneered more swims around famous land-marks than any other swimmer, and I am the only person to have completed a long distance swim in every ocean

of the world. But I'm probably best known for becoming the first person to undertake a long distance swim across the Geographic North Pole.'

Steve Price has swum the English Channel, the Bristol Channel, and, on his fourth attempt, the gruelling North Channel between Scotland and Northern Ireland. He is not tempted to leave it at that, but is looking round for more swims to add to his collection, studying maps, working out what crossings to try. He is considering swimming from the mainland out to Lundy Island:

'Apparently, you can claim 100 guineas or 3 live bullocks from the island if you swim from the mainland. You can't do Hartland because the tides are too fast. That's one I want to tick off. And round Manhattan, round the island. And Alcatraz.'

The new generation of wild swimmers also makes full use of the latest technologies, spreading the word and making connections across an ever expanding network. Today's swimmers tweet, text, blog and poke. They create Facebook pages, design websites and post interactive swimming maps.

The ritual swimmer

A number of water-based rituals are practised in Britain today, evidence of the vitality of the country's diverse faith groups. Orthodox Greek Church clergy cast an offering of a cross bound with herbs into the sea in Margate, which is then retrieved from the water by a young boy. The Rt. Rev Michael Langrish, Bishop of Exeter, performs baptisms in the cold waters of the River Tavy in Tavistock, West Devon, his cassock flowing down over a pair of fisher-man's waders. Water from the sacred Ganges has been mixed into a number of British rivers – including the Soar, the Thames and the Wye – now ready to receive the ashes of deceased Hindus. Some contemporary rituals, both public and private, may provide links back to pre-Christian Britain. People sprinkle themselves with the water from sacred wells and leave tokens, flowers, coins, photos and ribbons nearby. Worshippers place posies by the bubbling spring of Aquae Sulis within the Cross Bath at the sumptu-ous Thermae Spa in Bath. In Berwick-on-Tweed, a Salmon Queen is still crowned every July, to celebrate the return of the fish to the river.

Although not linked with organised religion, ritual swims are of course quite a familiar sight in Britain, particularly around the Christmas and the New Year period. From Tenby to Broughty Ferry, people who would rarely consider entering open water during the rest of the year will dress up and take the plunge, often in fancy dress, in order to raise money for charity. Some of these festive swims have been going on for at least a hundred years, although, in a culture of litigation, they are becoming increasingly vulnerable to scrutiny on health and safety grounds. Although most may seem like wacky stunts put on for the media, they may well have more profound significance, perhaps echoing early ceremonies of cleansing, purification and renewal, as Daniel Start describes:

'With ritual swims, there is a link with cleansing and rebirth, a fantastic way to recognise the end of an old chapter and the beginning of a new chapter if you go back to the idea that water is the link in pagan philosophy between the overworld and the underworld. So it's not surprising that on New Year's Day or with a bad hangover people go and jump in the water. It's a process of revitalisation.'

Kate Rew is also very aware of the importance of ritual swims, and through her instigation the Outdoor Swimming Society has started to put on regular events such as full moon swims, swims to celebrate the start of the season and December dips:

'Full moon swims are very popular. People just have an instinctive desire to go swimming underneath the full moon, getting in touch with nature's calendar. You get to the river bank and have to wait for the moon to come up and see this huge harvest moon. It's actually very infrequently in life you get the time to just sit still waiting for the moon to rise.'

Some swimmers create their own very personal swimming rituals. In Shetland, Alan Price has reinstated the ancient ceremony of the Haagdyve as a way of reconnecting with his Welsh roots. And on Skye, Duncan MacInnes decided to mark his 60th birthday by swimming across 60 lochs on the island, with the aim of raising £60,000 for the Sleat Community Trust. He began his project in early April 2010 and continued through the year, clocking up several swims each week:

'I am staggered at some of the beautiful little lochs in Sleat that no-one goes to. I have found one bottomless infinity loch overlooking the Ord Glen and have shared others with various water birds.'

But for many open water swimmers, the simple, informal act of entering the water is like a religious ceremony and as such has become an essential part of their daily, weekly or seasonal routine. If for any reason they cannot observe their ritual, they feel ill at ease, out of sorts, and even unwell.

'What going into a church is like for a true believer is what going into the sea, entering the sea, is like for me.'
David Sawyers

'I'm so blessed, so happy I can do this, just get in this pond or lake and swim.'
Kes Aleknavicius

For Channel swimmer Steve Price, the physical and psychological challenge of distance swimming can also have a spiritual dimension, which is in part a result of sensory deprivation:

'You lose hearing because your ears are full of water, your goggles get salt in, so you're not seeing. Your mouth is cold inside. One sense left is smell which is massively acute. I don't think we understand our bodies properly. We've become cocooned from surroundings. Being in the sea you feel exposed, yet protected. There is something quite spiritual about being in the water for a long time, you start to adapt.'

In my daily summer ritual at Henleaze Lake, I engage in a sequence of actions that has become so familiar I could almost perform them in my sleep. I walk slowly to the ladder under the willow tree, then descend without pausing. As I enter the water and swim away from the ladder I give a long sigh, like an incantation. I always swim to the same place, Mermaid's Ledge. I perch there, up to my neck in water, look back at the lake, feeling blessed.

The scientific swimmer: Dr Karen Throsby training for her Channel swim © Nick Adams.

The swimmer as scientist

Nearly three hundred years after Sir John Floyer wrote his treatise on cold bathing, the practice of open water swimming continues to attract medical and scientific interest. There have been studies of the health benefits of immersion in cold water (lowering blood pressure, reducing weight, increasing libido and energy levels, lifting mood) and of the mechanisms involved in cold water tolerance and adaptation. Some swimmers embark on their own experiments. Lewis Gordon Pugh set up impressive medical and scientific support teams for his swims in extreme cold temperatures at the North Pole and Everest. He had a thermometer inserted into his anus in order to keep a record of his core temperature, which could not

be allowed to fall below 35 degrees and had to be continuously monitored during his swims. Lewis also managed to defy science by raising his core temperature prior to immersion in icy conditions through using psychological stimulation – a process called *anticipatory thermo-genesis*.

Pete Roberts is another cold water swimmer-cum-scientist. Based in Runcorn, Pete (known as Wildswimmer Pete) has worked on raising his tolerance of cold water immersion with a view to better understanding the swimmer's adaptive mechanisms. He writes:

The vascular system also undertakes changes primarily intended to protect the body's core from chilling, endangering vital organs. It develops the ability to very quickly reduce (but not completely close down) circulation to the outermost tissues, hence the cyanotic blue or purplish hue of a cold-water swimmer's skin after a few minutes immersion. It must be borne in mind that the longer the swimmer is immersed, the deeper the chilling which means that upon exit he has to behave as though he does in fact have hypothermia. The reason? The circulation to outer tissues is much reduced with the accumulation of significant quantities of pooled chilled blood. Should this cold blood suddenly enter the core circulation it can cause cardiac arrest.

And wild swimmers don't just know about physiology. Some, like Roger Deakin, Daniel Start and Robert Macfarlane inform and enrich their swimming with reference to the natural sciences: ecology, geology, botany, zoology and ornithology.

Dr Karen Throsby, a sociologist based at Warwick University, is another type of swimming scientist who has embarked on a project exploring the link between *embodiment and identity in an extreme sporting subculture.* Her project involves interviewing Channel swimmers, exploring their motivation for taking on such a challenge. Far from keeping her topic at an objective distance, Karen has trained to swim the Channel herself, changing her own body shape in the process and documenting her own and others' reactions to her metamorphosis, all as part of her research.

The swimmer as artist

At the other end of the scale, immersion can inspire art and creativity. Of course, the shape of the human figure in water has drawn the eye of established British artists like painter Ivor Abrahams and sculptor Anthony Gormley, whose work *Another Place* has 100 cast iron figures facing out over the Irish Sea, submerging and emerging twice a day as the tide ebbs and flows. More recently, artists have started to explore the boundary between sporting events, creativity and culture. As part of the build up to the 2012 Olympics, for example, the Huddersfield-based *Balbir Singh Dance Company* has been commissioned to develop a project involving synchronised swimmers and dancers trained in classical Indian dance.

Swimming has also inspired performance art. On July 12th 2007, live artist Amy Sharrocks mounted an event entitled *SWIM.* Fifty people travelled across London by Routemaster bus from Tooting Bec Lido to Hampstead Heath ponds, via swimming pools, lakes, rivers and lidos: a British

Balbir Singh Dance Company © Tim Smith.

SWIM by Amy Sharrocks © Ruth Corney.

version of *The Swimmer.* When she called for participants, Amy was overwhelmed by the response and had to turn people away:

'There is some kind of zeitgeist of feeling about water. People are longing for something, for some kind of stronger connection. Water seems to answer those needs. It really changed them, changed our sense of London and where we were and what it meant to us. It meant a lot to a great deal of people. Everybody lived with the memories of the water throughout their lives. If you'd been to any of the pools before, and a lot of people had, suddenly you were catapulted back to when you were 10. They would tell me all the stories about their

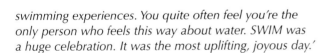
above: Photographer and swimmer Kevin Meredith in Brighton.
right: Kevin's photographs of David Sawyers swimming and catching mackerel.

swimming experiences. You quite often feel you're the only person who feels this way about water. SWIM was a huge celebration. It was the most uplifting, joyous day.'

Amy has created other work around London's waterways, for example dowsing for the capital's hidden rivers and tributaries. She plans to produce another piece in 2014, in which 100 people will swim in the Thames, under Tower Bridge, at high tide. When she talks about this project, the artist echoes the sentiments of Lewis Gordon Pugh and other campaigning swimmers:

'I want a legitimate swim, not a guerrilla swim. It's important that we open up the river in the city. To close it off seems not only morally wrong but philosophically wrong. I understand about health and safety and am not saying that you should just be able to jump in but I think one time a year we should have a mass swim across the river to celebrate our connection to it, a grand celebration of our city and our water.'

Kevin Meredith is a young photographer whose work has focussed, amongst other things, on the daily rituals of the Brighton sea swimming club, whom he joins as often as he can with his underwater camera. For the 2010 Brighton Festival fringe, Kevin posted his pictures of swimmers outside of the club changing rooms just near the North Pier.

The distance swimmer: Steve Price © Martin Parr/Magnum.

The distance swimmer

When Captain Webb crossed the Channel in 1875 he instantly became a celebrity, establishing the long distance swim as a symbol of daring and endurance within the British psyche. Since Captain Webb's feat, over 1,000 swimmers of all ages have successfully crossed the Channel, braving shipping, weather, sea sickness, shoals of jellyfish, tides, flotsam, sewage, and of course the cold. Many more swimmers have tried and failed, and at any point several hundred people are waiting for their chance. A small industry has built up around Channel swimming, with aspirant swimmers training at Dover while waiting for the correct weather conditions, placing themselves under the supervision of expert support boat teams and

The Channel Swimming Association. According to Steve Price, who now coaches others in their Channel crossing attempts, the distance swimmer's physical condition and psychological approach play an equal part in success:

'50% is fitness and 50% is doing it in your head, having the mental strength. I get that from my grandfather, who was very stubborn. There was a lady who recently swam the channel and broke the record for the longest time in water and I admire that because she's not a good, stylish or fast swimmer but there was no way she wasn't going to do that swim. She took 25 hours or longer than that. Captain Webb was 22 hours. Most people fall by the wayside after 12 or 13 hours. Not many people go on, really dig that deep. That was more impressive than someone who gets across in 8 or 9 hours. It's not about time. It's about completing the swim, about setting yourself this personal challenge.'

For Steve, distance swimming has brought a huge sense of personal achievement. He has become something of a local celebrity and regularly gives talks on his swimming feats:

'Whenever I go anywhere I look at the horizon and think "I've swum across there." That's such a great feeling. Because I was the school fatty and was brought up in quite a rough area, a rough council estate and you were continually told that you wouldn't amount to much. Suddenly finding a sport that I could do and others couldn't do, that was the drive for me. Swimming is something that just drove me on. You walk down the street or you go to a football match and there's thousands of people there and you think "I'm the only person in this stadium that has done what I've done." It's doing something that's so extreme and different, the satisfaction of doing it on your own.'

Extraordinary they may be, but Steve's feats of endurance took place within the strict conventions of a long established British tradition of distance swimming. But way beyond that discipline and structure, some swimmers are taking on more and more extreme challenges, for example swimming the length of the Amazon, or up the Yangtze River, or across the Atlantic.

The swimmer in search of healing

Research suggests that bathing in cold water has a number of benefits including reducing hypertension and boosting endorphins. Many people also find that swimming in cold water improves chronic conditions and helps to lift mood:

'I had a serious issue with blood pressure, meaning I had to either go on medication or lose weight and exercise more. So two years ago I started really doing the lengths. I do about a kilometre each session. It worked. I lost two stone and kept it off. My blood pressure came down. That is the unbelievable thing about it. The stamina built up. Swimming has changed my metabolism. I heard that you lose much more weight in cold water than warm water.' Brigitte Lardinois

'I like to use it as my form of exercise because I suffer from chronic fatigue, ME, life long. I'm also very health and exercise conscious. I like to look slim and fit. I have to in my job. I can't get fat. If I run or go to the gym I seem to get exhausted very quickly. The swimming seems to be fine if I don't overdo it.' Martine Watts

The psychological and mood boost that comes from swimming is as significant as the physical impact. It can lift depression, boost well being and promote a positive attitude:

'I leave my devils on the waves.' Roger Deakin

'You gain a lot of stamina and you gain a lot of confidence. If you do tournaments you're not afraid any more, you're not nervous. Not only with swimming, it's with school concerts, other sporting things, anything really. It helps you be confident.' Eliza Swinburn

'I get very, very low and withdrawn if I don't have a swim. I really, really need to have a swim. I need to be immersed in water at least twice a week. If I don't get that I just get so down, so depressed.' Steve Price

Perhaps Dr Robert Whittie was not so far off the mark when he claimed, nearly 400 years ago, that sea water is a most sovereign remedy against Hypochondriack Melancholly and Windiness.

The transformative swimmer

For some swimmers, immersion in water has a transformative effect – physically, psychologically and spiritually. The repetitive movement of the stroke during a long training or length swimming session can induce a sense of deep relaxation and elation:

'If all goes well, in a good long session sometimes I reach the point when the breathing is so pleasant, the breathing and the rhythm, that's the joy. I don't always reach that but when I do I feel absolutely fantastic. It's like really good drummers that get into a good rhythm, when the stroke and the breathing just seem to come so naturally that you don't have to think. The rhythmic movement is so thoroughly relaxing even though you're putting the effort in and burning the calories. It feels like you're floating without putting the power in.' Brigitte Lardinois

The belief that intense physical activity such as distance swimming or running a marathon can lead to a state of self transcendence was one tenet of the teaching of Sri Chinmoy, a spiritual leader who claimed that sport can unlock the potential of the human spirit. Followers of Sri

Chinmoy participate in and host endurance events across the UK and beyond:

The races are organised on the principles of self-transcendence, where each runner competes against himself and his own previous capacities rather than against his fellow runners. Endurance races allow each competitor to go deep within and truly find the best within themselves in order to persevere and finish, and even though there are trophies for the leading finishers, in truth every runner who completes such long distances is a winner.

Particularly with prolonged exposure, perhaps on a distance swim or in a training session, some swimmers feel almost as if they are changing state, adapting to their watery environment and moving through it with growing ease and efficiency. For Kate Rew, this moment of transformation comes when she trains, practising her front crawl:

'I don't do it because I want to beat people. I do it because I love the feeling of going really fast and I like occasionally to push myself to that endorphin threshold. There comes a point if you do front crawl continuously for an hour you kind of lose the sense of your joints. You become quite fish like. You feel like muscle just flexing your way through the water.'

Daniel Start is also familiar with such sensations. He looks on some swimming techniques and training as a form of meditation, yoga or tai chi in the water:

'You become like a dolphin through the water. You are more effective, you do less strokes. You're not fighting the water. The glide is as important as the stroke. To be a relief from going backwards and forwards it's imperative to draw out the full potential of this meditative process because it is about being free and with nature. The closest I've come to that is following white water courses like the River Dart. It's very exciting because you completely give up to the flows of the water. It's not like the sea where you might be battling the surf or the swell. You have to very much give yourself over to the forces and move like an eel or an otter with the way the water is flowing and with just a flick of your flippers or your hands you move in and out. Become part of the flow.'

It is not only the wild swimmers who experience this transition. Hard core athletes can also undergo moments of transformation:

'It's the first ten minutes when you go from being a land creature to a sea creature. You pull on the wetsuit and your environment is going to change, as soon as the hooter goes. Whoosh you're in. Suddenly you're a swimmer with lots of other swimmers.' Kes Aleknavicius

The idea that the human swimmer turns momentarily into a water creature – a fish, a dolphin, an otter or an eel is clearly an outcome of the physiological experience of immersion and repetitive movement. Some swimmers wonder if they are being drawn back to an earlier evolutionary stage. But perhaps the feeling of transformation is also a faint echo of ancient stories and legends about magical, shape shifting creatures. And even the seemingly fearless wild swimmers are wary, not just of the power of currents, waves and tides, but of less rational threats:

'I certainly like to swim with other people because I get spooked by myself. The more people in the water the safer I feel. Sea monsters, vortexes, creatures, funnels, siphons. I have a deep subconscious fear of dark unknown waters. Much more so when there might be possible man made things. Totally irrational. But it does make it more difficult for me to go swimming by myself.' Daniel Start

The literary swimmer

Moving through the water, most swimmers find that they start reflecting on the things that preoccupy them when on land. Going back and forth in her lane swimming sessions, Brigitte Lardinois thinks through conflicts at work. Training for hours in the cold sea, distance swimmer Steve Price mulls over professional issues and problems. Very often, solutions present themselves to the swimmer. For writers, swimming can be a similarly creative opportunity. In a piece for *The New Yorker* magazine, neurologist Oliver Sachs describes how his swimming helped him to write:

There is something about being in water and swimming which alters the writer's mood, gets his thoughts going, as nothing else can.

Sachs describes going up and down in a pool when working on a book and every so often getting out, dripping onto the page, to note down the ideas and insights that have occurred to him. Then, back into the water for more swimming and thinking.

Novelist Margaret Drabble also thinks about what she is writing when she swims, from a stony beach on the Bristol Channel, in a river on Exmoor or in a London pool. Sometimes her reflections take a more personal turn and her swimming becomes suffused with memory:

'When I'm swimming I don't worry about supper. It's liberating from every day worries. Increasingly I think about other years when I've been swimming. It's as if it becomes part of a long continuing process, of memory and swimming. As I walk along the coastline I see places where I've been swimming with different people. It's very Wordsworthian. When someone suggests a swimming place to me, that place is for ever associated with the fact that he or she told me about it.'

Margaret knew Iris Murdoch and John Bayley, both literary swimmers, who continued to bathe in rivers, ponds and the sea into old age, even when Iris was succumbing to dementia. Sometimes, being in the water would be the only way for her to be soothed, to become calm:

'Both Iris and John just loved swimming. She was very buoyant, the kind of physique just made for water. He was skinnier but he obviously did love it. I was having lunch with him at some literary event and he ordered scrambled egg and he said: "I can't eat because my false teeth are at the bottom of Lake Como". A friend of mine went swimming with them near Newhaven and Iris was getting to be a bit ill then. Iris rushed in and had a wonderful time. I think it is very calming. Like being in a different element. You return to the amniotic fluid.'

The reflective swimmer

While some people swim simply for fitness or pleasure, a few find that swimming offers an intellectual space, a chance to draw on their knowledge, experience and observations, to work out theories and build philosophies. I call these eclectic thinkers *reflective* swimmers, people for whom swimming is simultaneously a physical and a cognitive process. Each one is different, absorbed with his or her own intellectual preoccupations. Swimming out to a small island in Loch Coruisk in a remote valley on the Isle of Skye, Robert Macfarlane, Fellow of Emmanuel College Cambridge and seeker of Britain's last truly wild places, falls into a reverie on the subject of time:

I found myself struck by a sensation of inverted vertigo, of falling upwards. The air was empty of indicators of space or time, empty too of markers of depth. Lying there, with no human trace except the rim of my own eyes I could feel a silence that reached backwards to the Ice Age. To be in the Basin, even briefly, is to be reminded of the narrow limits of human perception, the provisionality of your assumptions about the world. In such a place, your conventional units of chronology (the century, the life-span, the decade, the year, the day, the heartbeat) become all but imperceptible and your individual gestures (the lift of a hand, the swimming stroke taken within water, the flash of anger, a turn of speech or thought) acquire an eerie quickness.

Swimming at the other end of the country, off the coast of the Isles of Scilly, Roger Deakin embarked on a similar form of time travel:

I felt myself sinking deeper into the unconscious world of the sea, deeper into history. I was going back 4,000 years, soaring above the ancient landscape like some slow bird and it reminded me how like a sea a field can be. I imagined ploughmen with seagulls in their wake tilling these fields and their first flooding by a spring tide storm, the crops ruined and the earth poisoned by the salt.

But for Brighton sea swimmer David Sawyers, the act of swimming in and managing the changing sea is in itself a form of thought, of thinking with your body:

'It's the whole body cross referencing sensory returns and co-ordinating them and producing an action plan. This fits so beautifully with modern ideas of neurophysiology, autonomous networks. Coping with the sea is not about being a strong swimmer but being a reflexive swimmer. Thinking literally with one's body and having the confidence and courage to let that happen.'

Wild swimming at The Port Eliot Festival

Whenever I am walking by rivers, lakes or the sea, I feel compelled to look for somewhere to swim. I know exactly what I like: clear, calm water; easy access to depth; and beautiful, wild surroundings that I can admire as I float about. If I find a place that meets those conditions I quickly assess potential problems. Are there weeds or obstructions? Does the water seem clean? What about tides, currents, waves and winds? If it feels safe and inviting, then I will go in. If I am not sure on any point, my confidence plummets. This is because, for me, swimming is usually a solitary pursuit. My partner can't swim and is baffled by my compulsion to get into water, especially when it is freezing cold. He has learned to tolerate the interruptions to our walks and sits resignedly on the shore, waiting. In these circumstances my swims are brief, almost embarrassed, as I wonder if I really am behaving as eccentrically as he seems to think.

Five years ago, we attended the Port Eliot Festival for the first time. The festival is set in the grounds of a fabulously dilapidated stately home in the village of St Germans in Cornwall. We arrived on a Friday afternoon in July, hot and sticky after slogging down the motorway. It was a relief to follow the shady pathways between rhododendrons and to sniff the cool river smell as we walked down through the estate to the boat-house on the banks of the Lynher. I could see the estuary gleaming in the late afternoon sunlight, curving under the magnificent viaduct that carries the railway line to St Germans station – amazingly still functioning. I had no idea what to expect, but was hoping for deep, clear water and a gravelly beach. As we got closer I could see that the tide was rising and that each bank was pasted with thick, slick, taupe-coloured mud. The water looked like hot chocolate: brown, with swirls of powdery residue eddying round as the level slowly rose. I was dismayed. Even the little stone slipway led straight into thick mud. I had no idea about the depth of the mud. I wasn't sure about the strength or height of the tide, and I knew nothing of possible currents. A few festival-goers were wandering along the river-side path, and a couple lay under trees in the shade, reading and dozing. But no-one else looked as if they were contemplating a swim and I didn't have the courage to try on my own. The idea was abandoned.

How different it is this weekend! The festival has grown, attracting several thousand people. I know that a wild swim is organised for the next day, so hurry down to the boat house in order to sign up. As I approach, I can hear shrieks of laughter coming from a group of people bathing in the middle of the river. A couple of women are swimming upstream, chatting, and other swimmers are changing on the bank. Signs reading 'Joy!' 'Adventure!' 'Freedom!' point towards the river, which looks sleek and brown. It is high tide and the festival river lido is open for business.

Near the slipway, the Outdoor Swimming Society stand is crowded with people. I ask a knowledgeable looking woman in a bathing costume about the easiest place to get in and am pointed in the direction of a good spot and reassured about the current. I change quickly then follow a young couple, watching closely as their feet sink into mud and they push themselves away from the grassy bank, laughing and chatting. I slide gently into the water, now knowing what to expect underfoot, and make my way across to the point where brown silk changes to grey silk, then on upstream.

Confident and calm, I have a long, peaceful swim, luxuriating in the cool, then float for a while looking at the trees on the hillside leading up to the estate, contemplating the pieces of river art along the banks and catching drifts of music from the different venues. As I swim back to shore, I watch people getting out at different spots, some with relative ease, others floundering and slipping as they try to stand up in the mud. Keeping my body flat on the very surface of the water, I manoeuvre myself towards a large rectangular stone that borders the slipway and pull myself out, surprised to see only the slightest trace of mud on one of my feet. I feel as if I have indulged in an expensive spa treatment.

The next day, over 400 wild swimmers take to the water.

Wild swimming at Port Eliot Festival © Martin Parr/Magnum.

Epilogue

My favourite time for a swim in Tenby is early evening, when there are fewer people around and I can walk peacefully towards my chosen spot. The choice of where to swim depends on the tide and the wind direction. Two of Tenby's three magnificent beaches – North Beach and Castle Beach – are separated by a small promontory surmounted by the castle ruins. Generally, the bather can find protection from the prevailing wind by choosing one side or the other.

Today, I walk along North Beach to the harbour, past children intent on crabbing, lowering clumps of bacon into the water to tempt nipping claws. Then along by St Julian's, the tiny fisherman's church on the harbour beach, where plastic lobsters flail, suspended in the netting that drapes the wall behind the altar. I reach Castle Beach and walk barefoot at the water's edge, where two plump starfish lie stranded by the receding tide, along with cuttlefish and razor clams. St Catherine's Rock (which will become an island again in a few hours time) shields me from the sharp east breeze and I feel warm in the late sun. This is the place to bathe today.

I change quickly, leaving my clothes and towel on a rock at the foot of the island, then enter the clear water. It is cold but I quickly acclimatise and swim along parallel to the shore looking up at the limestone cliffs that curve above the beach. Grasses, succulents and wild wallflower grow in the cracks and crevices above the dark mark of the high tide line. Over the centuries, Tenby's inhabitants have appropriated these cliffs, building them up into walls, turrets and towers, shaping steps leading down from town to beach, worn stone stairways that re-appear and disappear rhythmically, twice each day. From the water, the swimmer can also fully appreciate a more recent addition to the cliffscape. The restaurant constructed in the cellars of the Imperial Hotel, just by the town gate, boasts a plate glass window, suspended on the cliff face some fifty feet up, through which diners can enjoy a seagull's eye view of the beach.

As I swim, I can trace the lines of Tenby's history, the Norman walls, turrets and ruined arches as they rise and fall along the cliff line. These fortifications were begun around 1264 by William de Valence, Earl of Pembroke,

Plaque commemorating Peggy Davies, bathing woman
© Martin Parr/Magnum.

to make a living through fishing and trade. But the second part of the 18th century saw an extraordinary change in Tenby's fortunes. A plaque in St Mary's Church explains the reason.

Peggy Davies must have started her work as bathing attendant in 1767 – the same year that Sir Joseph Banks made his damning comments – making Tenby one of Britain's earliest sea-bathing resorts. Sea-bathing attracted aristocratic, rich and fashionable people to the town. Local residents must have been astonished by the sight of the first bathing machines drawn onto the sands, disgorging naked men (and shift clad women) into the waves, a scene captured in an oil painting by William Golding in 1799.

Tenby's sea and beaches rapidly became a more valuable asset than its harbour. As growing numbers of wealthy visitors arrived to bathe, exercise on the sands and contemplate the picturesque seascape, tall elegant buildings arose along the cliff edge, positioned to make the most of the spectacular views. The most exclusive of these houses and apartments – along St Julian's Terrace and, later, Castle Hill – enjoyed views on both sides, with drawing rooms and bedrooms looking out over North Beach to the rear and Castle Beach to the front. These buildings – so open to the elements – contrasted with earlier, lowlier dwelling places that, like their inhabitants, had sheltered from the wind and the sea.

Rescued from obscurity, Tenby was transformed into an elegant resort, a *fair and fashionable place*. Every facility was provided for the bathers: fine houses and apartments, theatres, coffee houses, inns, ballrooms, assembly rooms and a circulating library. Tradesmen, builders and businessmen were attracted by the opportunities offered by the resort. In 1805, Sir William Paxton, a wealthy Carmarthenshire banker, built a sea water bath house, which still stands today below Castle Hill. This provided sophisticated bathing facilities for ladies and gentlemen, private dressing rooms heated with warm air, a coffee room and an area in which servants could wait.

Tenby's natural assets, healthy atmosphere and clean seas gained a reputation across the United Kingdom. As roads leading to the town improved and it became possible to travel from Bristol by paddle steamer, the town started to attract middle class visitors from beyond Wales. Victorian artists, collectors, biologists, naturalists and intellectuals visited the town, including George Henry Lewes and his

in order to protect the town from attack by native Welshmen. The harbour, curled in the lee of Castle Hill, brought some prosperity to Tenby during the Middle Ages, but then the town went into decline. Wars with Spain and France caused trade to falter. The Civil War put an end to transactions across the Bristol Channel and the population of Tenby was decimated by an outbreak of plague in 1651. The impoverished and run-down state of the town led Sir Joseph Banks to describe it in 1767 as *the most complete ruin*. John Wesley reiterated this view in 1784, when he likened Tenby to Limerick: *once a large and strong city but now a heap of ruins*.

Such gloomy epithets convey a sense of a remote, impoverished and degraded settlement, its inhabitants struggling

North Beach, Tenby, by William Golding, 1799.

companion Mary Ann Evans (the writer George Eliot) who stayed for some months in a house overlooking the harbour beach. The railway arrived in 1863, significantly boosting the numbers of visitors and making Tenby accessible to trippers from the industrial heartlands of Wales and beyond. As more people descended onto the beaches, the question of propriety compelled local officials to set about regulating the practice of sea-bathing. They established an exclusion zone of 50 yards between ladies' and gentlemen's bathing machines and strongly recommended that gentlemen should wear drawers. Bathing without a machine was only allowed before 8.00am and after 9.00pm except on isolated stretches of beach.

But its remote, westerly position allowed the town to retain a certain exclusivity, an air of gentility that still pertains today, calming the bank holiday crowds, the hen and stag groups, and the coach parties that throng its streets.

And Tenby continues to value and look after its extraordinary assets, particularly its beaches. Each meets the strict criteria that earn it a Blue Flag and secure Tenby a place in any list of the top British beaches. The town looks after its bathers and swimmers. In the summer season, lifeguards keep watch and there is an inshore lifeboat ready to help those who get into trouble. Use of jet-skis and power boats is regulated. The water is clean. Every day, rubbish is meticulously cleared from the sand. The

South Sands, Tenby.

uncluttered expanse of South Beach, stretching for two miles towards Giltar Point has become a site for triathlon and other open water events, which attract hundreds of participants.

Today, looking out over the beach as the tide rolled up and the fingertips of water touched around St Catherine's Rock, I sat watching a young man in trunks, holding both hands of his baby daughter, whom I guessed was about a year old and barely able to walk. Patiently he helped her dip and kick her feet in the water, bent over her, his black trunks flapping. The baby's mother watched from where she sat on the sand, huddled beside the buggy in fleece and body warmer. After this gentle play, the baby was wrapped in a towel and placed in her mother's lap. The young man returned to the water, waded in, dived and

swam out for a few yards, then ducked his head under the surface of the water. Despite the warm holiday weather that has brought hundreds of people to picnic and doze on the sands, he was the only person I saw swimming.

Now, however, I am the only one in. I reflect upon the generally solitary nature of my swims, thinking about my collection of postcards showing groups of bathers, cheerful bands of friends and colleagues, clustered together for the photographer, enjoying the water together in their hired costumes.

This enviably communal approach to bathing largely died out during the latter part of the 20th century, other than in the few traditional swimming clubs that continued to operate despite declining numbers. But many of these

this page and following pages:
Postcards showing family, friends, colleagues
and communities enjoying bathing together.

THUMBS UP!!

371.

clubs are still going strong and now attracting growing numbers of new and younger members.

There are signs, too, that communal swimming may be undergoing a revival as The Outdoor Swimming Society and other associations extend their networks and enable swimmers to connect with each other and swim together once more. And there is encouraging evidence of a resilient collective folk memory of bathing across the country: on warm summer days, groups of young people continue to appear as if by magic at traditional swimming holes, like the river pool in Berriew, Wales.

I start to feel cold and move in towards the shore.

As I dry myself, I watch two children enjoying a late paddle in the shallows, supervised by their mother. Both are wearing suits with long legs and arms, designed to protect them from the sun's rays. Now we have become aware of the harmful effects of the sun, we are starting to cover ourselves up again, like the modest Victorian lady bathers for whom the slow transition to more rational and streamlined bathing attire accompanied the struggle to get the vote. And as Britain's different cultural groups seek to boost their fitness levels and have more of a presence at British beauty spots – as has been evident here today at Tenby – it is possible that modest bathing attire will make a reappearance on the beach, at the lakeside and on the river bank. Muslim women can now purchase swimwear that dries quickly, does not impede movement but fully covers legs, arms and hair. And photos of Nigella Lawson

River pool, Berriew, Wales © Martin Parr/Magnum.

The men's changing room, Brighton Sea Swimmers Club
© Martin Parr/Magnum.

on Bondi Beach may help to make the *burkini* a must-have fashion item for non Muslims too.

My baggy old bathing costume, worn thin through years of use, is good enough for me and I much prefer it to the tight rubbery feel of a wetsuit. The wetsuit still seems an anathema, a barrier between skin and water, reducing sensation and restricting movement. To me, it is the equivalent of swimming in a pool, immersed in tepid chemicals, breathing in chlorine. I have not tried a swimming wetsuit and feel no inclination to do so, just as I have no desire to race or to improve my technique. To me, that is not the point. I am more a bather than a swimmer. I love to dip, float, reflect and dream in true Romantic fashion. I do not compete, race or endure. I do not slog up and down in straight lines, urging myself to go faster. I prefer to be in the open, gazing at the landscape, twisting, turning and freely switching direction as I relish my buoyancy and my temporary transformation into a water creature.

But, having talked to swimmers who are focussed on speed, technique or endurance, like the Iron Man Wales competitors who will come to Tenby's South Beach in September, I realise that they too can experience a kind of transformation, a physiological and psychological change that comes about as they move their bodies through water. Working with the element rather than against it, maximising the efficiency of each stroke and the potential of each glide, they savour their speed and strength. Despite this

Susie Parr on Castle Beach, Tenby © Martin Parr/Magnum.

focus on technique, many open water competitors fully appreciate the natural environment they are swimming through. Swimmers rather than bathers, they are equally Romantic, albeit within the Byronic tradition, and their endurance and courage links them with Roman heroes and Anglo Saxon warriors.

There may, too, be a faint trace of Scandinavian heritage in my own swimming. Perhaps my compulsion to get into water, no matter how cold, re-connects me with my northern roots – my grandmother was Swedish and both my parents were born and brought up on the east coast of Scotland, where the sea is icy, the wind keen and the swimmers hardy.

And even though I swim in a cautious, profoundly un-athletic way, my cold water dips boost my fitness levels, counteract stress, release endorphins and make me glow with well being. As I do now, standing here, looking round at an historical – yet thoroughly modern – British beach.

Acknowledgements

A number of people have supported me in different ways over the ten year period it has taken me to write *The Story of Swimming* – sharing their knowledge, experience and insights, offering practical help, commenting on the text, or simply going for a dip with me. Needless to say, the errors, inaccuracies and omissions are all my own work.

Thank you to:

Kes Aleknavicius, Rozanne Barrow, Caroline Bowler, Peter Coates, Margaret Drabble, Rob Fryer, Tom Groves, Jonathan Hyams, Steve Joyce, David Kessler, Brigitte Lardinois, Liz Lee, Mairi MacArthur, Robert Macfarlane, Morag MacInnes, Kevin Meredith, David Mitchell, Simon Murie, Ellen Parr, Joyce Parr, Bob Pegg, Jean Perraton, Philippa Perry, Steve Price, Lewis Gordon Pugh, Kate Rew, Ellen Richardson, Pete Roberts, Georgina Rose, David Sawyers, Amy Sharrocks, Jenni Smith, Daniel Start, Gail Symes, Sara Tibbetts, Mark Thompson, Martine Watts

Heartfelt thanks to Dewi Lewis and Caroline Warhurst for their enthusiastic response to the proposal and their diligence and good humour throughout the process of bringing the book to publication.

And finally, my husband Martin Parr – a non swimmer – has never wavered in his belief in the project. Thank you Martin for the photographs, for the practical and emotional support and for sitting waiting patiently for me on sea shore, lake side and river bank.

References

Akhtar, M. and Humphries, S. (2000) *Some Liked it Hot: The British on holiday at home and abroad.* London, Virgin Publishing.

Ayriss, C. (2009) *Hung out to Dry: Swimming and British culture.* Lulu.com

Brand, J. (1883) *Observations on the Popular Antiquities of Great Britain: Chiefly illustrating the origin of our vulgar and provincial customs, ceremonies and superstitions.* London, George Bell and Sons.

Buxton, *A. Sea Change.* The Guardian, 26th July 2003.

Deakin, R. (2000) *Waterlog: A Swimmer's Journey through Britain.* London, Vantage.

Dutton, G. F. (1972) *Swimming Free: On and below the surface of lake, river and sea.* New York, St Martin's Press.

Fisher,S. (ed) (1997) *Recreation and the Sea.* Exeter, University Press.

Floyer, J. (1715) *The History of Cold Bathing both Ancient and Modern.* London, William Innes.

Fryer, R. (2011) *Rob Fryer's Wild Swimming Guide.*

Hammerton, J. (Ed.) (circa 1910) *Mr Punch at the Seaside.* London, The Educational Book Co. Ltd.

Hannavy, J. (2003) *The English Seaside in Victorian and Edwardian Times.* Princes Risborough, Shire Publications.

Hedges, S. (1930) *Swimming.* London, C. Arthur Pearson Ltd.

Klemperer, D. and J. (2007) *The Henleaze Lake Story.* Bristol, Redcliffe Press.

Love, C. (2008) *A Social History of Swimming in England 1800-1919.* London, Routledge.

Orme, N. (1983) *Early British Swimming 55BC-AD 1719.* Exeter, University Press.

Perraton, J. (2005) *Swimming against the stream: Reclaiming lakes and rivers for people to enjoy.* Charlbury, Jon Carpenter Publishing.

Pugh, L. (2010) *Achieving the Impossible.* London, Simon and Schuster.

Rew, K. (2008) *Wild Swim: River, lake, lido and sea. The best places to swim outdooors in Britain.* London, Guardian Books.

Sachs, F. (1912) *The Complete Swimmer.* London, Methuen.

Sinclair, A. and Henry, W. (1893) *The Badminton Library of Sports and Pastimes: Swimming.* London, Longmans, Green and Co.

Smith, J. (2005) *Liquid Assets: The Lidos and Open Air Swimming Pools of Britain.* London, English Heritage.

Sprawson, C. (1992) *Haunts of the Black Masseur: The Swimmer as Hero.* London, Jonathan Cape.

Start, D. (2008) *Wild Swimming.* London, Punk Publishing Ltd.

Start, D. (2009) *Wild Swimming Coast: Explore the secret coves and wild beaches of Britain.* London, Punk Publishing Ltd.

Titmuss, A. (Ed.) (1964) *Breaking the Ice. A publication to celebrate the centenary of the Serpentine Swimming Club.* London

Walton, J. (1983) *The English Seaside Resort: A social history 1750-1914.* Leicester, University Press.

Walton, J. (2000) *The British Seaside: Holidays and resorts in the twentieth century.* Manchester, University Press.

Open water swimming websites

British Long Distance Swimming Association
www.bldsa.org.uk

Channel Swimming Association
www.channelswimmingassociation.com

Henleaze Swimming Club
www.henleazeswimmingclub.org

Outdoor Swimming Society
www.outdoorswimmingsociety.com

River and Lakeside Swimming Association (RALSA)
www.river-swimming.co.uk

Swimtrek
www.swimtrek.com

Swimming Holes Wales
www.swimming-holes-wales.org.uk

Wild Swimming
www.wildswimming.co.uk

Tidal Pools
homepage.ntlworld.com/oliver.merrington/lidos/lidos4.htm

Facebook pages:
Wild water swimming in Scotland
Wet n Wild Open water swimming

Credits

Unless otherwise stated all images are from the author's collection.

Front cover: Venus's bathing (Margate). Side way or any way, by Thomas Rowlandson. Wellcome Library no. 35134i

p.12 London: The Capital that the Romans Built by Patrick Nicolle. Private Collection/ © Look and Learn/ The Bridgeman Art Library

p.16 Allegorical portrait of Sir John Luttrell, 1550 by Hans Eworth. Dunster Castle, Somerset, UK/ The Luttrell Collection/ National Trust Photographic Library/ John Hammond/ The Bridgeman Art Library

p.19 The Art of Swimming by Christopher Middleton © The British Library Board c13522-52.jpg & c13522-64.jpg

p.20 A Wanton Discovery, 1701 © The British Library Board c.40.m.10(1)

p.26 Coventina's shrine, Hadrian's Wall © English Heritage Photo Library

p.27 Mary Sutton being 'swum' in 1612. Private Collection/ The Bridgeman Art Library

p.28 Triton mosaic, Brading Roman Villa, Isle of Wight © Oglander Roman Trust

p.38 Sea-bathing at Scarborough, 1725, by John Setterington. Courtesy of North Yorkshire County Council Library Services

p.40 Bookshop, Scarborough. Courtesy of North Yorkshire County Council Library Services

p.43 The Court at Brighton a la Chinese, 1816, by George Cruikshank. Private Collection/ The Bridgeman Art Library

p.45 Venus's Bathing (Margate): A fashionable dip, by Thomas Rowlandson c.1800. Wellcome Library no. 35132i

p.50 Coniston by Joseph Arthur Palliser Severn © Abbot Hall Art Gallery, Kendal, Cumbria, UK/ The Bridgeman Art Library

p.51 George Gordon, 6th Lord Byron, by Charles Turner, 1815, after Richard Westall © City of Westminster Archive Centre, London, UK/ The Bridgeman Art Library

p.53 Portrait of Samuel Taylor Coleridge as a Young Man by Robert Hancock. Private Collection/ The Bridgeman Art Library

p.55 Hampstead Heath with Pond and Bathers, 1812, by John Constable © English Heritage Photo Library

p.58 The Funeral of Shelley, 1889, by Louis Edouard Paul Fournier © Walker Art Gallery, National Museums Liverpool/ The Bridgeman Art Library

p.59 Shelley Memorial, University College Oxford. Reproduced courtesy of the Master and Fellows of University College, Oxford © Martin Parr/Magnum

p.60 Lord Byron reposing in the house of a fisherman having swum the Hellespont, 1831, by Sir William Allan. Roy Miles Fine Paintings/ The Bridgeman Art Library

p.61 Portrait of Algernon Charles Swinburne by William Bell Scott. Balliol College, Oxford, UK/ The Bridgeman Art Library

p.62 Sketch of a Seated Boy, 1917, by Henry Scott Tuke. Royal Cornwall Polytechnic Society, Falmouth, UK/ The Bridgeman Art Library

p.63 Jacques Raverat and Noele Olivier, both members of the Neo-Pagans. Illustrations from The Neo-pagans courtesy of Paul Delaney.

p.68 The Railway Station, 1863, by William Powell Frith. New Walk Museum & Art Gallery, Leicester, UK/ Photo © Leicester Arts & Museums/ The Bridgeman Art Library

p.70 Bass outing railway timetable, 1914. Courtesy of The National Brewery Centre, Burton-on-Trent

p.71 Bass excursion programme, 1914. Courtesy of The National Brewery Centre, Burton-on-Trent

p.72 The beach at Ilfracombe with Professor Harry Parker in the water and Professor Harry Parker. Courtesy of Tunnels Beaches, Ilfracombe

p.73 The gentlemen's tidal pool and The Tunnels, Ilfracombe. Courtesy of Tunnels Beaches, Ilfracombe

p.77 Promenading along the pier. Mitchell & Kenyon, courtesy of BFI

p.79 Ramsgate Sands 1852-54 by William Powell Frith. The Royal Collection © 2011 Her Majesty Queen Elizabeth II/ The Bridgeman Art Library

p.93 Brill's Baths, King's Road, Brighton, built in 1869. James Gray collection/ The Regency Society. Reproduced with the kind permission of the Royal Pavillion & Museums (Brighton & Hove)

p.94 Posters advertising the Goulston Street Baths, London © Museum of London

p.96 Ladies' bathing fashion. Courtesy of Advertising Archives

p.107 Tenby, from Round the Coast, 1895 © The Francis Frith Collection

p.120 Whitley Bay, London and North Eastern Railway poster © NRM Pictorial Collection / Science & Society Picture Library

p.121 Hints for Holidays 1932. Reproduced courtesy of Bluebell Railway, Sussex

p.122 left: Jantzen logo © Gail Symes. Courtesy of the Fashion Museum, Bath and North East Somerset Council

p.123 Seaside comic series, Bamforth & Co Ltd, Holmfirth, Yorkshire

p.125 New Brighton Lido, London, Midland and Scottish Railway poster © NRM Pictorial Collection/ Science & Society Picture Library

p.127 Londoners relax on Tower Beach, 1952 © Henry Grant Collection/ Museum of London

p.132 Glamour at Butlin's c.1960 © NRM Pictorial Collection/ Science & Society Picture Library

p.133 Seaside comic series, Bamforth & Co Ltd, Holmfirth, Yorkshire

p.134 Glamour at Whitley Bay, 1957 © NRM Pictorial Collection/ Science & Society Picture Library

p.144 Swimming Free by Geoffrey Fraser Dutton. Published by William Heinemann Ltd 1972

p.154 Waterlog by Roger Deakin, 1999. Published by Vintage Books. Used by permission of The Random House Group Ltd

p.155 Wild Swim by Kate Rew and Dominick Taylor, 2008. Published by Guardian Books. Used by permission of Random House Group Ltd

p.155 Wild Swimming by Daniel Start, 2008. Punk Publishing Ltd

p.156 Rob Fryer's Wild Swimming Guide to Swimming in Rivers & Lakes in the UK, France & Overseas, 2011. Dry Hill Publishing Co.

p.179 North Beach, Tenby, by William Golding, 1799. Courtesy of Tenby Museum and Art Gallery